Interaction and the Standardized Survey Interview
The Living Questionnaire

This is the first study of its kind to investigate in detail the interaction between interviewers and respondents in standardized social survey interviews. Applying the techniques of conversation analysis, Hanneke Houtkoop-Steenstra reveals how certain rules of normal conversation fail to apply in interviews based on a standard questionnaire, and offers original empirical evidence to show what really happens. Her book demonstrates that interview results can only be understood as products of the contingencies of the interview situation, and not, as is usually assumed, the unmediated expressions of respondents' real opinions. Her conclusions have important implications for anyone interested in effective survey compilation and interpretation. The book is highly accessible, setting out the basic tools of conversation analysis simply and clearly, and suggesting ways of improving questionnaire design wherever possible. Its approach breaks new ground and will be of great interest to students and researchers of survey methodology.

Hanneke Houtkoop-Steenstra is lecturer in pragmalinguistics in the Dutch department of Utrecht University. She is author of *Establishing Agreement: An Analysis of Proposal-Acceptance Sequences* (1987) and co-editor with Harry Van den Berg and Margaret Wetherell of *Analysing Racist Discourse: Multidisciplinary Approaches*, a forthcoming book from Cambridge University Press.

Interaction and the Standardized Survey Interview

The Living Questionnaire

Hanneke Houtkoop-Steenstra

CAMBRIDGE
UNIVERSITY PRESS

PUBLISHED BY THE PRESS SYNDICATE OF THE UNIVERSITY OF CAMBRIDGE
The Pitt Building, Trumpington Street, Cambridge, United Kingdom

CAMBRIDGE UNIVERSITY PRESS
The Edinburgh Building, Cambridge CB2 2RU, UK   www.cup.cam.ac.uk
40 West 20th Street, New York NY 10011–4211, USA   www.cup.org
10 Stamford Road, Oakleigh, Melbourne 3166, Australia
Ruiz de Alarcón 13, 28014 Madrid, Spain

First published 2000

Printed in the United Kingdom at the University Press, Cambridge

Typeface Plantin MT 10/12 pt   *System* QuarkXPress™   [SE]

A catalogue record for this book is available from the British Library

Library of Congress Cataloguing in Publication data

Houtkoop, Hanneke.
Interaction and the standardized survey interview: the living questionnaire / Hanneke
Houtkoop-Steenstra.
    p. cm.
Includes bibliographical references and index.
ISBN 0 521 66202 8 (hardback) – ISBN 0 521 66571 X (paperback)
1. Interviewing in sociology.   2. Interviewing.   3. Social
surveys.   4. Questionnaires.
HM526.H68   2000
001.4′33–dc21   99–42112   CIP

ISBN 0 521 66202 8 hardback
ISBN 0 521 66571 X paperback

Contents

Preface

I have researched conversation since I graduated from the Department of General Linguistics at the University of Amsterdam. For the first seven years I studied everyday telephone conversations, and I then became interested in what I referred to as "interviewing techniques" in doctor–patient interaction. What did the textbooks say about how medical doctors should interact with their patients, and how did these interviewing techniques work out in real interactions? The advice these books provided was mainly based on psychological and socio-psychological theories of human interaction, and the real interactions often were not as successful as the textbooks predicted.

Being interested in interaction, and especially in the relationship between "how it should be done" and "how it is actually done," I chose the standardized survey interview as a uniquely interesting research object. A considerable amount of what we know about the social world comes from survey research that finds its way into books, articles, and the mass media. This survey research occasionally provides some general information about the questionnaire, the sample interviewed, and the statistical analysis, but it does not explain what actually happens in the interviews. In fact, the reader and/or user of survey research results is made to believe that interviewers read the questions exactly as they are scripted and respondents behave exactly as they are supposed to behave.

In order to learn what is going on in this part of the survey research procedure, we need to examine questionnaires and analyze recorded interviews. The questionnaires inform the analyst about what interviewers and respondents are supposed to do, whereas the actual interviews demonstrate what they are really doing. When a Dutch survey research organization permitted me to listen to their interviewers doing computer-assisted telephone survey interviews, I was surprised by what I heard. Respondents requested question clarification, interviewers asked questions respondents had previously answered, respondents answered "yes" or "no" although they seemed unsure of what the question meant, and interviewers asked questions that seemed irrelevant, not only to me, but to the respondent as well.

The research organization gave me the tape recordings of a number of these interviews and allowed me to use them for conversation analysis. My husband, a researcher in the sociology of education, provided me with the questionnaire that formed the basis of these interviews. I have studied several sets of these transcribed, tape-recorded, standardized survey interviews, and parts of these studies have been reported in various published papers. In this book I have tried to bring my published and new work together in a more coherent perspective.

This book brings the results of my research to the attention of those who, in one way or another, are interested in what happens in survey interviews. Students of survey methodology may want to know how questionnaires are enacted in real-life interviews and why interview participants may depart from the script and/or the rules of standardized interviewing. Though this book is not written as an instruction manual, survey methodologists and questionnaire designers may find it useful to learn how the principles of everyday conversation affect what happens in the survey interview. While some insights can be used to improve questionnaires, other insights show the in-principle restrictions of survey methodology.

Pragmalinguists, conversation analysts, and discourse analysts may be interested in the survey interview as a form of talk in its own right, to be compared with other forms of institutional talk (e.g., police interrogation, medical interviewing) and everyday conversation. Also, while linguistics tends to make a distinction between written language on the one hand and spoken language on the other, survey interviews constitute an intersection of the two forms of language, which linguists might find interesting.

Chapter 1 briefly mentions the methodological issues involved in the survey interview. The reader will be referred to other publications that discuss these issues in more detail.

The survey interview will be examined as a form of talk. Interview talk heavily relies on the practices and principles of ordinary conversation. These practices and principles are best understood through conversation analysis. Chapter 2 presents the current state of scholarship regarding how people organize and constitute mundane conversation. This chapter also forms the main theoretical framework for the analyses that are presented throughout the book.

The purpose of chapter 3 is to provide a description of the participation roles involved in the survey interview. I argue that the survey interview is a form of talk embedded in a broader framework of institutional or organizational activities. The scripted questions that constitute the basis of the talk and the pre-coded form used to record the respondents' answers are organizational requirements that have consequences for the various interactional roles the interviewer may take. The function of particular stretches of talk depends partly on the speaker's current interactional role. This insight has a special relevance for the methodology of interaction-coding studies.

Chapter 4 discusses how interviewers attempt to satisfy conflicting interactional requirements. The rules of the standard survey interview require that interviewers never deviate from the questionnaire; however, this inflexibility can result in a situation that is at odds with ordinary conversation. For example, asking the same question twice or not taking into account what the respondent has already said is a typical occurrence in standardized survey interviews. I show how such unconversational activities may lead to misunderstanding on the part of the respondent, and I also focus on the ways in which interviewers deal with these interactional problems.

Chapter 5 is devoted to problems that arise from poorly scripted questions. Sometimes questions are structured in such a way that they may result in respondents interrupting the interviewer and providing premature answers, which may in turn lead to interviewers omitting part of the scripted question and/or the response options. One possible effect of the pre-emptive answer is that the responses that are provided may be unformatted, which calls for the interviewers to probe for a formatted answer. Another possible effect is that serious problems in the sampling procedure may occur when interviewers omit part of the scripted questions during the introductory phase of the interview.

Chapter 6 discusses what interviewers do when respondents provide answers that do not match the pre-coded response options, as is especially common in the case of field-coded questions, where the respondents are not presented with the response categories. This chapter also discusses the fact that respondents are frequently asked to categorize their life experiences in technical terms. These technical terms, however, often do not match the respondents' ways of categorizing their world.

Chapter 7 presents a study of how interviewers build rapport with their respondents when the topic of the interview is a sensitive issue, such as respondents' serious lack of competence in literacy and numeracy. The study shows that building rapport often results in the interviewers revising neutrally formulated multiple-choice scripted questions as leading yes–no questions.

Chapter 8 is devoted to the analysis of interviews with learning-disabled persons living in sheltered homes. These persons were interviewed using a well-established Quality of Life questionnaire. I discuss how the interviewers revise the scripted multiple-choice questions upon discovering that the respondent has difficulty understanding the questions. The ultimate effect of this revision practice is that the respondents all end up with very high, though disputable, scores. This chapter is co-authored with Charles Antaki of Loughborough University, UK and Mark Rapley of Murdoch University, Australia.

The final chapter presents the methodological implications of these studies.

Acknowledgments

I carried out the main part of the work documented here while I was a research fellow with the Department of Social Research Methodology at the Free University in Amsterdam. I am especially grateful to the head of the department, Hans van der Zouwen, for his conviction that conversation analysis can benefit the study of survey interviews. I also worked on a portion of this research while at the Utrecht Institute of Linguistics at Utrecht University. I want to thank both departments for providing me with the opportunity to do this work.

I also thank Jürgen Streeck and Robert Hopper of the Speech Communication Department of the University of Texas at Austin for their support and hospitality during my stay in Austin in 1991. Sadly, Robert Hopper is no longer with us. Though his spirit lives on in our hearts and in the tremendous contributions he has made to scholarship, he will be sorely missed.

Further thanks go to Harry van den Berg, Wil Dijkstra, Paul Drew, Paul ten Have, Bregje Holleman, Gail Jefferson, Tom Koole, Douglas Maynard, Harrie Mazeland, Anita Pomerantz, Nora Cate Schaeffer, Emanuel Schegloff, Marja-Leena Sorjonen, Arie Verhagen, and the members of the Interdisciplinary Working Group on Interaction Analysis (IWIA) for their helpful comments during my work on survey interviews.

Special thanks go to Patricia Haegeman, Peter van den Bosch, and Kathryn Hickerson for correcting and editing the manuscript, and to the Netherlands Science Organization (NWO) for providing the funding for the correction work.

I gratefully acknowledge the support of the successive editors at Cambridge University Press, namely Catherine Maxwell, Sarah Caro, and Camilla Erskine, and the copy-editor Kay McKechnie.

Most of all, I thank my husband Willem Houtkoop. He is responsible for my realization that the standardized survey interview is a very interesting research object. Once I began to study the data, he never grew tired of discussing my work, reading drafts, and making very helpful comments.

I am grateful to the University Press of America for granting me permission to reprint the major part of chapter 4 section 5; to Kluwer for permission to reprint chapter 6 from *Quality & Quantity* 30 (1996): 205–30; to Elsevier Publisher for permission to reprint chapter 7 from *Journal of Pragmatics* 28 (1997): 591-623, and to Lawrence Erlbaum for permission to reprint chapter 8 from *Research on Language and Social Interaction* 30 (1997): 285-313.

Glossary of transcript symbols

⌈ ⌉ ⌊ ⌋	A single left-hand bracket indicates the point of overlap onset. A single right-hand bracket indicates the point at which an utterance (-part) terminates vis-a-vis another. For example:

A. I don't remem⌈ ber ⌉.
B.　　　　　⌊No.⌋

The brackets are also used when something happens during the talk, for example when a phone rings:

A. I⌈ don't remember ⌉
　⌊ ((phone rings)) ⌋

=	Equal signs, one at the end of one line and one at the beginning of the next, indicate no "gap" between the two lines.
(0.0)	Numbers in parentheses indicate elapsed time in silence by tenths of seconds. For example, (1.3) is one and three-tenths seconds.
(.)	A dot in parentheses indicates a tiny gap within or between utterances. It is probably no more than two-tenths of a second.
word	Underscoring indicates some form of stress, via pitch and/or amplitude.
wo::rd	Colons indicate prolongation of the immediately prior sound. The length of the colon row indicates the length of the prolongation.
.,?	Punctuation marks are used to indicate intonation.
↓↑	An arrow indicates a marked falling or rising intonation of the syllable that follows, for example, "word↓ing" and "word↑ing."
WORD	Upper case indicates especially loud sounds relative to the surrounding talk of the same speaker.
°word°	Talk between degree signs is relatively quieter than the surrounding talk of the same speaker.
wo-	A dash indicates that a word or phrase is cut off.

>word<	Right/left carats bracketing an utterance or utterance-part indicate speeding up.
<word>	Left/right carats indicate slowing down.
.hhh	A dot-prefixed row of "h's" indicates an inbreath.
(h)	A parenthesized "h" indicates plosiveness, associated with laughter, for example, "Yea(h)heah."
( )	Empty parentheses indicate the transcriber's inability to hear what was said. The length of the parenthesized space indicates the length of the untranscribed talk.
(word)	Parenthesized words are doubtful transcriptions.
((cough))	Doubled parentheses contain transcriber's descriptions rather than transcriptions.
(...)	Ellipses within parentheses indicates that some lines have been omitted.
#	The number sign indicates the sound of the interviewer working on the keyboard.

1   The standardized survey interview

1   Introduction

Social science research is primarily devoted to describing and analyzing peoples' actions and attitudes. In modern states, governments need this information in order to make well-founded policy interventions and evaluate their effectiveness. For example, governments may want to know parents' attitudes towards the schooling of their children and whether or not proposed changes will meet with approval. Also, political parties need to know what issues their prospective voters consider important in order to adapt the election strategies accordingly. In addition, industries may want to know what the trends in fashion will be in two years time, in order to purchase the appropriate materials and dyes.

To gather such information, researchers may send people a questionnaire to fill out and return. Another increasingly popular procedure is to interview people, either in person or, far more economically, by telephone. In the 1980s, personal computers led to the introduction and rapid development of computer-assisted telephone interviewing (CATI).

Among the different types of research interviews, the standardized survey interview is the most prevalent one in use in western societies. Large numbers of people earn an income in the survey research industry, enormous amounts of public and private money are spent in this field, and many important decisions made by governments and companies are based on the results of survey research. In fact our lives are ruled by survey research to a considerable extent.

The standardized survey interview is designed for gathering data with which to measure the intentions, actions, and attitudes of large numbers of people, usually representative samples of the populations being studied. Measurement must be carried out in such a way that measures can be aggregated to describe the population. According to Fowler and Mangione, "The standard for the success of a survey is how well the data measures the aspects of the population the researchers are trying to describe. The goal of a survey is to produce accurate statistics" (1990:

1

12). The quality of research methods depends both on validity and reliability. The research method is valid when it generates the research data that it is designed to collect. This means that the questions should measure the dimension or construct of interest (construct validity). In addition, the respondents should interpret the questions as the researcher intended, and the answers should correspond with respondents' actual perceptions (response validity). So, when we want to know what percentage of the research population visited a museum last year, we should make sure to define exactly what we mean by "museum" (do art galleries count as museums?) and by "visiting" a museum (does a visit count if we briefly drop in, or if we only visit when we accompany our grandmother?). Furthermore, the research method must be reliable. The concept of reliability refers to the degree of variation among responses in repeated trials and with different interviewers. All respondents should understand the concept of museum in the same way, irrespective of the conditions under which they were interviewed.

2   Measurement error

Survey measurement is carried out by applying the same procedure to each respondent, so differences between responses can be attributed to real differences in the studied population. Differences in measures should not be attributable to characteristics of either the measurement instrument or measurement procedure. In order to reduce such measurement errors, the survey interview must be maximally standardized across all aspects of the measurement process.

- The interview setting, for instance either in person or over the telephone, should be the same for all respondents in order to avoid mode effects. For an overview of these so-called mode effects, see Lyberg and Kasprzyk (1991) and Czaja and Blair (1996).
- Characteristics of the interviewers should not influence the respondents' behavior. Research shows that interviewer characteristics such as sex, race, age, level of experience, or motivation can have an effect on response behavior (Schuman and Presser 1981; Fowler and Mangione 1990).
- All respondents must be presented with the same stimuli. Thus, every interviewer should present the questions exactly as scripted in the questionnaire, without omitting or adding anything.
- Interviewers should probe answers in a neutral way. They must follow the rules of standardized interviewing behavior in order to reduce interviewer-related errors.

The need for standardized interviewer behavior is partly related to the careful design of the questionnaire. Ideally, questionnaires are designed so that they take into account the various insights that survey methodology research has generated over the years. Since questionnaires are, ideally, designed so that maximum validity is guaranteed, interviewers should not decrease this.

Standardized interviewer behavior is also necessary for reasons of reliability. Survey methodology works from a stimulus-response model of interaction (Foddy 1993), in that every respondent should be presented with the same verbal input. For that reason, interviewers should read aloud each question exactly as worded, preserve the order of the questions, and probe in a non-leading manner. This consistency ensures that differences in responses can be related to respondent characteristics, rather than to characteristics of the interviewing procedure.

In section 3, I will briefly discuss how question format, wording, and order, as well as the order in which response options are presented, may have an effect on response behavior. For a more detailed discussion, see Schuman and Presser (1981), Belson (1981), Biemer et al. (1991), and Schwarz and Sudman (1992). At the end of this section I will make some remarks on the assumption that standardized question wording equals standardized meaning, even though the studies under review point in a different direction. Next I will focus on aspects of standardized interviewing techniques (section 4), and how to probe inadequate answers (section 5). In section 6, I propose that the concepts of interviewer effect and interviewer error are misleading and unfair. In fact, many supposed interviewer effects and errors should be seen rather as questionnaire effects and errors. Questionnaires, I claim, often do not live up to their intended use in interaction. Section 6 also points out why survey methodology may benefit from conversation analysis studies on survey interviews.

3   Question characteristics

3.1   Question format

Survey methodology distinguishes between different question formats. An important distinction is whether or not respondents are free to formulate their own answers. Question formats also differ depending upon who will do the final coding of the respondents' answers.

Open questions do not limit response alternatives. Respondents are free to formulate their own answers. The interviewers are instructed to copy the answers verbatim. Later in the research process, trained coders will translate the copied answers into a restricted number of response codes.

In the case of closed questions, also known as fixed-choice questions, the interviewers read the questions and a list of response options from which respondents are to choose their answers. When respondents formulate their answers in a way that differs from the response options, interviewers are supposed to probe for a formatted answer (Schaeffer and Maynard 1996),[1] that is, an answer that matches one of the pre-coded response options that can be recorded. In these cases, it is crucial that interviewers use neutral probes. A special type of closed question is the yes–no question. Unlike ordinary conversation (Churchill 1978), the yes–no question constrains respondents replies, permitting only "yes" or "no" answers.

Survey questionnaires may also contain field-coded questions. These questions are presented to respondents as open questions. However, the interviewers are given a list of response options, and they must translate the respondent's answer into a coded option before checking one of the response boxes.

Face-to-face interviews provide the possibility of using show card questions. Response options are written on a card that is presented to the respondents. After hearing the question, they select the pre-coded response of their choice. Whether or not the response options are presented on a card, closed questions require that respondents provide the information they have in mind in terms of the pre-coded response categories. Thus respondents are doing the coding work.

3.2   *Question-order and context effects*

The way a question is interpreted may depend on what precedes it. This holds true especially when successive questions concern the same topic. When the prior question provides a context for interpretation of the next one, we may speak of "question-order effect" or "context effect." For example, if a person is asked how his wife is doing and is next asked how his family is doing, this person may not include his wife in the second answer. He could assume that the questioner would not request information already provided.

Context effects may also arise when respondents try to appear consistent by putting a response to a later question in line with an earlier one (the part–part consistency effect). See Schuman and Presser (1981) for an extensive discussion of several types of question-order effects. See also Schwarz and Sudman (1992).

3.3   Response options and response order

Closed survey questions present two or more response options from which the respondent is supposed to choose. Several experiments show that the presenting order of these options may influence the respondent's choice. This type of context effect is referred to as the "response-order effect." Respondents who read the response options themselves will be more likely to choose the options they see first. When options are read to them, however, respondents are more likely to endorse the ones they hear last (Krosnick and Alwin 1987). In order to reduce response-order effects, computerized questionnaires may randomize the order in which the response options are presented across respondents (Schwarz and Hippler 1991).

Behavior-coding studies by Oksenberg and others (1991), Loosveldt (1995), Dijkstra, Van der Veen and Van der Zouwen (1985) and Smit (1995) show that closed questions may easily lead to interviewer effects. Smit found that in 42 percent of the cases where interviewers had to read a list of response options, they presented fewer than all options. As suggested, this may be partly because respondents begin to answer before the interviewer is able to read the entire list of options. When a respondent answers the question before the interviewer presents all the options, the interviewer tends to read only a selection.

In chapter 5 we will see that closed questions as found in survey interviews are often formulated such that they implicitly cue respondents to take their turn before the interviewer reads the response options. The questionnaire tacitly guides both interviewer and respondent to speak at the same time.

As Fowler and Mangione (1986) point out, open questions also offer a potential for interviewer effects, caused by possible ambiguity concerning the kind of answer that will suffice. I will show that survey questions in general are scripted such that they create a response expectation that runs contrary to what the researchers had in mind.

If Fowler and Mangione are right, that open questions tend to be ambiguous with respect to the way respondents should deal with them, then field coded questions must be even more problematic. From the respondent's perspective, field coded questions are just open questions. For the interviewer, however, they are similar to closed questions. The significant difference is that field coded questions may generate answers that do not match the hidden response options. When receiving an unrecordable answer, the interviewer must probe for an answer that will match the pre-coded options. In Smit's study (1995) two field coded questions led to a high degree of directive interviewer behavior, such that Smit advises against using field coded questions in survey research.

3.4   Question wording and the interpretation of questions

Belson (1981) convincingly shows the difficulty in phrasing questions that will be interpreted as intended by the researcher. He presented the following question to fifty-nine individuals: "How many days of the week do you usually watch televison? I mean weekdays and Saturdays and Sundays, of course, and daytime viewing as well as evening viewing?" After respondents completed the questionnaire, a second interviewer tested the respondents' understanding of the question, producing the following results:

- Fourteen out of fifty-nine failed to interpret this question as a request to mention a numerical answer.
- A large majority did not interpret "days of the week" as meant by the researchers.
- Five persons out of fifty-nine did not interpret "you" as referring to themselves only. They turned out to have treated "you" as "you and your wife," "you and your family" or "your family."
- Fifteen persons interpreted "watch televison" as "have the TV set on," rather than actually paying attention to a program.
- Twenty-eight out of fifty-nine did not interpret the term "usually" as intended.

Groves et al. (1992) asked respondents the closed-ended question, "Would you say your own health, in general, is excellent, good, fair, or poor?" It turned out that 43 percent of the men and 28 percent of the women rated their health condition as "excellent." When respondents were asked via an open follow-up question whether they had compared their own health to that of others, it turned out that 12 percent said "yes," and 88 percent said "no." Asked whether they had compared their health now to it at an earlier age, 43 percent said "yes," and 56 percent said "no." These answers show that respondents evaluated their health condition from at least two different perspectives, which makes their answers incomparable.

Experimental studies show that small changes in question wording sometimes produce very large changes in response distribution. Butler and Kitzinger (1976) asked British people, "Do you accept the government's recommendation that the United Kingdom should *come out of* the Common Market?" The difference between pro and con response was only 0.2 percent in favor of the Common Market position. However, when the question read "Do you accept the government's recommendation that the United Kingdom should *stay in* the Common Market?" the difference was 18.2 percent in favor of the pro position.

Rugg (1941) found a 21 percent difference in response distribution depending on whether the verb "allowing" or the verb "not forbidding" was used in a question on supporting freedom of speech. For other studies in the forbid/allow asymmetry, see Schuman and Presser (1981) on American data; Waterplas, Billiet, and Loosveldt (1988) on Belgian data; Hippler and Schwarz (1986) on German data; and Holleman (1996) on Dutch data.

The list of response options may contain a "don't know" or "no-opinion" option. An experimental study by Schuman and Presser (1981) shows that 90 percent of the sample chose the "no opinion" option when it was offered to them. When this option was not offered, 69 percent volunteered they had no opinion on the issue. When interviewers vary in presenting this option, they create a bias.

Several studies show that vague quantifiers like "usually," "many," "some," or "a few" are interpreted differently by different respondents (Bradburn and Miles 1979). Schaeffer (1991b) found a significant difference in the interpretation of phrases containing vague quantifiers for race, age, and level of education. The meaning of vague quantifiers differs also concerning the verbs and nouns that they quantify. The meaning of "many" in "having many children" and "having many books" may very well differ for one and the same respondent. Similarly, "watching television often" may well refer to more times than "going out often." Similar problems exist for vague qualifiers, for example, "excellent," "good," "fair," and "poor."

Experimental evidence suggests that respondents often answer questions having little or no knowledge at all of the topic. In his review of the literature, Smith (1984) mentions the following findings: 96 percent of a sample offered opinions on the importance of a balanced federal budget. Only 3 percent of them had enough information on which to base an opinion. Ferber (1956) studied attitudinal questions and found that people expressed opinions they were not able to define. Converse (1970) would later refer to such opinions as non-attitudes. In fact, this notion may not quite cover the entire issue, as a Dutch field experiment by Van der Sloot and Spanjer (1998) makes clear. They presented respondents with a number of topically related opinion questions, some of which contained non-existent objects. The analysis of the transcripts makes clear that respondents may use the context to try to make sense of these terms (Schwartz 1996). In response to the question whether the (non-existent) "televiewer" was a practical telecom service, one respondent replied, "Is that a picture phone, or something?" Respondents may also think they misheard the interviewer. When the interviewer asked a question about the non-existent "NPM," one person assumed the interviewer said, or meant to say, "NPB, the Netherlands Press Bureau." This study also shows that respondents are willing to give an opinion about things they have no opinion about. Some of the respondents were very explicit about this. One person said, "I have no clue what it is, but just put no."

3.5   Standardized wording versus standardized meaning

Fowler and Mangione (1990:136–7) state that questions should meet at least the following standards:
- Questions are fully scripted.
- Questions mean the same to every respondent.
- Answer options are read to all respondents.

The combination of the first two requirements suggests that standardized question wording and standardized meaning go together. However, when we look at the many studies on respondents interpreting survey questions, it will be clear that almost any word or concept used in questionnaires may be interpreted in more than one way. The main problem for survey methodology and for questionnaire designers is that these studies do not tell us how to phrase questions in an unambiguous way right from the start. This is because unambiguous questions hardly exist, due to the intrinsic ambiguity of language. The best that authors can come up with are pieces of advice on what questionnaire designers should avoid doing (e.g., Moser and Kalton 1978, Belson 1981).

The general advice to questionnaire designers is to pre-test their questions. However, when we look at, for example, Belson's work, it is clear that a serious pre-test of a questionnaire is too difficult for most research because of time and money constraints. But suppose serious pre-testing were feasible, what could its practical use be? We might decide to explain one problematic question in more detail. A problem could then be that the question becomes far too long and complex. Molenaar (1982), who reviewed the relevant literature, found that longer questions increase the chance that response effects occur. Furthermore, explanation of the ambiguous question would contain ambiguous language too. The same problem appears when we decide to use filter questions.

The only sensible conclusion with regard to this issue, then, is that standardization of question wording does not necessarily imply standardization of meaning. The first person to point this out may be Lazersfeld (1944), and since that time it has been stated again and again (Nuckols

1953; Cicourel 1964, 1982; Briggs 1986; Mishler 1986; Suchman and Jordan 1990a; Schaeffer 1991a; Foddy 1993). Remarkably, the ocean of studies in question interpretation has not led survey methodology to give up the idea of presenting respondents with standardized question wording. Standardization is, after all, the heart of survey methodology and market research, and for that reason it would not be easy to give it up.

In the next section I will discuss how survey methodology sees the role of the interviewer in the standardization of the measurement process. Since Fowler and Mangione are well-known protagonists of standardization, I will make extensive use of their 1990 study.

4   Standardization of the interviewer–respondent interaction

Because a change in the formulation or the order of questions and response options can have an effect on the responses, it is crucial that interviewers do not alter anything in the questionnaire. Interviewers, therefore, are to follow the rules of standardized interviewing. Fowler and Mangione (1990: 33) formulate the rules of standardized interviewing as follows:

- Read the questions exactly as worded.
- If the respondent's answer is incomplete or inadequate, probe for clarification or elaboration in a non-directive way.
- Record the answers without interviewer's discretion.
- Do not provide any positive or negative feedback regarding the specific content of respondent's answers.

Several studies in which interviewer–respondent interactions were coded show that interviewers often do not act according to these rules. For example, Brenner's (1982) analysis of tape-recorded interviews shows that more than 30 percent of all questions were not asked in the required manner. In a Dutch study, Dijkstra et al. (1985) found that interviewers altered the essential content or the meaning of the written questions to the extent that 40 percent of all answers are not to be trusted. For similar findings, see Belson (1965), Bradburn and Sudman (1979), Cannell, Fowler, and Marquis (1968), Fowler and Mangione (1986), Cannell and Oksenberg (1988).

Why are interviewers often not rule-obedient? Fowler and Mangione (1990: 33–4) summarize the obstacles to carrying out an interview in a standardized way. One is that interviewers like to be considerate and responsive to respondents, and feel this to be in conflict with standardized behavior.

Another possible problem is that the questionnaire may be inadequate.

For example, a question may be ambiguous or difficult to read aloud. Such potential problems can, to some degree, be solved by pre-testing the questionnaire (see Czaja and Blair 1996 on pre-testing procedures). Furthermore, respondents may not understand what they are expected to do. They often do not act their roles as prescribed. Fowler and Mangione advocate that interviewers explain clearly to respondents the rules of the game, and they present the following text to be read:

> Since many people have never been in an interview exactly like this, let me read you a paragraph that tells a little bit about how it works. I am going to read you a set of questions exactly as they are worded so that every respondent in the survey is answering the same questions. You'll be asked to answer two kinds of questions. In some cases, you'll be asked to answer in your own words. For those questions, I will have to write down your answers word for word. In other cases, you will be given a list of answers and asked to choose the one that fits best. If at any time during the interview you are not clear about what is wanted, be sure to ask me. (1990: 51)

Cannell et al. (1981) found that reporting improves when the respondent's role is made clear by explicit instruction. In this book it will become clear that such an introduction will hardly solve the problem of respondents failing to do what is expected from them.

5   Probing inadequate answers

When respondents do not provide satisfactory answers, interviewers must probe for more adequate or more complete ones. And they should do this in a non-directive way, that is, interviewers' probes should not increase the chance of one answer over another. As Fowler and Mangione (1990) say, each probe that can be answered by "yes" or "no" is directive. They propose a number of rules that interviewers should follow when probing answers:

- When respondents miss part of the question, interviewers should reread the entire question.
- When respondents do not understand a term or concept in the question, for example, because a term turns out to be ambiguous, interviewers are not allowed to provide an explanation. They can reread the definition, if the questionnaire provides one. Otherwise respondents must be told to interpret the question to their own liking and answer the question.
- When probing answers, interviewers should make sure that answers meet the questions' objectives. It is the interviewers' task to make sure that respondents indeed provide a numerical answer, or choose one of the response options read to them.

How should interviewers probe answers in Fowler and Mangione's perspective? Regarding numerical answers, respondents may answer with an approximation. When this happens, interviewers should repeat the question, "since the real problem with the respondent's answer was that the question was not answered" (1990: 41). They give the following example of a correct way of probing an inadequate answer:

QUESTION: In the last seven nights, how many times have you gotten fewer than eight hours of sleep?
RESPONSE: I usually get eight hours of sleep.
PROBE: In the last seven nights, how many times have you gotten fewer than eight hours of sleep?

This solution, I believe, creates the problem of the interviewers not being responsive to the interviewees, treating them as if they have not answered the question. It is not surprising that interviewers hardly ever repeat the question when it has not been answered adequately.

When respondents fail to choose one of the response options, interviewers should read the list of responses again, according to Fowler and Mangione (1990). Interviewers should not accept an answer that does not exactly fit one of the options and code the answer themselves, because "When the respondent chooses an answer, it does not guarantee zero error, but it should make the answer dependent only on the respondent and unrelated to the interviewer" (39). As we will see in chapter 6, interviewers frequently disobey this rule. They often accept answers that don't exactly fit one of the scripted options.

Another mistake interviewers can make in probing closed questions is to repeat only part of the alternatives. According to Fowler and Mangione, "Respondents respond to the number of categories and the position of a category on a scale, as well as to the words, when classifying themselves. A truncated version of a set of responses is not the same stimulus, and it will affect the answers" (1990: 40). I will return to this topic later.

6   Interviewer effects or questionnaire effects?

It is clear that all question formats used in standardized survey interviews constitute to some degree interview problems of some kind. Survey methodology literature tends to see these problems in terms of interviewer effects and errors. The often-mentioned remedy is to give interviewers more and better interview training.

However, it seems unfair to the interviewers to use the term "interviewer effects." This term places blame on the interviewer instead of the designer of the questionnaire. A more appropriate perspective might be to speak of "questionnaire effects." This shift in perspective regarding the actual responsibility for the undesirable effect of a question on the ensuing interaction and the quality of the final data is not an ideological issue, but a very practical one.

In this book I will present a perspective that differs from what we usually find in the literature on survey methodology. Many of the problems that occur in survey interviews are related to the design of survey questions, which are frequently unfit for their purposes. When interviewers are supposed to read scripted questions, the designers of the questionnaire should take into account that the questions are meant for use in an interactional setting. The survey interview is a form of verbal interaction, and we should be aware of the fact that interaction participants are normatively oriented toward a specific set of rules. Although the survey interview differs from mundane conversation, I will show that the participants in survey interviews orient toward many of the same interaction rules as participants in conversation (see also Suchman and Jordan 1990a). For this reason questionnaires should be designed in a conversationally adequate way. That is, they should take conversational constraints into account. In order to be able to design questionnaires in a more conversationally adequate way, we need a thorough understanding of interaction and how it works, and how interactants use certain linguistic forms for specific interactional purposes.

Survey methodology, and especially questionnaire design, can benefit from conversation analysis. As will be discussed in chapter 2, conversation analysis is a relatively new field of research that takes naturally occurring interactions as its research object, both mundane conversations and interactions in various sorts of institutional or organizational settings.

Like medical consultations, police interrogations, psychotherapy sessions or classroom interactions, the survey interview can be investigated as a form of talk in its own right. We can study the survey interview as a "living questionnaire," as Michael Lynch referred to it during a workshop on interviewer–respondent interaction in 1995.

One could study the standardized survey interview and conclude that it does not work (e.g., Mishler 1986; Briggs 1986). This may be a justified conclusion. Conversation-analytic studies make visible the weak basis of the results of quantitative research. Nevertheless, I adopt a more pragmatic view and believe that modern society cannot and will not do away with this efficient and relatively inexpensive measurement instrument. We should therefore try to improve its quality.

Conversation-analytic research can be used as a diagnostic instrument for interactional problems in a specific set of interviews. Such problems frequently turn out to be clearly related to features of the scripted text that forms the basis of the interview interaction. Conversation-analytic research on survey interviews, therefore, will offer useful insights for improving the design of a questionnaire. On other occasions, it will become clear that standardized interviewing may put interviewers and respondents in a problematic situation that cannot be solved. This study may, for a part, be seen as a form of error analysis. It describes problematic instances in order to show the interactional principles that participants in the interview seem to be orienting toward, and how these interactional principles may cause problems for standardized survey interviewing.

When discussing the "standardized/non-standardized interviewing controversy," Beatty (1995: 154) suggests that Suchman and Jordan (1990a) present worst-case scenarios, "rambling, undirected interactions in which the interviewer follows no observable conventions for clarification of misunderstandings and keeping the respondent focused." He also says that "training interviewers to perform these tasks is essential for successful standardized interviewing," suggesting that the interviewers Suchman and Jordan present act so poorly because they are not trained properly.

In this study too, the reader may find what look like worst-case scenarios: ambiguously worded or structured questions, and interviewers who depart from the rules. However, both the questionnaires and the interviewers in this study are of average, or better than average, quality. These interviews were carried out by trained interviewers, and the questionnaires were designed by professionals in the field of social science research, who often work with universities and market research companies. Most of the research data collected from these interviews were statistically analyzed and published in books that are well respected in their fields. No one ever questioned the basis of the facts and figures presented in these publications.

There may well be a large gap between what is known in the field of survey methodology and what occurs in the everyday practice of survey research. As long as the quality of empirical research continues to be judged primarily by the quality of the statistical analyses performed on the output of standardized survey interviews, there is little reason for researchers to improve the quality of the data collection process. A possible criticism of qualitative studies of survey interviews such as the present one is that they discuss problems without quantifying the occurrence of these problems (Beatty 1995: 157–8). I will not make any claims to quantification either. Instead, my work may be considered a form of error analysis. I describe problematic instances in order to show how going against conversational principles may cause interactional problems, which in turn may cause interviewers to depart from the rules of standardized interviewing. My focus on problematic instances proves productive because conversational rules become most apparent when they are being violated.

Let me give one example. In a series of Dutch interviews the question occurs whether or not respondents have "completed" a certain level of education ("Have you completed this education you just mentioned?"). Respondents may say either "yes" or "no," and there seems to be no problem at all. However, one respondent answered this question by saying, "Yes. With certificate." Even though this happened only once in the series of about ten transcribed interviews, this instance is extremely relevant. This answer points out the ambiguity of the term "completed education." When these researchers talked about "having completed some school," they meant to imply that one got the certificate. But the term may not necessarily be interpreted by the respondents in this way. So, one such instance may be a reason for questionnaire designers to want to find out what people mean by "completing an education." And it seems to make sense to ask all respondents who say "yes" the follow-up question, "And did you or did you not get the certificate?"

This book is not a plea for abandoning standardized interviewing. Solutions should first be sought within the constraints of standardized methodology. Detailed conversation analytic study of actual survey interviews may provide insights for the improvement of questionnaire design in general. Conversation analysis may also be used as a diagnostic instrument for specific questionnaires. In that respect it may be viewed as an alternative to cognitive interviewing procedures, which ask respondents how they have interpreted certain questions or encourage respondents to think aloud while answering questions (Belson 1981; Studman et al. 1996; Willis and Schechter 1997). However, this study, as well as the numerous studies in question-wording effects, convinced me that not all problems can be solved within the constraints of standardized methodology. I therefore especially plea for "avoiding overzealous enforcement of the smallest letter of the law when clear answers are obtained through generally acceptable means," to use Beatty's words (1995: 166). In this book I attempt to make transparent the means interviewers employ to obtain recordable answers. I leave it to the reader to decide whether or not these are "generally acceptable means."

7   The data used in this book

The interview data in this book come from different sets of U.S., British, and Dutch interviews. The U.S. and Dutch questionnaires contain a few open questions, but consist mainly of closed questions. The British questionnaire contains only closed questions. In all cases, the interviewers were neither the designers of the questionnaires nor the researchers. They were hired for the interviewing job only.

The fragments presented in the book contain the following identification headings: USA CATI; USA CATI, Wisconsin; Schober and Conrad 1997; Adult Education CATI; Culture P&P Survey; Literacy Survey; Dutch CATI Survey, Van Gerven; Quality of Life Interview; and Conversation. Below I give information on the data.

The USA CATI is a U.S. computer-assisted national opinion telephone survey on various topics. The questionnaire was designed by Nora Cate Schaeffer from the University of Wisconsin. The interviews were performed by interviewers trained in applying the rules for standardized interviewing. They worked from the University of Wisconsin's survey research center with monitoring facilities. The USA CATI fragments used in this book are taken partly from a set of interviews that were recorded and transcribed for the "Workshop on Interviewer-Respondent Interaction in the Standardized Survey Interview" that was held in Amsterdam in 1995. These fragments are referred to as USA CATI, Wisconsin. Other USA CATI fragments are taken from papers by Schaeffer and Maynard. In the headings of these fragments it says, for example, USA CATI, (Maynard and Schaeffer 1996: 36).

Other U.S. fragments concern telephone paper-and-pencil survey data that are referred to as "Schober and Conrad 1997." These fragments are taken from a paper by Michael Schober and Frederick Conrad (1997) that reports on a laboratory experiment in standardized versus flexible interviewing. The interviewers were professional Census Bureau interviewers.

The Adult Education CATI is a Dutch computer-assisted telephone survey interview on respondents' possible interest in adult education. The interviews were carried out at a leading Dutch survey research center. The interviewers were instructed to use standardized interviewing techniques and were monitored. The written questionnaire was designed by the sociologists Willem Houtkoop and Charles Felix. An employee of the survey research center adapted the written questionnaire for CATI-use.

The Culture P&P Survey is a Dutch paper-and-pencil telephone interview, examining the influence of people's upbringing on their present participation in cultural life. The respondents were asked questions about their own cultural interests and activities, as well as those of their family members. The interviews were carried out by telephone from the interviewers' private homes. The interviewers were trained, although perhaps less than those who carried out the other Dutch sets of interviews.

The Literacy Survey is a Dutch face-to-face, paper-and-pencil survey. The respondents were adults who took a basic course in literacy. This set of interviews is primarily used in chapter 7, and further details will be given in that chapter.

The fragments labeled "Dutch CATI Survey, van Gerven" come from a nationwide survey carried out by one of the leading Dutch survey research centers. The interviews were recorded for a quantitative analysis of the effects of different forms of introductions to survey interviews on response rates (Houtkoop-Steenstra and Van den Bergh forthcoming). Daniëlle van Gerven transcribed some of these introductions.

Chapter 8 is devoted to the British face-to-face, paper-and-pencil Quality of Life Interview. As the cover sheet of the questionnaire makes clear, this questionnaire is meant for interviews with people with learning disabilities. Further details of these data will be found in chapter 8.

In the review of conversation analysis in chapter 2, I present several fragments of American, British, and Dutch mundane telephone calls. These conversational fragments are labeled "Conversation," followed by the name of the person who collected and/or published the fragment. The fragments of the Dutch conversations and survey interviews are reproduced only in translation. It should be stressed, however, that the data were analyzed before they were translated.

All data presented here are transcribed according to the conventions used in conversation analysis and developed by Gail Jefferson. These conventions are explained in the glossary of transcript symbols.

The fact that this book focuses on American, British, and Dutch interview data might suggest cultural or national comparisons as a research topic. However, I want to stress that this is not the case. It will become clear in this book that the American interviewers presented here seem to follow the rules for standardized interviewing more strictly than the Dutch interviewers. For the time being, I assume that this is the case because the USA CATI data were generated in a more interviewer-controlled setting than the Dutch data. Whereas the focus of the Dutch interviews was the gathering of information from the respondents, the American interviews were also strictly monitored for methodology research purposes.

2   Interviewer–respondent interaction

1   Introduction

When an interviewer and a respondent are engaged in a survey interview, they are performing communicative actions. The interviewer asks a question, and sometimes presents the answering categories, by reading the questionnaire. The question is answered by the respondent, and the interviewer acknowledges that the answer has been received. This results in the following action sequence:

Interviewer: asks a question
Respondent: answers the question
Interviewer: accepts the answer

In survey methodology the question-answer-acceptance sequence is considered the "prototype sequence" (Schaeffer and Maynard 1996) or "norm sequence" (Van der Zouwen and Dijkstra 1995) in standardized survey interviews. Interviewer and respondent are considered as behaving "adequately" if they act according to the script; that is, if the interviewer reads the question (and response options) exactly as written, and the respondent provides an answer that matches the question or selects one of the presented answer categories.

Behavior coding studies of recorded survey interviews show that all participants often behave "inadequately." Interviewers rephrase questions, change the order of the questions, probe in a leading manner, fail to read the answer options, or read only parts of the questions (Smit 1995). Respondents, for their part, provide answers that do not match the options, say more than just "yes" or "no" in response to a yes–no question (Molenaar and Smit 1996), and behave in other "inadequate" ways.

When both interviewers and respondents behave inadequately from a stimulus-response perspective, they do not act in the way that the questionnaire designer expects. The dominant attitude in the present book is that so-called inadequate interviewer and respondent behavior is primarily an artefact of incorrect theoretical assumptions about the nature of conversational interaction. Interviewing and being interviewed means that participants perform an interactional task far more complex than the stimulus-response perspective on survey interviewing presupposes.

1.1   The survey interview as a speech exchange system

Suchman and Jordan (1990a), who studied recordings of survey interviews, show that survey participants rely heavily on a wealth of communicative resources that find their base in mundane conversation. Conversation is the most basic form of interaction with which individuals are familiar. In addition to conversation, other speech exchange systems or speech events (Hymes 1972) exist, such as doctor–patient interaction, classroom interaction, research interviewing, and the like. Whereas all these institutional speech exchange systems differ in some respects, they share most of their features with mundane conversation. The modifications of a few conversation characteristics alert participants to the fact that some form of interaction is being constituted as classroom interaction, interrogation, or research interviewing (Heritage 1984b: 239–240). In this book standardized survey interviewing is seen as a form of talk that is both similar to, and different from, conversation (cf. Suchman and Jordan 1990a; Schaeffer 1991a).

In this chapter I will discuss the regularities of mundane conversation. This discussion provides the theoretical basis for my description of the standardized survey interview and its relation to mundane conversation. This discussion also serves as a starting point for my analysis of the differences between conversation and the standardized survey interview, and what consequences these differences have for the survey interview interaction process.

2   Conversation Analysis[1]

Conversation Analysis (CA) is deeply rooted in ethnomethodology, a research tradition within sociology developed in the sixties by Harold Garfinkel. Ethnomethodology views social acts not as manifestations of fixed social structures, but as the results of human action (including linguistic action) and interaction, that is, as "social accomplishments." In Garfinkel's words, ethnomethodology studies "the rational properties of indexical expressions and other practical actions as contingent ongoing accomplishments of organized artful practices of everyday life" (1967b: 11). These practices are also called "methods" or "procedures." The focus of ethnomethodology is on the methods people use in order to make sense of other people's behavior, and to render their own behavior understandable to others. CA is more specifically concerned with the methodical construction of social action in and through talk-in-interaction (Schegloff 1987).

Heritage and Atkinson (1984: 1) regard the basic goal of CA research as "the description and explication of the competencies that ordinary speakers use and rely on in participating in intelligible, socially organized interaction. At its most basic, this objective is one of describing the procedures by which conversationalists produce their own behavior and understand and deal with the behavior of others." The analyses of large collections of mundane conversations exhibit order, and they do so because mundane conversations are methodically produced by participants for one another. Conversationalists have a set of methods at hand which they apply for solving conversational problems. Conversing is not a mechanistic and determined business, however. A conversation is not determined by structural provisions only, but also by what conversationalists do with them.

Studies of conversations between different people with various kinds of relationships and backgrounds show that these conversations overwhelmingly exhibit the same basic patterns of openings and closings, of how topics are developed, changed and closed, of how stories and jokes are initiated, told and terminated, and of how compliments and invitations are accepted or rejected, for example.

CA studies demonstrate that conversationalists are normatively oriented to such regularities. This becomes exceptionally clear from the analysis of what may look like deviant cases or counterexamples. For example, if a question goes unanswered, this is not an instance that calls into question the fact that conversationalists are normatively oriented toward questions receiving answers. Instead, CA uses such instances to show that the answer is "noticeably" or "observably absent" (Sacks 1992a: 97), which becomes clear when the questioner repeats the question.

The premise of CA is that ordinary conversation incorporates the broadest range of possible resources for interaction. Institutional forms of interaction, for example classroom interaction or research interviewing, are characterized by particular limitations, modifications, or extra constraints. Most types of institutional interactions differ from ordinary conversation (see Zimmerman and Boden 1991, Drew and Heritage 1992) on the following points:

- Institutional interaction is, to different degrees, agenda-based.
- Topics are pre-specified.
- The length of the interaction is more or less fixed.
- The interaction is often organized in terms of question–answer sequences.

- The institutional identities are given as well as who will do what. The agent of the institution asks the questions, the client (or lay person) answers them.

For example, a telephone survey interview is based on a written questionnaire that sets the agenda for the interaction. It takes about 25 minutes, and the topic is local politics. The interviewer asks the questions, and the respondent answers them. I will discuss the differences between mundane conversation and institutional interaction in more detail at the end of this chapter.

2.1   The need for natural research data

CA avoids the use of research data generated by experimental methodologies that involve manipulation of behavior. It makes use of neither introspection nor interviewing techniques. Such techniques involve processes in which the specific details of naturally situated interactional conduct are irretrievably lost, and replaced by idealizations about interaction and its working (Heritage 1984b: 236).

One reason for using actual interaction is that there is "more out there than we can imagine," as Sacks says:

We will be using observation as a basis for theorizing. Thus we can start with things that are not currently imaginable, by showing that they happened. We can then come to see that a base for using close looking at the world for theorizing about it is that from close looking at the world we can find things that we could not, by imagination, assert were there. We would not know that they were "typical". Indeed, we might not have noticed that they happen. (Sacks 1984: 25)

Since it is very difficult to specify in advance the relevant aspects of the interaction, and since research shows time and again that very small details may have an interactional function, interactions are transcribed in great detail. We could compare it to biologists studying interaction between animals in their natural habitat. Primatologists make video recordings of animal behavior and play the tapes at low speed over and again. Only then will they discover how and under what conditions the one animal moves its fore paws, and how this effects the behavior of the other animal.

2.2   Meaning and interpretation

Speakers do not usually state explicitly what they mean when they say something. Talk receives its meaning from the context in which it is produced, among other things. That is, meanings are "indexical." Let me illustrate the indexicality of meaning by giving an example.

The meaning of the personal pronoun "we" can only be established in its context. Interviewers use "we" (or "us") with different meanings. It may refer to "you and I" (e.g., in "Okay, let's get started"), or to "we, the research group" ("We'd like to ask you"). It is left to the respondent to look at the context and construct a plausible interpretation of "we." Interpretations are not definite. Later occurring talk may provide reasons to change the initial interpretation.

A complicating factor is that context is not an unambiguous framework for interpretation. What the context is indeed depends on the meaning and interpretation of the talk. One needs to understand first that "let's get started" is meant to say "let's get started with the interview," in order to understand that "us" refers to "you and me." In this way, context and meaning each provide grounds for the other. This is referred to as "reflexivity."

The interpretative context for an utterance consists of several aspects, including:

• What was said so far (the sequential or conversational context).
• The ethnographical particulars of the speaker. If we know that the speaker who says, "We went to New York for the weekend" is married, we may interpret his "we" as the speaker and his wife. But if this speaker is homosexual, the pronoun "we" may be the speaker and his male partner.
• The relationship between the participants.
• The social context or setting. The interpretation of "Do you smoke?" in a survey interview differs from that in a medical interview.

Traditionally, the survey interview tends to be seen as a single social context or setting. But as we will see in the next chapter, the survey interview appears to consist of different settings. Here the interviewer not only interacts with the respondent, she also "interacts" with the questionnaire. Chapter 3 will discuss the standardized survey interview as a document-based form of interaction, that is, a form of talk embedded in the framework of a written text.

Context is not a stable and fixed entity. The particulars that make up the context are assembled by the hearer in order to decide the specific meaning of the talk, and anything can be used as part of the contextual particular. A methodic consequence of the context-sensitivity of the meaning and interpretation of talk is that it does not suffice to study isolated question–answer sequences, as is sometimes found in behavior-coding studies. CA studies examine larger fragments of conversation that contain the instance-to-be-described. Thus, the analyst provides the context he or she thinks is relevant for the conversationalists; the particular fragment is the analyst's interpretation of what is relevant for the conversationalists' interpretation of the utterance under discussion.

3   The sequential organization of conversation

What participants in standardized interviews do and say is highly pre-organized by the questionnaire and the rules for standardized interviewing. This is quite different from ordinary conversation, in which who says what and when is locally and collaboratively organized by the participants themselves (Sacks et al. 1974). Detailed analysis of standardized survey interviews, however, shows that they too are characterized by a high degree of local and collaborative organization by the participants. This organization by participants is partly due to the fact that it is impossible to totally direct respondents in the way they act. Another reason is that in some respects, questionnaires are not designed for the fluent and flawless interaction that the quest for standardization requires.

An utterance occurs within a sequence of other utterances. It often follows a prior utterance, and is followed itself by a next utterance. This next-positionedness of utterances has a large influence on how they are produced and interpreted. Speakers design their utterances so that they fit the immediately preceding talk. For example, an answer is designed in relation to the preceding question. When a speaker asks, "How many children do you have?" the answer can be formulated as succinctly as "three." This "three" may be interpreted as "I have three children," since it was produced in response to that question.

Talk is also designed in such a way that it fits what speakers expect will be said next, either by themselves or their co-participants. The two utterances "Do you like X?" and "You like X, right?" differ because the speaker displays a different expectation as to how the recipient will respond. Speakers design their talk for their specific recipients, which is known as recipient design. When designing their talk, speakers take into account what they know that their recipients know, and what they believe are the recipients' needs. When the speaker knows or believes that the recipient knows who the speaker's friend Maud is, she will refer to her friend simply as "Maud," rather than "this friend of mine."

3.1   Adjacency pairs

Many conversational actions come in "adjacency pairs," for example, question and answer, request and acceptance, greeting and return greeting. An adjacency pair is characterized by Schegloff and Sacks (1973) as a sequence of two actions or utterances that form the first pair part and second pair part of a sequence. The two parts of the sequence are adjacently positioned and produced by different speakers. The production of a first pair part, for example a question or an invitation, by a first speaker makes the production of the type-connected second pair part (the answer, the acceptance) by a second speaker expected, or "conditionally relevant" (Schegloff 1972: 364). Worded differently, a first pair part projects a type-connected second pair part as the relevant next action. This phenomenon is referred to as "sequential implicativeness." According to Schegloff and Sacks, "Given the recognizable production of a first pair part, on its first possible completion its speaker should stop and a next speaker should start and produce a second part from the pair type the first pair part is recognizably a member of" (1973: 296). On first possible completion of the utterance, "Do you have the time, please?" the next speaker is expected to take the floor and produce the requested answer. Before answering the question, he may request more information. In that way a second pair part can be postponed by an "insertion sequence." But once this information has been given, the second speaker is still expected to answer the initial question.

The fact that a recipient is expected to produce the second pair part of an adjacency pair makes it possible to observe when this second pair part is absent. It is not "just not there," but absent in a non-trivial way; it is observably absent. When an answer is absent, the questioner will try to learn the reasons for this absence, for example, the recipient did not hear the question, did not understand it, or found it to be a delicate question. Depending on the questioner's "candidate analysis" of the possible problem, he or she will present a "candidate solution" (Pomerantz 1988). For example, the questioner may ask the question again in a louder voice, rephrase the question, explain the reason for asking the question, or just leave it at that and change the topic.

As we will see, survey interviewers sometimes treat respondents' "don't know" answers as absent answers. Rather than accepting a "don't know" as an appropriate response to the question and moving on to the next question, interviewers may provide a candidate analysis of the reason why the respondent did not answer.

3.2   Displaying understanding of the prior talk

Due to the sequential organization and the next-positionedness of utterances, speakers display their understanding of the prior talk in their own, next-positioned turn. They display this not only to their co-participants, but also to the analysts of the talk.

Suppose speaker 1 says, "Do you have a watch on you?" and speaker 2 says, "It's four." In his response speaker 2 displays a variety of understandings.

- Speaker 1 has completed his turn at talk.
- He (speaker 2) is the addressee.
- He is expected to respond to the prior utterance.

• Although the prior utterance is formatted as a yes–no question, he (speaker 2) interprets it as a request to tell the time.

When speaker 1 takes the next turn and says "Thanks," he displays that speaker 2 provided the sort of information solicited in the first turn.

One problem in survey interviews is that they usually contain many yes–no questions. All that respondents need to know in order to provide a recordable answer is that the prior utterance is a yes–no question and that a "yes" or a "no" will suffice as an answer. As long as respondents are not given the opportunity to elaborate on their yes–no answers, the interviewer has no way of knowing if the question has been understood. The Dutch interviews show many examples of respondents revising their yes–no answers after the interviewer further explains the question once the initial yes–no answer has been provided. As a consequence this means that the use of yes–no questions in survey interviews poses an inherent threat to the validity of the responses (Suchman and Jordan 1990a).

A second turn displays the recipient's understanding (or misunderstanding) of the first turn. When a speaker finds that the recipient is misunderstanding the first turn, the speaker can use his next turn to remedy the trouble. This "next-turn repair" will be discussed at the end of this section.

3.3   Receipting the answer

An adjacency pair may be followed by a third turn. This "third turn option" (Heritage 1984b: 257) is reserved for the producer of the first pair part. It provides the first speaker with the possibility of displaying his reception of the response to the first turn.

A question–answer sequence is an action structure built of sequence positions. Each position provides a slot for a turn in which an action can be performed. The third slot is for the receipt of the response.

Turn 1 position: Speaker 1: question
Turn 2 position: Speaker 2: response
Turn 3 position: Speaker 1: receipt of response

Different types of receipt tokens exist, each type performing a different operation on the second turn. The first speaker may display that he is surprised at the second speaker's response, or that he would like to hear more, or that enough information has been given. I will briefly discuss acknowledgment tokens, (partial) repeats, assessments, "oh"-receipts, and formulations, and I will show what interactional work these receipt tokens do. I will also discuss how survey interviewers restrict themselves regarding the types of receipt tokens they use, in this way displaying their neutrality towards respondents' answers.

Acknowledgment tokens are items like "okay," "right," and "I see." The speaker does not provide any evaluation of the prior talk.

(1)   USA CATI, Maynard and Schaeffer 1997: 59
       1 I.   and (.) we're doing a national (0.4) public
       2   opinion study?
       3   (0.5)
       4 R.   oh no I don- I'm not interested
       5 I. → OH: okay =
       6 R.   = thank you
       7 I.   alright⌈bye bye⌉
       8 R.   ⌊bye bye⌋

An acknowledgment token can also signal the satisfactory termination of the prior sequence (Jefferson 1972: 317) and pave the way for the initiation of another action. It is therefore closure implicative, as Jefferson phrases it. Indeed, we usually find interviewers producing a further question right after an acknowledgment token.

Unlike acknowledgments, assessments evaluate the information that is provided in the prior talk. They usually contain contrast-class terms, such as good/bad, right/wrong, true/false, and the like (Frankel 1984). For example,

(2)   Conversation, Jefferson 1984c: 196
       1 G.   I'm gonna do some spaghetti an:d (.)
       2   n-eh::m meatballs for tea for this lot now,
       3 L. → oh lovely.

Although assessments do occur in standardized survey interviews, they are rare. This infrequent occurrence of interviewers' assessments is consistent with the rules for standardized interviewing, which say that interviewers should not show their evaluation of respondents' answers. From an interactional point of view, interviewers, by refraining from assessments, also display to the respondents that they only "collect" the requested information.

Another way of displaying the reception of the answer is by fully or partially repeating it. By repeating the answer speakers show that they heard the answer, but they do not give any indication whether or not they understood it. In mundane conversation displaying one's understanding of the prior talk is crucial for its further continuation. The fact that repeats display only a proper hearing of the prior talk and not necessarily a proper understanding may explain why they are not a preferred practice in mundane conversation. However, repeats are extremely common in research interviews, for example,

(3)   Schober and Conrad 1997: 592
    1   I.   how many people ((pause)) live in this house.
    2   R.   three.
    3   I.   → three.
    4   okay, ((continues))

This fragment tells us more about the nature of the interactional work that interviewers do, as well as the specific type of interaction that is standardized survey interviewing. The progress of standardized interviewing is, to some degree, pre-organized by the questionnaire. In principle it is not relevant for the interviewers to really understand the information they receive. All they need to understand is whether or not the respondent's talk is an appropriate response to the question, and its appropriateness is dictated by the response categories in the questionnaire. Answer repeats give the analysts of interviews the opportunity to learn what may be recorded as the answer. As will be discussed in more detail in chapter 6, these repeats also suggest that interviewers sometimes transform a respondent's answer into an answer that better matches the pre-coded response options.

We find partial answer repeats especially when interviewers copy down the answer, rather than just ticking off a box. For example,

(4)   Adult Education CATI 85
    1   I.   how did you kno̲w about that course?
    2   how did you learn about it. =
    3   R.   = u:h from a u:h so:cial uh worker with us.
    4   I.   social work. =
    5   R.   = yes. =
    6   I.   → °°so-ci-al wo:rk°° ((at dictation speed))

By repeating the answer in this way, the interviewer shows the respondent that he is temporarily engaged in a non-conversational activity. In survey interviews carried out by telephone, respondents cannot see that the interviewer has to write, causing a short timeout for the interaction. By repeating respondents' answers, interviewers also fill up the silence while they are writing.

A speaker may also use the third-turn option to produce an "oh"-receipt. Heritage refers to an "oh"-receipt as a "change-of-state token." The speaker demonstrates that "he or she has undergone some kind of change in his or her locally current state of knowledge, information, orientation or awareness," Heritage writes (1984a: 299). He states that "oh"-receipts often follow the response to a request for clarification. In the telephone call fragment below, speaker M's "oh" displays he has been informed by the clarification he requested.

(5)   Conversation, Houtkoop-Steenstra 1987: 174
        1   F.   hey, will you be coming too?
        2   M.   where?
        3   F.   here.
        4   M. →   oh.
        5   that's all right.

"Oh"-receipts in survey interviews are primarily produced by respondents. They use them especially after receiving a response to their request for clarification. For example,

(6)   Culture P&P Survey 23A
        1   I.   what is your civil status.
        2   R.   what do you mean?
        3   I.   are you single, or marr↑ied or living togeth↑er
        4   R. →   oh.
        5   R.   no single.

"Oh"-receipts are hardly ever found in standardized survey interviewers' talk. By refraining from "oh"-receipts, interviewers display their position in the interaction as persons who collect information on behalf of someone else. Interviewers do not speak for themselves, nor do they collect information for themselves. They are neutral intermediaries between researcher and respondent. Thus, they rarely display any change in their state of information or awareness.[2]

The sequential environment where we do find interviewers producing "oh"-receipts is in the introductory phase of the interview when the candidate respondent declines the request for the interview. In their paper on declinations of the request to participate in a telephone survey interview, Maynard and Schaeffer (1997) provide several fragments where the declination or the account for the declination is receipted with "Oh: okay." In these instances interviewers do display that they have undergone some change in their orientation.

A further way of displaying the receipt of the answer is to formulate co-participant's talk. Garfinkel and Sacks (1970: 350) describe a formulation as the following:

A member may treat some part of the conversation as an occasion to describe that conversation, to explain it, or characterize it, or explicate, or translate, or summarize, or furnish the gist of it, or take note from its accordance with rules, or remark on its departure from rules. That is to say, a member may use some part of the conversation as an occasion to formulate the conversation.

Heritage and Watson (1979) show that formulations play a role in the topical organization of the conversation. A speaker's formulation of the gist of the prior talk may function as the result of the co-participants' negotiation about what that gist is. When the co-participant accepts this agreed gist, the formulation completes the current topic.

Given the fact that respondents in standardized interviews are expected to select one of the response options read to them, one would not expect formulations to occur in these data, but they often do. Below, a Dutch survey interviewer reads a statement on modern art. The respondent is requested to agree or to disagree. Rather than saying "agree" or "disagree," the respondent expresses his attitude towards modern art. The interviewer then formulates this talk as, "So: u::h you agr<u>ee</u>, say." When the respondent accepts this formulation, the interviewer proceeds to her next statement.

(7)   Culture P&P Survey 26A
```
      1   I.      I'm n<u>o</u>t interested in modern art because most
      2           often you can't see what it's supposed to m<u>ea</u>n.
      3           (1.0)
      4   R.      w<u>e</u>ll, I think (.) well, I d<u>o</u> think, modern
      5           art (.) if modern art is <u>a</u>rt indeed
      6           (. . .)
      7   I.      hahahah.
      8   R.      yeah, cause I mean, in that case everybody
      9           can make something,
     10           (0.5)
     11           I think. in that case uh <u>e</u>verybody makes art.
     12   I.  →   so: u::h you agr<u>ee</u>, say.
     13   R.      yes.
     14   I.      ((next statement))
```

Chapter 6 will discuss in more detail how interviewers formulate respondents' unrecordable answers such that they will match the pre-coded response options.

Acknowledgments, assessments, repeats, and formulations accepted by the respondent propose to terminate the prior talk or sequence. "Okay" is perhaps the clearest example of a form of receipt that indicates that the prior speaker has said enough (Beach 1993). This holds true for both Dutch and American conversations. In the interview data we usually find the interviewer moving on to the next question after having receipted the prior response.

3.4   Withholding third-turn receipt

The fact that recipients display their reception and understanding of the prior talk through the third-turn receipt has its implications when such an action is absent. Rather than receipting the prior talk upon the turn's completion, a recipient may keep silent or produce a continuer ("hm mm"). The prior speaker analyzes the absence of a receipt as an indication that the recipient evaluates the answer as unclear, not yet complete, or inappropriate. The prior speaker may then take the next turn in which she or he attempts to deal with the possible problem. When the invitation in the fragment below gets no response, the speaker takes the next turn and adds something to her invitation:

(8)   Conversation, Davidson 1984: 150
         1   S.   well yih c'n both sta:y.
         2   (0.4)
         3   S. → got plenty a´ roo:m

I will show that interviewers make heavy use of this device when respondents' answers are not fit to record. Let me give one example here. After the respondent has said that he works with an "insurance company", the interview proceeds as follows:

(9)   USA CATI, Schaeffer and Maynard 1996:73
         1   I.   and what kind of business or industry is this? =
         2   R.   = the insurance industry
         3   (7.0) ((typing))
         4   I.   is this business or organization mainly
         5   manufacturing retail trade wholeta-
         6   wholesale trade or something else?
         7   (1.0)
         8   R.   it's a service industry
         9   →   (1.8)
         10 I.   so it'd be under::?

When the respondent does not choose one of the response options that are presented to him, the interviewer keeps silent for 1.8 seconds (line 9). When this pause does not generate a recordable answer, the interviewer prompts, "so it'd be under::?" (line 10).

4   Repair

When a speaker of a first pair part observes that the second speaker did not treat the first turn as intended, the first speaker may use the third turn option to initiate repair. Schegloff (1992) provides an account of the forms that such third position repairs recurrently take in conversation. The repairs are constructed out of four main types of components.
• The A component (generally "no," or "no no") initiates the repair.
• The B component is the agreement/acceptance component. This occurs primarily when the first turn is treated as a complaint.

- The C component is the rejection component, by which the speaker overtly rejects the understanding of the first turn.
- The D component is the repair proper that carries out some operation on a prior turn, so as to address its problematic understanding.

This last component, the repair proper can adopt the following forms:

- Repeating the turn that caused the trouble more clearly, for example pronouncing it louder or enunciating more.
- Using a repair marker ("I mean") followed by a contrast with the understanding of the prior turn. This is the most common form Schegloff found in his data.
- Reformulating the trouble source turn. The same is said in different words, again framed by "I mean."
- Specifying the first turn. Rather than producing the same more clearly or in different words, the speaker introduces candidate specifics included within the earlier formulation of the trouble source.

Schegloff provides the following example that occurs in an American radio call-in:

(10)   Radio Call-in, Schegloff 1992: 1313 (C = caller, H = host)

1	C.	I have fears a'driving over a bridge.	
2		((pause))	
3	C.	a:nd uh seems I uh- just can't	
4		uh (sit)- if I hevuh haftu cross	
5		a bridge I jus', don't (goan' make-	
6		uh- do the) trip at all.	
7	H.	whaddiyuh afraid of.	TROUBLE SOURCE
8	C	I dun'kno:w, see uh	
9	H.	well I mean watam'n.	REPAIR MARKER
10		wat amn' what kind of fear izzit	REFORMULATION
11		'r you afraid yer gunnuh drive	CAND. ANSWER I
12		off the e:dge?	
13		'r afraid thet uh yer gonnuh	CAND. ANSWER 2
14		get hit while yer on it? =	
15	H. →	= what	
16	C. →	= off the edge 't somethin	

When the caller begins his answering turn with "I dun' kno:w, see uh" (line 8), the host initiates repair. He does so with an "I mean," followed by a reformulation, "what kind of fear izzit" (line 10) and offers two candidate answers: "'r you afraid yer gunnuh drive off the e:dge? 'r afraid thet uh yer gonnuh get hit while yer on it?" (lines 11–14). Next, the caller takes the turn and answers the question.

When the Dutch survey interviewers employ third-turn repair, they prototypically use the repair proper, and do so by means of specification. Standardized interviews contain mainly closed questions, consisting of the question proper, followed by its response options, from which respondents are expected to choose. These response options are not always read aloud, with the effect that respondents may not know how to answer the question. They keep silent or say they do not know the answer. When this happens, interviewers frequently take the next turn and present candidate answers. In doing so, they repair the troublesome question. In other words they are clearer about the type of answer expected. For example,

(11)   Culture P&P Survey 12
        1   I.   with whom did you <u>go</u> to your first concert.
        2   (2.3)
        3   R.   >I don't remember.<
        4   I.   → ehm fr↑iends, sch↑ool,
        5   R.   just fri̲ends. (yes.)
        6   I.   °hm hm.°

When the respondent indicates that he does not know the answer (line 3), the interviewer presents the first two response options on the questionnaire. In doing so, she repairs the troublesome question so that the repair "is built to provide for an opportunity to respond to the trouble source, as it is newly understood," as Schegloff (1992: 1315) puts it. This way of dealing with respondents' problems in answering survey questions will be discussed in more detail in chapter 6.

Even when interviewers read response options, respondents frequently fail to provide answers that match the options. In such cases interviewers rarely employ third-position repair. Instead they choose one of the alternatives for repair described by Schegloff. He points out that, when a response turn (e.g., the answer) is understood as displaying a misunderstanding of its prior turn (the question), the questioner may decline to initiate repair of the misunderstood turn. He can treat the response turn as if it were sequentially appropriate and correct. The questioner may later redo the misunderstood talk of the trouble source as a new utterance. The first speaker thus may adopt non-repair ways of dealing with the misunderstanding.

When a respondent's answer is not formatted as requested, survey interviewers often treat the answer as if it were an appropriate answer and then produce a follow-up question. For example:

(12)   Culture P&P Survey 42b
        1   I.   I'll mention a list of: Amsterdam museums. =
        2   = could you i̲ndicate whi̲ch of these museums

```
3           you have ever visited, (.) a:nd how long
4           ago that was, the last time.
5  I.       the Van Goghmuseum?
6  R.       pf:::, that was when I was small.
7  I.   →   u:h fifteen?
8  R.       yes↑
```

Or the interviewer reformulates the answer so that it does not look like a correction:

```
(13)    Culture P&P Survey 23a
        1  I.       a:nd about how old were you when you for
        2           the first time visited a museum.
        3           (1.0)
        4  R.       well, that was primary school uh (1.2)
        5           right sixth grade or so (you know)
        6  I.   →   abou:t ten. say.
        7  R.       yes.
```

The interviewer treats the answer "well, that was primary school uh (1.2) right sixth grade or so (you know)" (lines 4–5) as an appropriate answer to the question "about how old were you." In mundane conversation this would be an appropriate answer. The interviewer, who needs to fill in the respondent's age, reformulates the answer in terms that match the requirements of the questionnaire, "abou:t ten. say." (line 6). This reformulating takes the form of a concluding statement, confirmed by the respondent.

In the USA CATI data we find a different way of dealing with this type of respondent's "misunderstanding":

```
(14)    USA CATI, Wisconsin AW-1:160
        1  I.       and how much have you heard or REA(GH)D about
        2           the issue: of federal agencies sharing
        3           information about individuals?
        4           .hh a gr⌈eat DEAL some not very much or
        5  R.                ⌊none
        6  I.       nothing at all?
        7  R.       none.
        8  I.   →   nothing at all?
        9           (1.0) ((typing))
        10 I.   →   would that be nothing at all?
        11 R.       YES
```

When the respondent says "none" (line 7), the interviewer initiates repair with "nothing at all?" (line 8). When the respondent does not respond to this obvious question, the interviewer becomes more explicit, asking, "would that be nothing at all?" What was the problem with the respondent's "none"? When the interviewer read the three response options, the respondent was supposed to understand that this contained two answer instructions: select one of the response options, and use exactly the same wording rather than synonyms or descriptions.

5   The preference organization of responses

Several types of adjacency pairs have two alternatives as their relevant responses. For example, an offer may either be accepted or declined. If we look at conversations, it becomes clear that the two types of responses are not of equal standing. One of them is preferred, the other dispreferred. For example, a request or an invitation generally invites acceptance as its preferred next action.

Recipients are normatively oriented to produce responses that will be in agreement with the projected response. Sacks (1987) and Pomerantz (1984a) show that even when recipients produce responses that are in disagreement with the prior utterance, they design their response turns so that they are structurally in agreement with the prior utterance. They may begin their response turn with an agreement component, adding disagreement components such as qualifications, exceptions, additions, and the like (Pomerantz 1984a: 74). The fragment below is an example:

(15)   Conversation, Pomerantz 1984a: 75
     1   R.   butchu admit he is having fun and
     2   you think it's funny.
     3   K.   I think it's funny, yeah.
     4   but it's a ridiculous funny.

Sacks relates the preference for agreement to the preference for contiguity, the preference for a response to start immediately after completion of the prior utterance.

When the response is in agreement with the first action's preference, it tends to occur immediately on or after the completion of the prior utterance. When the response is in disagreement, it tends to be produced noncontiguously, "it may well be pushed rather deep into the turn that it occupies" (Sacks 1987: 58). Preferred and dispreferred responses are put into so-called preferred and dispreferred action turn shapes (Pomerantz 1984a: 63).

Preferred actions are usually produced straight after completion of the prior turn, and without delay. Dispreferred actions have one or more of the following characteristics:

- Delay by pre-turn pauses.
- Delay by hesitations ("u:h," "we:ll").
- Delay by means of repair initiators ("What?").
- Prefacing by token agreements ("That's right, but . . .").
- Appreciations, in the case of offers and invitations ("I'd really love to come, but . . .").
- Apologies, in case of requests and invitations ("I'm terrible sorry, but . . .").

The following fragment contains several features of dispreferred turn shapes. Two friends Mick and Peter are on the phone, discussing Peter's new job:

(16)   Conversation, Houtkoop-Steenstra 1987: 173
       1   M. I think it'll be an incredibly,
       2   unbelievably tough job.
       3   (1.0)   PRE-TURN PAUSE
       4   P.   what? it's a?   REPAIR INITIATOR
       5   M.   an unbelievebly tough job.
       6   P.   we:ll nice, ⌈I think.   HESITATION
       7   M.   ⌊sure, very nice,   AGREEMENT TOKEN
       8   but uh with i:ncredibly many   QUALIFICATION
       9   hooks and eyes.

The fact that speakers orient toward the preference for agreement is very relevant in survey methodology. Interviewers who request a confirmation should be aware that the response may be put in a dispreferred turn format. Interviewers must carefully attend to what respondents do and how they structure their talk, paying close attention to possible dispreferred actions.

When the interviewer in the example below does not get an affirmation after her proposal that New Age music is a sort of house music in 0.4 of a second, she interprets this silence as having made a wrong assumption:

(17)   Culture P&P Survey 48a
       1   R.   I don't know about wha- what you make of
       2   it on categories, there's new age music.
       3   I.   that fits just (.) a bit into direction
       4   of hou:se and that sort of stuff doesn't it?
       5   →   (0.4)
       6   I. →   or does it.
       7   R.   no, no. that really is all uh very
       8   ⌈uh much exalted and uh idyllic and
       9   I.   ⌊totally different. yet.
      10   R.   harp and er I don't know.

Right after the interviewer's "or does it" (line 6), the respondent displays that the interviewer's initial assumption was incorrect indeed.

6   Turn construction and turn taking

Sacks, Schegloff, and Jefferson (1974) propose a model of how ordinary conversationalists construct turns and how they organize the allocation of turns. The end of a turn at talk may constitute a Transition Relevance Place (TRP). When a turn has reached a TRP, the roles of speaker and recipient change. After the interviewer asks a question, the turn goes to the respondent, who is expected to provide the answer. However trivial this observation may seem, most questionnaires do not take this rule for turn taking into account, thereby causing interactional problems in the interview.

Turns are built out of Turn Construction Units (TCUs): full sentences or single words like "what?" When speakers construct a TCU, they project where this TCU will end, and so they project the first possible TRP. Because of their linguistic knowledge, co-participants can predict when the current turn-in-progress will be completed and arrive at a possible TRP, where they may take a turn as the next speaker. For example, when a first speaker says, "How many children do you", the recipient will guess that the utterance only needs the verb "have" to be complete. Rather than waiting for the utterance to be complete, he or she may decide that the utterance is complete enough to respond, and may say "three," creating an overlap.

Note that an overlap differs from an interruption. The latter occurs when the next speaker starts a turn not at or near a TRP of the current turn. Unlike an overlap, an interruption is considered a violation of a current speaker's right to complete his or her turn.

Many of the respondents' interruptions in survey interviews are caused by the fact that the same list of response options may be read again and again. Once the respondents know that this list is going to follow the question, they do not necessarily wait for the interviewer to (fully) present it. This inherent redundancy of questionnaires thus creates what survey methodologists see as inadequate respondent behavior. From the perspective of mundane conversation however, these respondents just take the turn at or near a TRP.

As we know from CA research, speakers who want to take a multi-unit turn have ways to make clear to the recipient that the current TCU will be followed by more talk, for example, "which of the following options apply to you?" projects mentioning a number of options. In this way interviewers can make clear to their respondents in which stage of completion the current turn has reached (see Schegloff 1980, Houtkoop and Mazeland 1985, Ford and Thompson 1996).

7   The collaborative construction of talk

The traditional view of language production is that talk is produced by the speaker only. As it turns out, however, conversational talk tends to be constructed collaboratively. When a speaker is speaking, the recipient is not a passive participant waiting for the speaker to be finished. Recipients play a far more active role in the construction of the speaker's talk. Recipients do so to a great extent by using silences and continuers.

7.1   Continuers

While listening, recipients monitor the ongoing talk by both nodding and producing continuers. Continuers are "objects with which a recipient indicates that he sees that a prior speaker has more to say, and inviting him to go on with" (Jefferson 1981a: 60). Continuers often bridge the end of one TCU and the beginning of a next (Schegloff 1982, Goodwin 1986). The following is an example from the introduction to a Dutch survey interview:

```
(18)     Dutch CATI Survey, Van Gerven
    1   I.        your opinion is is important indeed because
    2             we want to form as clear as we can a picture
    3             of the Dutch consumer.
    4   R.  →    ye:s. =
    5   I.        = .hh we'd like to know for instance which
    6             programs you watch, and which not,
    7             .h u::h also of course why not.
    8   R.  →    hm⌈mm
    9   I.             ⌊mm.hh the interview will take about
   10             a quarter of an hour . . .
```

Continuers do not respond to the content of the talk. They primarily function in the organization of the turn. They also display the lack of any trouble in the understanding of what is being talked about.

A continuer can be used strategically in that its producer encourages the other speaker to elaborate, even though the latter seems to have completed his turn. Regarding survey interviews this means that an interviewer can employ a continuer when the response is not, or not yet, the one sought for. The interviewer may act as if she sees that the respondent is still in the process of producing his answer. In the fragment below the respondent is requested to mention the number of records, tapes, and cds she owns (line 1–2). When she does not provide a number but instead says, "Oh no idea! (2.2) I've got more cassette tapes" (line 5), the interviewer produces a continuer ("°yah°") (cf. Jefferson 1984a on misfitted passive recipiency). She then waits 1.2 seconds for the respondent to continue (line 7). When this does not happen, the interviewer asks, "you think over a hundr⬆ed or less." After the answer "<less>, less." (line 9), the interviewer produces another continuer, and next receives an answer she can record: "about thirty."

(19)   Culture P&P Survey 67a
    1   I.   a::nd how many records tapes cds have
    2   you got in tot⬆al.
    3   R.   ohm no idea!
    4   (2.2)
    5   I've got more cassette tapes.
    6   I.   °yah.°
    7   (1.2)
    8   You think over a hundr⬆ed or l⬆ess.
    9   R.   <less>, less.
    10 I.   °yah.°
    11 R.   about thirty
    12 I.   yah.
    13   ((next statement))

7.2   Volume

In the last fragment the two continuers (°yah°) in lines 6 and 10 are both produced low volume, whereas the "yah" in line 11, following the answer "about thirty" and preceding the next interview question, is produced with the average volume the interviewer generally uses in this interview. It often happens that conversationalists, including survey interviewers, lower their voices when they produce recipient talk, such as continuers (Houtkoop-Steenstra 1986, 1994; cf. Goldberg 1978). In shifting her volume from the soft "°yah°" to the louder "yah," the interviewer displays shifting from recipient to speaker.

7.3   Silences

As was pointed out in the review of third-turn receipts and of the preference for agreement, silences play an important role in interaction and should not be neglected in the analysis of survey interviews. When a conversationalist keeps silent, her or his co-participant can analyze this as a meaningful action. When a speaker has completed his turn and the recipient does not take a response turn, causing a silence to occur, the speaker may analyze the silence as a cue to continue talking. When interviewers keep silent after an answer, respondents usually take another turn in which they add more information to the initial answer or provide a revised answer. This happens in the last fragment above. It can also be seen in the fragment below.

(20)   Culture P&P Survey 23A
        I.   and what's your profession?
                (1.0)
        R.   well, I don't actually have a diplom↑a.
        → (1.4)
        → I don't have a steady profession.

Jefferson (1989) showed that in mundane Anglo-American and Dutch conversation, the standard maximum silence after which a speaker will resume talking is about 1.0 second. Looking at interview data it is clear that Jefferson's finding does not hold for survey interviews. As the data presented in this study show, pauses in survey interviews may be much longer. The fragment of an American CATI interview below shows several long pauses. In some cases the interviewer is working audibly on her keyboard, in other cases she may be heard waiting for the respondent to talk.

(21)   USA CATI, Schaeffer and Maynard 1996: 80
        1 R.   Jack's (.) Refrigeration
        2   →   (5.2) ((typing))
        3 I.   .hh what kind of business or industry is this?
        4   (0.6)
        5 R.   uh::: 's a refrigeration (.) company
        6   →   (1.6)
        7 I.   .hh would that be for retail sale wholesale
        8   or manufacturing?
        9   (0.8)
        10 R.   uh::: retail
        11 →   (4.0) ((typing))
        12 I.   and (.) what particular products do they sell
        13   would that be a refrigerator?
        14 R.   uh: n- air conditioning (.) uh
        15 →   (1.5)
        16   and refrigeration
        17   (0.7)

```
18          repair products
19      →   (13.5) ((typing))
20  I.      .hh alright and your believe you said
21          this (in-) uh (.) business organization
22          was mainly b- retail trade is that correct?
23      →   (1.2)
24  R.      uh retail and service
25          (0.7)
26  I.      alright
```

This fragment also shows that interviewers may use silences in a strategic way. When the interviewer asks what kind of business or industry Jack's refrigeration is, she gets the answer, "uh::: 's a refrigeration (.) company." (line 5). From the interviewer's perspective this is an inadequate reply. Had she presented the question as scripted, the respondent would have known that the response options to choose from are "mainly manufacturing, retail trade, wholesale trade, or something else." When the interviewer waits for 1.6 seconds (line 6) following the answer "Jack's (.) refrigeration," she seems to be giving the respondent the opportunity to extend his initial answer and present one of the pre-coded response options. When the respondent keeps quiet, the interviewer presents the response options to him.

Just like continuers, silences may be used as an alternative to an explicit request for more talk or a different answer. By employing a continuer or a silence after a respondent's answer, interviewers display that the respondent may give it another try. In that respect, producing continuers or silences after a non-recordable answer may be seen as what Schegloff (1992) refers to as a non-repair way of dealing with troubles.

8   Mundane conversation and institutional interaction

In mundane conversation both turn taking and turn construction are locally controlled by the participants. What the participants will talk about and how long the conversation will take is, by and large, not known beforehand. Institutional interactions differ in these respects. The turn-taking system in the courtroom (Atkinson and Drew 1979) differs systematically from the one in ordinary conversation. The same holds for interaction in the classroom (McHoul 1978), for news interviews (Greatbatch 1988, Heritage and Greatbatch 1991), as well as for research interviews, standardized or not.

These types of interactions are organized in terms of question–answer sequences. The questioning is done by the agent of the institution (e.g., judge, teacher, journalist, interviewer), and the answering is performed by the client (witness, student, interviewee, respondent). Institutional interactions may differ from one another with respect to what is done after producing the answer. While in classroom interaction answers are evaluated in terms of correctness (McHoul 1978, Mazeland 1995), in the courtroom they are evaluated in terms of truth (Lynch, fc). In research interviews answers are evaluated in terms of relevance and completeness (Mazeland 1992a), and subsequently recorded by the interviewer, who writes them down, ticks off a box on the paper questionnaire, or strikes a key.

One might say now that judges, teachers, interviewers, and their respective clients perform these subsequent actions because these are their prescribed tasks. However, as Drew and Sorjonen (1997) correctly observe:

> Even if the turn-taking system is pre-determined by an external prescriptive organization, nevertheless the task of analysis is to specify how it is locally managed, in ways which display the participants' orientation to what they should properly be doing in a setting, and hence to their institutional identities and roles. Thus we can view any specialized institutional turn-taking system as the product of participants' orientations to their task-related roles. (102–3)

Many forms of institutional talk are agenda-based. The agenda may be rather loose, as in doctor–patient interactions (Ten Have 1987), or rather strict. Meetings, for example, may have an agenda that informs the participants which topics will be addressed and the order in which they will be discussed (Boden 1994). Standardized and non-standardized research interviews are agenda based in a very strict and particular way, in that they are questionnaire based. This has some crucial consequences for the interaction. As in many other expert–lay interactions, there is an unequal distribution of knowledge of the agenda (cf. Beckman and Frankel 1984; Heritage 1995). The interviewer knows which questions are on the questionnaire, the order in which they will be presented, and the approximate time the interview will take to be completed. The respondent, on the other hand, usually has only very general knowledge of the topic. For example, the interview will be about "local politics," or "consumer goods," or "your personal situation." He may also be informed about how long the interview generally takes.

When it comes to standardized interviews, rather than asking questions, the interviewers read the questions as scripted on the questionnaire. Because the questions in standardized interviews are most often closed questions, the interviewers are also expected to read the list of response options. Although respondents may not realize it, they are not expected to answer survey questions as they answer questions in ordinary conversation. They are supposed to provide formatted answers (Schaeffer and Maynard 1996), or answers that are formulated so that they will match one of the response options on the questionnaire. When interviewers present the set of response options, respondents are supposed to make a choice. This is why survey methodology sometimes refers to closed questions as "fixed choice questions." However, the fact that the response options are read to respondents does not automatically make clear to the respondents that they are supposed to answer in this specific wording.

Most respondents do not know that the standardized interview is standardized to the extreme degree that it actually is. They may know that the topics to be discussed are pre-specified, but they may not be aware that they will need to provide information the interviewer already knows or answer questions that seem irrelevant. They might be aware that they should choose from a set of answers, but they may not realize that they have to uphold this requirement very strictly. In short, respondents are not aware of the interactional rules that guide the interview.

In chapter 4 we will see that survey interviewers tend to orient toward two different sets of interactional rules: conversational rules and the rules for standardized interviewing. Respondents, however, seem to primarily orient toward conversational rules, both in the production of their talk and in the way they try to make sense of the interviewer's talk.

3   Participant roles

1   Introduction

Survey methodology considers the standardized survey interview to be an interaction involving two participants: the interviewer and the respondent. Survey methodology then analyzes the utterances of these participants in terms of their functions in a question–answer sequence. We can see this approach at work when we study coding schemes for the analysis of verbal utterances in survey interviews, for example Dijkstra's elaborate and elegant coding scheme (forthcoming). According to Dijkstra: "Such an interaction sequence generally starts with the posing of a question from the questionnaire by the interviewer and ends at the moment the interviewer indicates that the question is sufficiently answered by the respondent, for example, by posing another question from the questionnaire." Dijkstra's coding scheme contains three possible actors, namely, the interviewer, the respondent, and a possible third party who actively participates in the interview, usually the respondent's spouse or child. The second variable in Dijkstra's model is the type of information exchange that occurs:

- A "question" is a request to the other person for information related to the questionnaire, for example, a request for information, a probe, a repeat of the question, or an elucidation.
- An "answer" is the requested information.
- A "repeat" is the repetition of an answer by the same speaker.
- "Perceived" is a remark indicating that an utterance is received and/or understood. It includes utterances like "hm mm," "fine," "OK," or "yes."
- A "request" is a request for repetition.
- A "comment" is a remark on former talk, for example, "Difficult question!"
- "Unintelligible" is an utterance that cannot be understood.
- A "detour" is an utterance that departs more or less from the main stream of information exchange, though it may be topically related to the interview, for example, when respondents ask what will be done with the information, or how many questions are left.

In this chapter I will argue that a standardized survey interview is more complex than a series of information exchange sequences, and it contains more parties than just the interviewer, the respondent, and a possible third party. Standardized survey interviews cannot simply be looked at in terms of oral communication. They are embedded in the context of a written text (the questionnaire) and the actions this text assigns. As I will demonstrate, interviewers may perform actions that are not included in Dijkstra's coding model, and these actions are related to the broader context in which the interview is carried out.

The main purpose of this chapter is to analyze a series of Dutch paper-and-pencil interviews in order to learn more about what standardized survey interview participants really do, and how their talk is to be interpreted. The questionnaire series discussed in this chapter contains mainly closed questions and pre-coded response options about the respondent's participation in cultural life, currently and as a child: visiting museums, reading art books and articles, watching televison art programs, listening to music, playing musical instruments, and the like. The interviewers have been informed about the research to the extent that they have a general idea about its purpose. They carry out the interviews by telephone from their private homes. Although they are trained in how to conduct a standardized interview, they apply the rules of standardized interviewing relatively flexibly.

The concepts of interviewer and respondent are "task-related" or "institutional concepts" (cf. Wilson 1985, Mazeland 1992). The interview participants have different tasks in the research data measurement procedure that is the survey interview. The interviewer reads the questions from the questionnaire, and the respondent provides the requested answers, after which the interviewer records these answers on the questionnaire.

If we want to analyze the survey interview as a form of conversation, we need to distinguish between different levels of analysis. Following Mazeland (1992), I specify three orders of participant identity. There are institutional or situation-specific identities, which in this case consist of interviewer and respondent. There are also the permanently shifting conversational identities of speaker and recipient, which exist on a local level. In addition, there are interactional identities, for example questioner and answerer (cf. Jefferson and Lee 1981, Mazeland 1992). When the interviewer is asking a question she is the current speaker, and the respondent is the recipient of the interviewer's talk. Upon completion of the question, the conversational and interactional roles change. The turn goes to the respondent who is expected to answer the question, and thus becomes the speaker. The interviewer, as a result, becomes the recipient of the answer.

In order to better understand what is going on in survey interactions, we need even more refined concepts than speaker/recipient and questioner/answerer. When people talk to each other, they have ideas about what they are doing. They may be joking, collaboratively solving a problem, seeking and providing help or information, or a number of other activities. Tannen and Wallat (1993: 59–60) refer to these participant definitions as "interactive frames." Interactive frames are related to the members' mental models for understanding situations, actors, and actions, known as knowledge schemes. Interactive frames and their related knowledge schemes provide participants with expectations of what may happen, and how actions and utterances will be interpreted (Goffman 1974). That is, they provide an interpretive frame.

Interactive frames are accomplished by the participants themselves. In the process of framing events, participants negotiate the alignments that constitute these events. Goffman refers to these alignments as "footing" (1981a). Footing is primarily effected through linguistic and paralinguistic cues and markers, as Goffman points out (1981a). For example, when someone makes a pun in the course of the conversation, he or she may mark this talk as a pun by producing it with a different pitch and/or speech rate, with laugh particles, and/or by using a dialectic variation (cf. Gumperz 1982, Auer and Di Luzio 1992 on "contextualization cues"). Through the negotiation of alignments, participants may change or shift the interactive frame, and/or embed one interactive frame inside another. Goffman refers to this process as "footing shift" (1981a).

The survey interview is usually considered to occur within a single interactive frame, providing a relatively clear outline for the interpretation of the ongoing talk. This chapter will discuss the survey interview as a complex form of talk, consisting of alternating or embedded interactive frames. These different interactive frames are accomplished by the participants', especially the interviewers', shifts in footing.

Speakers in ordinary conversation generally speak for themselves, and design and vocalize their own text. As pointed out by Ten Have (1995c) and Mazeland (1995), this is not the case for survey interviewers. They speak on behalf of someone else and read a questionnaire aloud. The interviewer is "the sounding box from which the utterances come," as Goffman says, the "animator" (1981b: 226). Clark uses the term "vocalizer" to refer to someone performing a similar function (1996: 20). Rather than using Goffman's notion of animator, Levinson (1988) distinguishes between "relayer" and "spokesperson."[1] Whereas a relayer reads a text designed by others (172), a spokesperson speaks for the author of the text (166). As we will see, this distinction proves useful for the description of the interviewer's participant roles in the standardized survey interview.

Behind the interviewer is a person who has written the questions for the interviewer to read. This may be the researcher or someone who designed the questionnaire for the researcher. In Goffman's terms, the designer of the questionnaire is the "author" of the talk, "the agent who puts together, composes, or scripts the lines that are uttered" (1981b, 226). Clark uses the phrase "formulator" to refer to this agent (1996: 20). Using Goffman's terms, the questionnaire designer is also the "principal," the party "to whose position, stand, and belief the words attest" (226). For the sake of clarity, I list below the labels used for the various production roles of interviewer and questionnaire designer:

Goffman	Clark	Levinson
principal		
author	formulator	
animator	vocalizer	relayer and spokesperson

In survey methodology interviewers are considered either animators/vocalizers or relayers of the scripted questions only. They are not the ones responsible for the text, and the meaning that is at issue is not their meaning. Interviewers do not mean anything, they merely relay the author's text to the respondents.

In section 2, I will first show how interviewers make clear to respondents that the assigned role of interviewer is that of relayer. Then I will show that interviewers do not restrict themselves to this role. In section 3, I will discuss the interviewers' roles accomplished during their task of entering the respondents' answers on the questionnaire. In section 4 the focus is on reception roles, that is, the roles of the parties that are recipients of the talk. It will become clear that more recipients exist than only interviewer and respondent.

2   Interviewers' production roles

2.1   The interviewer as relayer of questions

In Levinson's terms, interviewers take the role of relayers when they ask the scripted question and declare not to be responsible for the question. When respondents request clarification of the question, interviewers may indicate that they merely read the questions. The two fragments below come from a series of related questions that ask whether the respondents like to listen to various sorts of music "not at all, a little or very much". When it comes to "hardrock, punk, house," several respondents have difficulty with considering this as one category. When the respondent below asks whether these three go together, the interviewer refers to the questionnaire:

(1)   Culture P&P Survey 12B: 201
         1 I.   hardrock punk ↑ho̲u̲se
         2   (1.5)
         3 R.   uhm do these three belong together? =
         4 I. →   = yes, it says here o̲ne: category.

In the next fragment we see how another interviewer explicitly distances herself from the responsibility for this odd category.

(2)   Culture P&P Survey 23A: 230
         1   I.   u:h hardrock punk house and the l↑ike
         2   R.   oh. ju̲st ho̲u̲se.
         3   I.   that- yes according to me they should change
         4   this divi̲sion, because a lot of people don't
         5   like hardrock at a̲ll, but they do quite like
         6   ho̲u̲se a lot. =
         7   R.   = yes house and hardrock you can't compare. ( )
         8   I.   no̲. as one can se̲e now.
         9   well fortunately I didn't design thi(h)s
         10   que(h)stionnai(h)re, so(h).
         11   they can't ho(h)ld i(h)t against me̲.

By saying "according to me they should change this divi̲sion," (lines 3–4) the interviewer reveals that other people ("they") are responsible for the questionnaire and its categories. Later on she becomes explicit about who is responsible, when she says, "well fortunately I didn't design thi(h)s que(h)stionnai(h)re, so(h). they can't ho(h)ld i(h)t against me̲" (lines 9–11).

When respondents display that they think they are being asked odd or redundant questions, the interviewer may refer to the technical requirements of the interviewing processes, as happens in the following American CATI interview. After the respondent is asked where she works, she replies:

(3)   USA CATI, Schaeffer and Maynard 1996: 80
         1   R.   children's hospital
         2   (6.8)
         3   I.   what kind of business or industry i̲s this
         4   (1.2)
         5   R.   it's a it's a hospital eh heh heh =
         6   I. → = uhkay I have to ask the question
         7   as ⌈they⌉ come up on the screen
         8   R.   ⌊( )⌋

```
 9   R.      tha(h)t's fine.
10   I.      uhkay:
```

When the interviewer inquires as to what kind of business or industry a children's hospital is, the respondent says, "it's a hospital" after which she laughs, "eh heh heh" (line 5). This laughter may well be about the fact that the interviewer asks a rather self-evident question here. The interviewer joins in with the laughter and accounts for this question by referring to the technical requirements and the interviewing rules she has to follow.

2.2   Interviewers as spokespersons for the researcher

Interviewers may also take the role of spokespersons for the designer of the questionnaire/researcher when they engage in explaining and clarifying the scripted questions to the respondents. After the interviewer informs the respondent of fragment 1 that the questionnaire contains only one category for hardrock, punk, and house, she explains what "they" mean by this:

```
(4)      Culture P&P Survey 12B
         1   I.      hardrock punk ↑house
         2           (1.5)
         3   R.      uhm do these three belong together? =
         4   I.      = yes, it says here one: category.
         5      →    what they mean is uh >let's say<
         6           specialisms within the pop music.
         7   R.      °I see°
         8           ye:s, I do like to listen to that.
```

Whatever the researcher/designer may have meant by making hardrock, punk, and house one category of music, this explanation creates an answer that is at least potentially invalid.

   In the next fragment, the interviewer finds herself confronted with a situation that the researcher/designer has not foreseen. The questionnaire contains a large number of questions that inquire whether the respondents "listen to particular types of music not at all, a bit or very much." The current respondent turns out to be a sound engineer, and he therefore listens to various types of music, whether he likes it or not.

```
(5)      Culture P&P Survey 26a
         1   I.      I mention a number of types of music,
         2           could you tell if you not at ↑all listen
```

```
3            to it, a ↑bit or very much so with pleasure. =
4            (. . .)
5   I.       music↑al
6   R.       and well I do uh yes, I myself am a sound
7            engineer and uh I work a lot with sound,
8            and uh then uh I do musicals too. so.
9            (.)
10           I actually do listen indeed but⌈ ( )
11  I.  →                                   ⌊okay fine,
12      →    but out of any free will. it's about when
13      →    you do it yourself and with pleasure.
```

In saying "I actually do listen indeed but (   )" (line 10), this respondent seems to imply that he listens to musicals for professional reasons only. He does not listen to them privately for his own amusement. Next the interviewer speaks on behalf of the researchers when she explains what is meant by "listening." Rather than saying, "I mean," she explains what the question she relays to the respondent refers to by saying, "it's about when you do it yourself and with pleasure" (lines 12–13).

When we look at the way the interviewers make use of personal pronouns, we can see that they usually present themselves as a member of the research group. Most often they use the organizational pronoun "we" (Sacks 1992a: 713), for example:

(6)   Culture P&P Survey 32b
        1   I.   u:hm no that's all we need to know.

Whether the interviewer is responsible for the research project or whether she merely speaks on behalf of the researcher usually becomes clear when problems arise with the scripted questions. As we have seen in fragment (2), the interviewer may then shift the responsibility from "we" to "they." In fragment (3) she implicitly distances herself from the responsibility for the problematic category by referring to what is written on the questionnaire. She implies that she is not the person who wrote this questionnaire; she just reads it.

In the following fragment a respondent wants to know why "you guys" only ask a few questions about the theaters that he visited (lines 1–3). He thereby suggests that the interviewer is responsible for the content of the questionnaire. The interviewer distances herself from this suggestion of responsibility when she explains why she "thinks" that "they" proceed this way. She ends her explanation with a very explicit account of her role in the research process in lines 13–15: "I I haven't drawn this up. I ju(h)st ca(h)rry this ou(h)t, nothing m(h)ore."

(7)   Culture P&P Survey 26a
   1 R.   I thought I'll ask after all. what few
   2   theatres you guys mention by the way (0.9)
   3   that I have been to.
   4 I.   yes. yes ⌈I-
   5 R.   ⌊there have been ple:nty of course
   6   ⌈where I've been to.
   7 I.   ⌊yes: I I think that it also uh particularly
   8   it concentrates this investigation on these
   9   lessons at school. so I think that they
 10   particularly uh put things down where they
 11   uh have gone to with that school.
 12   (...)
 13 I.   I don't know ei:ther. I I haven't drawn
 14   this up. I ju(h)st ca(h)rry this
 15   ou(h)t, nothing m(h)ore.
 16 R.   no:, yes: no: you're right.

2.3   Interviewers as principals and authors

Sometimes interviewers speak for themselves. A recurrent sequential context in which they do so is after respondents report something noteworthy, as in the next two fragments.

(8)   Culture P&P Survey 32ba
   1 I.   next we'll come to any possible brother
   2   or sister, have you got any?
   3 R.   yes, one brother.
   4 I.   how old is he at this moment.
   5 R.   he turned uh thirty this week.
   6 I. → congratulations

(9)   Culture P&P Survey 71a
   1 I.   HAVE you any brothers or sisters?
   2 R.   u:h I have one sister °still°,
   3 I.   a sister and ⌈
   4 R.   ⌊>I had a brother but he died.
   5 I. → °ah° my condolences, sorry. .hhh

Reportings of birthdays and deaths are usually met with assessments. Assessments are also provided when respondents report other special or extreme facts, especially if these facts are presented as being special or extreme, as in the fragment below. In response to the question regarding whether he watches art programs on television, the respondent states that he is "awfully" busy and that he works "thirteen to fourteen hours a day." (line 6). The interviewer then provides an assessment in line 7 by saying, "you didn't."

(10)   Culture P&P Survey 63B
        1   I.   do you watch arts on television?
        2   R.   .hh uhm to uh be honest I am awfully uh
        3   b↑usy it now now it is, this is it really (.)
        4   the second week that I'm a bit (.) quieter,
        5   putting it like that. you see I worked uh
        6   f- (.) thirteen to fourteen hours a day. =
        7   I. → = you didn't.

As will be discussed in chapter 7, interviewers are expected to be friendly towards respondents (Fowler and Mangione 1990). They accomplish this by providing assessments when the situation seems appropriate. When interviewers provide assessments, they speak for themselves. As assessments are not, and cannot be, scripted, the interviewer is both author and principal of the assessments.

3   Interviewers as spokespersons for respondents

Interviewers not only speak for the researcher/designer of the question-naire, but also for the respondent. After the respondent has answered a question, the interviewer must record it. We may consider a questionnaire a written document consisting of two parts. One part is the set of ques-tions to be read by the interviewer, which may contain the response options. For example, question 16 of the culture survey reads, "Do you possess reproductions of works of art, and if so, how many do you have?" The other part of the questionnaire consists of a registration form, that contains the set of pre-coded responses for the interviewer to mark off. The set of responses to question 16 is:

    1. no
    2. 1 or 2
    3. 3 to 5
    4. 5 to 10
    5. 10 to 50
    6. more than 50

When questions are open-ended the interviewer is supposed to copy down the answer on an open space on the questionnaire.

The written questionnaire as a whole constitutes the input for, as well as the output of, the interaction (cf. Smith and Whalen 1995, Whalen 1995). On the level of the questionnaire are scripted questions and pre-coded responses. On the interactional level are the interviewers' questions and the respondents' answers. The respondents' answers to the interviewers' questions are recorded as responses to the questionnaire's questions. In this perspective respondents do not provide responses but answers. The interviewer transforms the interactionally generated answers into written responses. In the same way the interviewer talks the written questions into being. By using sound, prosody, intonation contours, volume, accent, speech rate, and the like, and designing this for the recipient, the interviewer turns the written questions into interactional activities (cf. Lynch forthcoming).

Let us return to the transformation from answer to response. A respondent's answer may vary in the degree to which its formulation matches the corresponding scripted response option. In the case of a closed question, where not only the question but also the response options are read, a respondent may provide a formatted answer, that is, an answer that matches the read response options. In the case of a formatted answer the interviewer can simply relay it to the questionnaire. The respondent in the fragment below makes clear that he understands the interviewer's dual role as the presenter of the scripted questions and the collector of formatted responses.[2]

(11)   Culture P&P Survey 48
        1 I.   modern art I'm not interested in, because
        2   most often one cannot see what it is
        3   supposed to mean.
        4   (1.5)
        5 R.   u::hm (1.8) well, I don't agree with the
        6   first one, but I do agree with the second one,
        7   →   still just say that I don't a(h)gree.
        8 I.   do no(h)n't a(h)gree

The respondent makes clear that this statement about modern art consists of two parts. She disagrees with the first part and agrees with the second. She next displays that she knows the interviewer wants only one response to be entered on the form by saying, "still just say that I don't a(h)gree" (line 7).

Respondents frequently make clear that they are providing the interviewers with a response to be recorded. At the same time, they display or explicitly state that they are not quite sure about the truth of this response. In the next fragment, the respondent, who is being asked if he ever visited the NINT Museum, provides a formatted answer, adding that this is just a guess because "I really don't know."

(12)   Culture P&P Survey 81b

```
1  I.    the nint. =
2  R.    = but oo:ps gosh how- got me there.
3         year or: (.) about three?
4         I just guess you know. I really don't know. =
5  I.    = ye:s. maritime muse↑um
```

In adding that his answer is just a guess, the respondent distances himself from the truth of it. Respondents frequently provide a response that is formulated in Dutch as "doe maar X," which roughly translates as "just put down X." When a respondent says, "just put down X," he or she indicates that X is not quite correct, but good enough as a response to be recorded.

After the respondent below has been presented with a numerical question, he says in line 6, "make that also ten years." A little later on he says, "just put down no(h)" (line 12).

(13)   Culture P&P Survey 81a

```
 1  I.    Rembrandt h↑ouse.
 2  R.    uhm well that's been ten years ago
 3        (. . .)
 4  I.    Rijks museum? ((the Dutch National Gallery))
 5  R.    uhm gosh that's also a long time ago,
 6     →  make that also ten years.
 7  I.    also ten years.
 8        (. . .)
 9  I.    antiquities' r↑ooms. authentically furnished
10        old monuments.
11        (1.8)
12  R. →  just put down no(h)
```

Rather than providing true answers to the questions, he provides "responses" when he tells the interviewer what she can put down. A little later he indicates that his answer is either the "Tropical Museum" or the "Municipal Museum" (line 4) and that he leaves it to the interviewer to make a choice.

(14)   Culture P&P Survey 81a

```
1  I.    the last time that you went to a museum,
2        what kind of museum was it?
3  R.    uh let me think, what do I think?
```

4   uh well either the Tropical or the Municipal.
5   I.   myes:
6   R.   so you just check anything

It also happens that interviewers and respondents negotiate what should
be put down as a response. This happens especially in cases where
respondents are presented with a numerical question. When respondents
have difficulty in providing an exact number they give an approximation
in terms of round numbers, as happens below in line 4:

(15)   Culture P&P Survey 12a
    1   I.   about how old were you when you attended a
    2   classical concert for the first time.
    3   (3.2)
    4   R.   u:h between fifteen and twent↑y or s↑o.
    5   (0.9)
    6   I.   seventeen. ⌈ha ha.
    7   R.   ⌊yes.
    8   (1.8)
    9   °that's fine°

When the interviewer suggests that a number between fifteen and twenty
is seventeen (line 6), the respondent accepts this as an adequate response
by saying "°that's fine°" (line 9). The interviewer's short laughter in line 6
that follows her suggestion of "seventeen" supports the assumption that
she is well aware she is illegitimately constructing an exact number here.[3]

The striking detail about approximate numbers is that they turn out to
be culturally specific. In Dutch interviews we often find "about ten." In
American interviews, however, we find as an approximate number "a
dozen." Although there is no reason to assume that the approximate
number "a dozen" is used by respondents to represent more than "about
ten," this difference in language use has an effect on what is recorded on
the questionnaire. Whereas Dutch interviewers treat the answer "about
ten" as ten, American interviewers take "a dozen" to mean twelve and
"half a dozen" to mean six. It goes without saying that such approximate
numbers end up as exact numbers in the final statistics.

A respondent may provide an answer that does not match the formulation of the response options, but is close enough to be treated as if it were
formatted. For example, a respondent may say "none," whereas "nothing
at all" is a possible response. In such a case we may speak of a "near-formatted answer." The interviewer may translate this near-formatted answer
into a provided response category. In the first fragment below the answer
"seldom" (line 7) is translated into the response option "occasionally." In

the second fragment, the answer "no occupation" is translated into ""°housewife°.""

(16)   Culture P&P Survey 12a

    1 I.   and next I like to know if you ne̲ver,
    2   occa̲sionally, or re̲gularly joined. =
    3 R.   = yes.
    4 I.   the school paper?
    5 R.   uhm y↑es
    6 I.   was this regular⌈1↑y or occa̲sionally.
    7 R. →   ⌊no, no, se̲ldom.
    8 I. →   °so occa̲sionally.°
    9 R.   uh yes.

(17)   Culture P&P Survey 12a

    1 I.   and how about your moth↑er
    2 R. →   uh no occupa̲tion
    3 I. →   °housewife°

Respondents also provide "unformatted answers"; rather than wording the answer in terms of the response categories, they provide talk that must be translated in order to fit into one of the response options. Schaeffer and Maynard (1996) refer to such answers as "descriptive answers." If an answer is unformatted, the rules of standardized interviewing require that the interviewer probe for a formatted answer. This means that interviewers must speak for themselves, since the questionnaire does not contain such probes. As we will see in more detail in chapter 6, interviewers may also choose to speak for the respondent and record the descriptive answer in what they believe to be the matching response category.

4   Reception roles

So far we have discussed the production roles of the different actors in the survey process. In the present section the focus is on reception roles. In "participant reception roles" the respondent is the recipient of the interviewer's question and the interviewer is the recipient of the respondent's answer. These roles seem obvious with regard to the standardized interview interaction, but "non-participant recipients" are also involved in the interview. Although the interviewer is a recipient of the respondent's answer, the ultimate recipient is the written form, which is in turn received by researchers who will further process the data gathered in the interview.

In addition, ratified overhearers (Goffman 1981a) of the interview may exist. Research interview centers usually have supervisors who may listen to telephone interviews and monitor that the interviewers are properly conducting the interview. Although the interviewers are usually not in the position to actually hear or see whether the monitor is listening in or not, they know it may happen. Depending on the monitor's ideas about how strictly the interviewers should follow the rules for standardized interviewing, we can expect monitored interviewers to be relatively more rule obedient. Kovar and Royston (1990) write that their observations of and conversations with interviewers of the National Health Interview make clear that interviewers who are observed by a monitor tend to apply the rules of the center more strictly.

It is likely, though difficult to prove, that interviewers who are monitored will perform certain activities that are at least partially meant to be overheard by the monitor. That is, while the addressee of the interviewer's talk is the respondent, the "targetted overhearer" of the talk (Levinson 1988: 173) is the monitor.

In the following fragment from an American CATI interview (Schaeffer and Maynard 1996), where the interviewer is monitored, we see that the interviewer presents the respondent with a question that is not only very hard for the respondent to answer, but also redundant regarding the context. After the respondent has said where he works, the following question plus its response options appear on the interviewer's screen:

> Is this business or organization mainly manufacturing, retail trade, wholesale trade, or something else?
> Manufacturing
> Retail trade
> Wholesale trade
> Something else
> [blind] Don't know
> [blind] Refused

Given that the respondent works for an insurance company, the interviewer could infer that the correct answer is "something else," but the rules of standardized interviewing require that she let the respondent give the answer. Schaeffer and Maynard (1996) show that respondents to whom the category "something else" applies feel that they are supposed to fill in this category with a specification, for example "service industry," as the following example illustrates:

(18)   USA CATI, Schaeffer and Maynard 1996: 73
        1   R.   insurance company
        2   (13.0) ((typing))

```
 3  I.    and what kind of business or industry is this? =
 4  R.    = the insurance industry
 5        (7.0) ((typing))
 6  I.    is this business or organization mainly
 7        manufacturing retail wholeta- wholesale trade
 8        or something else?
 9        (1.0)
10  R.    it's a service industry
11        (1.8)
12  I.    so it'd be under::?
13        (2.0) ((3rd voice whispers "something else"))
14  R.    well: it wouldn't- wouldn't be manufacturing
15        or retail or
16        (0.9)
17  R.    or anything like that it's:
18        (0.7)
19        I don't know how- I don't know what you'd (.)
20        classify it =
21  I.    = under something else =
22  R.    = yeah:
23        (1.0)
24  I.    and what kind of work do you usually do at
25        this job that (.) what is your occupation.
```

It is clear that the respondent does not realize he is supposed to say "something else." He fills in this broad category with "a service industry" (line 10). The interviewer pursues a formatted response when she asks in line 12 "so it'd be under::?" Someone in the interview center, most likely the monitor, then whispers to the interviewer "something else." Rather than using this information and asking "would this be under something else?" the interviewer lets the respondent continue to search for the appropriate answer. He then says which of the categories presented do not apply. When he finally says in line 19–20, "I don't know how- I don't know what you'd (.) classify it," the interviewer makes clear that she knows the answer already: "under something else."

In a series of monitored USA CATI interviews, we find cases where the interviewers, after receiving an unformatted answer, seem to record the answer on the form. They then proceed with the interview and verify the answer. For example in line 9 below:

(19)   USA CATI, Wisconsin AW-1
```
 1  I.    how many days of last week did you
 2        feel BOthered by things that usually
```

```
 3              don't BOTHer you?
 4              (2.1)
 5   R.         uh::m (2.6) I really didn't.        UNFORMATTED
                                                    ANSWER
 6   I.         .hhh okay N⌐O?
 7                         ⌊#                       RECORDING RESPONSE
 8              (.)
 9   I.    →    no days?                            VERIFYING RESPONSE
10              (0.4)
11   R.         no days
12   I.         ↑okay good ↑week
```

In cases like this one, the interviewer seems to participate in two activities at the same time. After the respondents' unformatted answer, the interviewers deal with the registration form and enter the response. At the same time they verify the correctness of the recorded response. When we schematize the last fragment we get the following:

    I.   asks question
    R.   provides unformatted answer
    I.   accepts answer
         ENTERS TRANSLATED ANSWER/RESPONSE ON
         FORM
         verifies translation of answer
    R.   confirms verification
    I.   receipts confirmation

In fact this is a very time-effective way of operating. In most (if not all) cases respondents agree with interviewers' translation of their unformatted answers. And just in case the respondent indicates that the interviewer was mistaken, the interviewer can correct her entry.

The presence of ratified overhearers impacts on interviewers and respondents differently. Interviewers must complete interviews and do so by following certain standards if they wish to keep their jobs. Respondents do not have such worries. Even if they realize that they are being requested to provide pre-formulated answers, they may not see any reasons to restrict themselves to these requested formulations. They are in a power position. They know they can stop the interview at any moment.

Ratified or unratified overhearers may also be present for the respondent, usually the respondent's partner or child. In survey methodology literature, these overhearers are sometimes referred to as "third parties present," who may influence the respondent's answers. As the data used here do not document whether or not third parties are present, we will not discuss them here.

5   The survey interview as a complex interactive frame

Interviewers and respondents may take different participant roles in the interview. This is partly due to the fact that a standardized survey interview is composed of a series of "text-to-talk-to-text" sequences, with the text highly regulating the talk. Smith and Whalen (1995) speak of "regulatory texts," or texts that regulate the production of other texts.

When it comes to standardized interviews, two different written texts exist, which both have an influence on what will occur in the interview and how it will be accomplished. First we have the scripted question (plus its response options) and the interaction that follows. Whereas the respondent deals with the interviewer only, the interviewer deals with both the respondent and the scripted question. Since the question is designed by someone other than the interviewer, she is often not in the position to explain the intended meaning of the question. If the rules of standardized interviewing are to be followed strictly, all that the interviewer is allowed to do after the respondent asks for a question clarification is to read the question again.

The other written text that plays a role in the actual interview is the registration form that contains a set of response options to each question. This form is often the source of the seemingly odd and redundant sequences that result from the answers the respondent provides. The respondent may not realize that the interviewer is not allowed to accept answers that do not match the scripted response options on her form. The respondent also may not know that the interviewer's talk could be oriented to a targetted overhearing monitor.

The standardized survey interview thus can be seen as a complex interactive frame, consisting of a number of embedded or alternating interactive frames. This holds especially true for the interviewer. While in most cases the respondent interacts with the interviewer only, the interviewer interacts with more parties than just the respondent.

An interviewer may present some text, for example the response options, for no other reason than that they are on the questionnaire. The rules of standardized interviewing may require her to read these response options, regardless of the respondent's need to hear them. Furthermore, an interviewer may reject a conversationally appropriate answer to some question for no other reason than that this answer does not match the scripted response categories. When the interview is held at a survey center, an interviewer may also have to interact with a monitor who is listening in on the interview.

Since each answer has to be recorded immediately after its production, answers are followed by an interviewer's activity on her keyboard or on the written questionnaire. While the interviewer enters the answer, or just before, she often repeats or reformulates it. These answer repeats and reformulations are often produced with a low volume, which signals that they are not meant for the respondent, for example in fragment 17 where "no job" is softly reformulated as "°housewife°."

Sometimes interviewers explictly announce that they will temporarily step out of the interaction. This happens in lines 1–2 of the fragment below. While entering the text, interviewers often work aloud for a period of time, as in lines 10–11 and 13–14 below. Note that after the interviewer announces that she will put a note in her computer she works silently for 2.5 seconds. The respondent begins to talk then, which results in a brief interaction in lines 4–8. The interviewer markedly returns to her work on the keyboard in line 9, and she then works aloud for some time. She begins this activity by saying, "okay so you" in line 9, by which she makes the respondent the ratified overhearer of her writing activity. Note that the respondent keeps silent while the interviewer says in a dictating voice, ".hhh okay so you got pai:d but (.) di:d (.) n:OT (.) WORK (0.6) beCAUse o:f summer:: V:CA::CAtion." The respondent also does not confirm this summary. She keeps silent until the interviewer has posed the next question. This fragment thus consists of alternating interactive frames.[4]

(20)   USA CATI, Wisconsin AW-1: 771

| 1 | I. | I'm just gunna (0.2) PUT a note | ANNOUNCEMENT |
| 2 | | in my computer to exPLAIN this: | OF TIME OUT |

| 3 | | ((2.5 seconds sound of typing)) | WORKING SILENTLY |

4	R.	I mean did a LOT uh work at ↑home	
5	I.	.hh⌈o↑kay	
6	R.	⌊huh huh	INTERACTION
7		(0.5)	
8	I.	I- we all DO °y'know°.	

9		.hhh Okay so you got pai:d	
10		⌈but (.) di:d (.) n:OT (.) WORK⌉	WORKING ALOUD
11		⌊s o u n d s o f t y p i n g⌋	

| 12 | | ((0.6 seconds of typing)) | WORKING SILENTLY |

| 13 | | ⌈beCAUse o:f summer::⌉ V:CA::CAtion | WORKING |
| 14 | | ⌊s o u n d s o f t y p i n g⌋ | ALOUD |

| 15 | | ((2.5 seconds of typing)) | WORKING SILENTLY |

16	.hh (0.2) ↑Oh kay(gh):::	CLOSING OFF
17	((0.8 second of typing))	WORKING SILENTLY

18	a(gh)::::nd i:s this: thee	RETURN TO INTERVIEW
19	uh(gh):: (0.4) uh >i this the	
20	number of hours that you usually work	

As this fragment makes clear, we would make a serious mistake if we were to treat all talk in an interview as part of an interaction between interviewer and respondent. What activity is being performed by some stretch of talk, and how it is interpreted, depends on the interactive frame in which it is produced. This fragment makes clear that coding schemes for interactional analyses have to take into account that not all talk is part of the interviewer–respondent interaction.

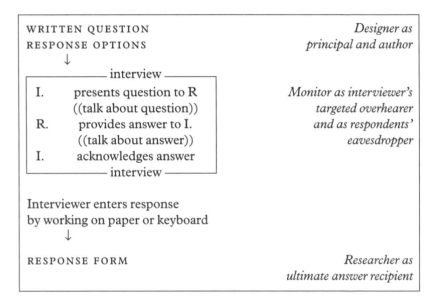

Let me make a last remark on the role of the interviewer according to survey methodology. One of the participant roles that an interviewer may take is that of the relayer of both the scripted question and the respondent's answer. When an interviewer acts as a relayer, no difference exists between the scripted question and the interviewer's question, and the answer is formulated by the respondent such that it will match one of the response categories.

For survey methodology, this is the ideal realization of the standardized survey interview. As is usually the case with ideals, everyday interview practice often does not live up to expectations. Departures from the ideal are primarily caused by respondents who do not always understand the scripted questions. When a respondent requests clarification of a question, the interviewer may decide to change her role from relayer to spokesperson and clarify what she thinks "they" mean.

Interviewers thus often play a role in connecting a respondent's understanding of a question with the reseacher's intended meaning of this question. Because all respondents are supposed to answer the same question as intended by the researcher, rather than the same question as written, interviewers play a crucial role in the stability of question meaning across individual respondents. As Suchman and Jordan (1990b) say, validity of inference about individuals is a prerequisite to comparison across groups of people. I agree with Suchman and Jordan (252), when they say that the interviewer should be:

in the position to facilitate negotiations effectively about the meaning of the question whenever necessity arises. We believe that the critical requirement for competent interviewing is not (only) knowledge of the correct stance to take towards the various systems of rules involved, but fully informed participation in the survey research process.

In terms of participation roles, this means that a competent interviewer should be allowed to act as a spokesperson for the researchers. In order to make this possible, interviewers should not only be trained in applying the rules for standardized interviewing, but they should also be informed about the research and the questionnaire to the extent that they are able to actually speak on behalf of the researcher when necessary. In addition to improving the validity of responses, this may also prevent interviewers from providing incorrect explanations. Even when interviewers are not supposed to discuss the questions, they will do so at times, and because they are often not informed about the questionnaire and the research, they run the risk of providing incorrect information. In the next chapters we will see examples of this.

Fienberg (1990: 242) quotes a psychologist, who attended a workshop on non-sampling error, as saying:

Look, the trouble is the whole interview situation. The statisticians simply don't understand the dynamics. What we need to do is have the interviewer talk with the respondent about events and issues relevant to completing the questionnaire and then say, "Now let's fill out the questionnaire together so that the people in Washington can get the answers to questions important for national health policy."

Statisticians may not be fully aware of the fact that interviewers, to a certain extent, already do it this way.[5] In the chapters to follow we will look at how they do this in more detail.

4   Recipient design

1   Introduction

This chapter examines how talk in standardized survey interviews differs
from talk in ordinary conversation, and how this departure may confuse
respondents. Section 4 provides an analysis of an extensive American
interview fragment that illustrates how the interviewer strictly follows the
rules of standardized survey interviewing and thus simultaneously disre-
gards the principles of ordinary conversation. Section 5 discusses some
interview fragments that show how interviewers try to follow the principles of ordinary conversation, thereby seemingly departing from the rules
of standardized interviewing. The two preceding sections provide the
theoretical basis for the analyses.

Although this book is written from a conversation analysis perspective,
in this chapter I also make use of the conversational maxims of the language philosopher Paul Grice. I chose to use Grice's maxims in this
chapter partly because these maxims are more specific than the related
CA concept of recipient design. Also, although recent survey methodology literature has come to refer to Grice, especially in its discussion of
context effect, I chose to make use of his work because I believe that he
has more to offer the field than is usually acknowledged.

In his Lecture Notes of 1971 (published in 1992), Harvey Sacks discusses the concept of "recipient design." This concept refers to the fact
that participants in ordinary conversation design their talk for its specific
recipients (Sacks 1992b: 438). Speakers are expected to orient toward
what they know their co-participants know (564). Consequently, this
means that "if you've already told something to someone then you
shouldn't tell it to them again" (438). This recipient design rule is similar
to the conversational maxims formulated by Paul Grice (1975).

Working in the tradition of ordinary language philosophy, Grice's
theory is one of speaker's meaning and recipient's interpretation procedures. Grice's purpose is to describe a type of meaning, or "implicature"
in his terms, that goes beyond the semantic meaning of the words uttered.

Speakers often do not explicitly say what they mean: for example, when joking or being ironic they may mean something entirely different than what they say. In fact, speakers hardly ever say exactly what they mean.

Grice explains how we manage to adequately understand the implied meaning, or the implicature, of such utterances. He distinguishes two types of implicature: "conventional implicature" and "conversational implicature." Conventional implicature is always conveyed, regardless of context. For example, the word "therefore" always has the same implicature. Conversational implicature, on the other hand, depends on the particular context of the utterance.

Grice says that in order to interpret conversational implicature, participants employ four conversational maxims to construct inferences about a speaker's meaning, the characteristics of the situation, and the immediate conversational context. His theory starts from the general "co-operative principle":

Make your contribution such as is required, at the stage at which it occurs, by the accepted purpose or direction of the talk exchange in which you are engaged.

This principle means that speakers are expected to design their talk to satisfy the accepted and immediate requirements of the current interaction. Speakers are expected by their recipients to follow four maxims and their sub-maxims. In Grice's words the "maxim of quantity" says, "Make your contribution as informative, and no more informative than is required (for the current purpose of the exchange)" The second part of this maxim means that a recipient will expect the speaker not to ask or say things he has already asked or said. The "maxim of quality" says, "Do not say what you believe is false, or for which you lack adequate evidence." The "maxim of relation," sometimes referred to as the maxim of relevance, calls for talk to be relevant. For example, when A asks B a question, A may expect B's talk following that question to be the response to that question. This maxim also requires that if the current topic of the conversation is pets, for example, a co-participant's next turn will also be about pets. If a co-participant wishes to talk about a different topic, he or she is expected to mark this new utterance as a topically unrelated utterance, for example by prefacing this utterance with a topic change marker. In survey interviews this is usually accomplished by the interviewer saying something similar to "the next question is . . .", or "we now want to . . ." Finally, Grice's "maxim of manner" says, "Avoid obscure expressions and ambiguity. Be brief and orderly".

Contrary to what the imperative formulation suggests, the maxims are not prescriptions for speakers. Recipients listening to the speaker are operating under the assumption that the speaker is co-operative and that he or she is observing the maxims, unless indications are to the contrary. When recipients are faced with an utterance that seems to fall short of meeting the requirements of the maxims, they will change the conventional interpretation of the utterance. So when a speaker says, "I called you a thousand times, but you didn't answer the phone," she will be seen as violating the maxim of quality. However, because the recipient considers the speaker to be co-operative, he will assume that the speaker means to imply that she called a large number of times.

Grice's implicature theory, with its conversational maxims, and Sacks' recipient design rules can both be used to describe the aspects of standardized survey interview interactions that differ from ordinary conversations. When Sacks and other conversation analysts speak of rules for recipient design (and other conversational rules), they are using "rules" in the sense of "principles" or "maxims." In order to construct a well-formed sentence, a speaker follows language-specific grammatical rules. Such rules are constitutive in character; they define what is a well-formed sentence. Conversational rules, or rather principles/maxims, are not constitutive in character, but regulative. They manage the conversation. Conversationalists follow conversational principles/maxims in various degrees. According to CA, conversationalists are normatively oriented toward these principles/maxims. I will therefore use the terms "conversational maxims," "principles," and "rules" interchangeably. (See Thomas 1995 on the status and characteristics of rules versus principles/maxims.)

I will first discuss the difference between survey interviews and conversations from the perspective of both Grice and Sacks. I will then turn to a number of actual survey interviews and show that the participants may, nevertheless, be following these conversational maxims under specific circumstances.

2   Survey interviews versus ordinary conversations

According to Sacks and Grice, conversation participants have, to some extent, a shared or common purpose. As Grice (1975: 45) says:

Our talk exchanges do not normally consist of a succession of disconnected remarks, and would not be rational if they did. They are characteristically, to some degree at least, cooperative efforts: and each participant recognizes in them, to some extent, a common purpose or set of purposes, or at least a mutually accepted direction.

In survey interviews, the purpose of the interaction is not quite the same for interviewers and respondents. They do share the purpose of collecting the information that the questionnaire seeks, however, on the local level of successive questions their purposes may differ.

Whereas a respondent may believe that he or she is to provide the information requested, the interviewer's local purpose may be to collect a response that matches one of the scripted response categories. For example, interviewers occasionally ask questions that require yes–no responses, but in ordinary conversations recipients tend to provide more than just a "yes" or "no" in response to yes–no questions, in the spirit of being co-operative. If someone is asked, "Do you have any children?" he or she may say, "Yes, three," or "Yes, two boys." Respondents, however, are not supposed to say more than "yes" or "no" in response to a yes–no question. As will be discussed below, respondents frequently do not formulate their answers the way the questionnaire designer had in mind.

Grice and Sacks refer to a type of interaction where co-participants speak for themselves. In survey interviews, however, only respondents speak for themselves. As discussed in chapter 3, interviewers usually speak for the researcher (Clark and Schober 1992: 26–7),[1] and the researcher's intentions and meanings are at issue. Whereas a conversation recipient may ask, "What do you mean?" such a question is, strictly speaking, irrelevant in a survey interview setting. Interviewers mean nothing; they merely read the questions. In addition, they are often trained not to provide the requested clarification. Clark and Schober (1992) state that interviewers and respondents understand these restrictions, and they recognize that an interviewer has little or no authority. This statement may not necessarily be true, however. Respondents do sometimes request clarification of questions, and interviewers sometimes provide explanations, as the next section will illustrate. Whether or not these clarifications coincide with the researcher's meaning is not always obvious.

Both Sacks and Grice talk about interactional situations where the participants have, or assume that they have, some degree of shared knowledge, also referred to as "common ground" (Clark 1992; Jucker and Smith 1996).[2] Common ground consists of the co-participants' shared knowledge, beliefs, and presuppositions. When the co-participants have the same cultural background, part of their common ground is based on culturally specific activities or "scripts" (Schank and Abelson 1977). For example, a culture may have the script that, when invited for dinner at someone's home, one should bring flowers for the host, and these flowers should be (or should not be) unwrapped before presenting. A substantial part of the co-participants' common ground usually consists of specific knowledge about one another's lives, circumstances, and attitudes. For example, co-participants could know one another's birthdays, marital status, religious denomination, level of education, and the like.

An important site for establishing common ground is the interaction between the parties. In the interaction process, the participants add to their common ground. What initially is exclusively participant A's or B's knowledge, also known as an "A-event" or a "B-event" (Labov and Fanshel 1977), becomes shared knowledge, or an "AB-event," once this information is shared with the co-participant. As soon as some piece of information is added to the common ground, the participants can treat this information as mutually known.

When a speaker is not sure if a recipient is knowledgeable about some fact, the speaker may present this fact with a "try-marker" (Sacks and Schegloff 1979: 18), for example, a rise in intonation. A try-marker tends to be followed by a brief pause that gives the recipient the opportunity to display his or her knowledge through such tokens as a nod, an "uh huh," or a "yeah." When the recipient displays that he or she is not already informed, the speaker will provide more information until the recipient displays that he or she is adequately informed. This process occurs twice in this fragment of a mundane conversation:

(1)   Conversation, Sacks and Schegloff 1979
                     (editing slightly changed)
     1   A.   ya still in the real estate business, Lawrence
     2   B.   wah e' uh no my dear heartuh ya know Max
     3   Rickler .h
     4   (0.5)
     5   uh whom I've been associated since I've
     6   been out here in Brentwood ⌈has had
     7   A.   ⌊yeah
     8   B.   a series of um – bad experiences uhh .hhh
     9   I guess he calls it a nervous breakdown .hhh
    10   A.   yeah.
    11   (. . .)
    12   B.   well I was the only one other than the uhm
    13   tch Fords?,
    14   uh Mrs. Holmes Ford?
    15   you know uh ⌈the the cellist?
    16   A.   ⌊oh yes. she's she's the cellist.
    17   B.   yes.
    18   A.   well she and her husband (. . .)

When A does not produce an acknowledgment in response to B's "ya know Max Rickler .h" in line 3, B provides more information about him. It is only after A displays knowledge of who Max Rickler is ("yeah" in line 7) that B tells what happened to Rickler. Also, it is only after A displays knowledge of who the Fords are by saying, "Oh yes, she's she's the cellist" in line 16, that B continues his reporting about the Fords.

The more knowledge conversationalists share, the less explicit they will be.[3] Thus, whether or not speakers can be seen as observing Grice's maxim of quantity is closely related to the information that is a part of the participants' common ground. The same holds true for Grice's maxim dealing with ambiguity and obscurity of expression. What may seem an ambiguous or unclear expression for an overhearer of a conversation may be perfectly clear to the conversationalists themselves.

Survey methodologists suppose that participants in standardized survey interviews communicate without the benefit of a common ground. As a result, questions are designed toward a degree of explicitness that hopefully guarantees that any respondent can grasp the meaning as intended by the researcher. Therefore, standardized survey interviews seem to be characterized by a preference for maximization instead of a preference for minimization. But, as we will see below, this preference for maximization also applies, at least at times, to the answering of survey questions.

Not only do interviewers speak on behalf of another, rather than for themselves, but they also speak in someone else's words. They are primarily oriented toward reading a text. This script is not designed for each individual respondent, but for a large anonymous group. The researcher may have some general knowledge of the respondent group, for example their age, sex, level of education, and the like, depending on the research sample. But whereas conversational talk is recipient designed, when interviewers are strictly following the rules of standardized survey interviewing their talk is audience designed.[4] In principle, interviewers only produce recipient designed talk when acknowledging the respondents' answers and when probing for an answer.

Sacks' principle that speakers are expected to design their talk with an orientation toward what they know their co-participants know (1992b: 564) does not hold true for standardized survey interviewers. The interviewer/researcher assumes certain knowledge on the part of the respondent, despite the fact that the respondent may not realize this. A respondent is expected to know that an interviewer merely reads someone else's script and that this script is not especially designed for him or her, but for a large number of respondents. Recipients are also supposed to know that the interviewer should act as if no common ground is being accumulated in the process of the interview. For example, when a respondent mentions "my wife," he should not expect the interviewer to act as if she knows from that point forward that he is married.

Interviewers do not observe Grice's maxim of relation or Sacks' maxim "If you've already told something to someone then you shouldn't tell it to them again." They must read whatever is written in the questionnaire, even when a respondent needs to hear only part of the question in order to understand what is meant. Interviewers may also repeat the same response categories over and over again. This repetition often leads to interruptions by respondents, who do not wait for this redundant talk to end.

Interviewers, furthermore, act as if respondents would not be oriented to this maxim. A respondent may be asked a question for which he has already provided the information. When this happens, he may get confused and believe that the interviewer must mean something other than she seems to mean.

As will be discussed below in this chapter, respondents again and again are confronted with interviewers flouting the maxim of quantity. Rather than acknowledging that this is what interviewers often do, respondents have trouble understanding what interviewers are up to when asking "known-answer questions" (Searle 1969) or "exam questions," meaning questions to which the answerer realizes the questioner already knows the answer. Respondents may first try to see the conversational implicature of a known-answer question, and if they fail to do so, they will decide that the interviewer did not follow the maxim of quantity. (See also chapter 6, "The changing meaning of redundant questions" in Schwartz 1996).

Respondents, furthermore, are sometimes requested to provide information they may not have at all. In other cases they may only have a vague knowledge of the topic at hand. As pointed out by other authors (e.g., Clark and Schober 1992), respondents tend to provide answers, whether or not they possess the required knowledge. Respondents, apparently following the maxim of quality (Do not say that for which you lack adequate evidence), frequently hedge their answers with expressions such as "I guess" or "probably." They also use vague quantifiers and approximate numbers like "a dozen" or "about five, say." We will see in chapter 5 that interviewers tend to reformulate vague answers to fit the response categories, which are usually formulated in exact terms.

Grice's maxim of manner says that a speaker should avoid using language that is unfamiliar to the recipient. Questionnaire designers solve this potential problem by providing an extended explanation of a concept. Even when specific respondents display that they know the meaning of the concept, the rules of standardized interviewing require that interviewers read the entire explanation.

The interviewer's purpose is to generate responses that will match the pre-coded response categories. One might think that this is a clear and easy task for respondents, since the response categories are usually presented to them. All they need to do is select one of the options and copy the wording. However, respondents often provide answers not formulated in the pre-scripted wording. They may say "not at all" where "no" or "zero" was expected, or they may provide a "descriptive answer" (Schaeffer and Maynard 1996; cf. Drew 1984 on "reportings"), that is, a description that could count as, for example, a "yes" or "no." If the interviewer asks, "Do you play any sports?" the respondent may say, "I play tennis," rather than "yes," or "I used to play tennis," rather than "no."

When respondents provide descriptive answers, interviewers must either translate the answer into the option that seems to match the answer or probe for an answer that will match the formulation of one of the pre-scripted options.

3   How conversational is standardized interviewing?

In the next two sections I will discuss some standardized interview fragments from the perspective discussed above. I will demonstrate that both interviewers and respondents, to a certain extent, are oriented toward conversational maxims and practices, such as the preference for recipient design and minimization.

Two sets of data will be discussed. In section 4 we examine a long fragment of an American CATI survey, where the interviewer follows the rules of standardized interviewing to a very high degree and also tends to refrain from following the conversational maxims. It will become clear that this may lead to several types of interactional problems.

In section 5, I will discuss fragments taken from a set of Dutch standardized interviews. These interviewers follow the interviewing rules less strictly. They seem to try and find a compromise between the rules of standardized interviewing on the one hand, and the maxims of ordinary conversation on the other.

Although American and Dutch interviewers may generally differ in the degree to which they standardize their interviewing practices, this possibility is not at issue here. Rather than comparing American and Dutch interviewers, the purpose is to compare interviewers who generally apply the rules for standardized interviewing more strictly and less strictly.

4   Redundant interview questions and their uptake

In this section I will discuss a long fragment that illustrates what may happen when interviewers do not follow the conversational maxims and when they refrain from recipient design. There are several indications that the respondent, a young man, expects the interviewer to follow the

maxims. The first impression we get from this fragment is that the interviewer does not follow the maxims at all, but it will become clear that she
follows two sets of rules. Sometimes she acts according to the rules of
standardized interviewing, yet in other cases she engages in recipient
design.

The fragment is part of a computer-assisted telephone interview. It will
be presented in parts (fragments 2a–2f), which will be discussed separ-
ately.

(2a)   USA CATI, Wisconsin AW2: 64, 795, 813
    1   I.   we need to select one adult to speak with in
    2   your household
                (. . .)
    3   how may WOMEN? eighteen or older >LIVE
                THERE<
    4   (0.8)
    5   R.   n:one
    6   I.   .hhh how many MEN eighteen or older live in
    7   your household
    8   R.   uh:: TWO
    9   I.   .hhh TWO okay we've randomly selected the
   10   YOUNger man of the household as the person we
   11   would like to ↑interview for our important
   12   national study. .hh is that you:?
   13   (0.6)
   14   is he home? =
   15   R.   = uh well it'd have to be me cause my
   16   roommate's currently in haiti.
   17   I.   .hhh oh K(H)AY-
   18   R.   = we're in the military so hh huh =
   19   ((INT asks permission to record the interview))
                (. . .)
   20   I.   oh kay a:::nd FIRST how many persons live in
   21   your household counting all adults AND children
   21   and yourself
   22   (0.5)
   23   R.   two
   24   I.   two

The interviewer knows by now that two males over eighteen years old live
in this household: the recipient and his roommate. They both work in the
military. No women of eighteen or older live there. The interview proceeds as follows:

(2b)   continued
        25   I.   .hhh how many persons live there who are NOT
        26   re↑lated to you?
        27   (1.3)
        28   R.   uh:: j'st- (0.3) ⌈MARK (.) with (uh) one
        29   I.   ⌊#
        30   okay j's:' your roommate ⌈.hhh a:nd
        31   R.   ⌊yeah

Despite the fact that the interviewer knows that only the respondent and
his roommate live in this household, she reads the scripted question,
".hhh how many persons live there who are NOT re↑lated to you?" (lines
25–6). It takes 1.3 seconds and an "uh::" before the respondent takes his
turn. As we have seen in chapter 2, pauses are often associated with problems. The delay in lines 27–8 may be explained by the fact that the
respondent knows that the interviewer has the requested information
already. He then repeats, "j'st- (0.3) Mark" (line 28). This descriptive
answer to a question that literally asks for a number is a conversational
way of dealing with questions. The respondent now continues his turn
and provides an answer that meets the requirements of the interview: "(.)
with (uh) one.".

When the respondent mentions Mark, he demonstrates to the interviewer that he expects her to take into account what he told her before.
The formulation "Mark" is an example of what Sacks and Schegloff
(1979: 16) refer to as a "recognitional." Recognitionals are recipient-
designed forms of reference to persons. They invite and allow the recipient to identify the person who is being referred to. In Sacks' Lecture
Notes (1992b: 445–6) recognitionals are called "type 1 identification
selections." "Nonrecognitionals," or "type 2 identifications," on the other
hand, are identifications that a speaker uses to indicate that the recipient
should not employ them to attempt to identify who is being referred to,
for example, "a guy," "someone," "a friend of mine." Sacks and Schegloff
say that, on occasions when reference is to be made, it should preferably
be done with a recognitional. This is exactly what the respondent does.
The interviewer, although she acted as if she had no information about
the number of people living in the household, now demonstrates she
knows who Mark is.[5] When she acknowledges the answer, she displays
that she recognizes Mark as "your roommate" (line 30). In doing so she
demonstrates to the respondent that she does make inferences, just like
ordinary conversationalists do.

Given that the respondent has said that this household consists of only
him and Mark two times by this point, and also given that the interviewer

acknowledged his last answer with "okay j's:' your roommate," the next episode is even more remarkable:

(2c)   continued
    30 I.   okay j's:' your roommate ⌈.hhh a:nd how many
    31 R.   ⌊yeah
    32 I.   others- PERsons live there you ARE
    32   related to you?
    33   (0.9)
    34 R.   z⌈ero
    35   ⌊#

Again, it takes the respondent a rather long time before answering this question. The interview proceeds as follows:

(2d)   continued
    36 I.   .hhh ↑okay now we'd like to ask about your
    37   employment ↑STATUS (.) did you do any work
    38   for ↑PAY last week?
    39   (1.3)
    40 R.   did i do any work for pay? ⌈yeah
    41 I.   ⌊mmhmm

After having heard the question, it takes the respondent 1.3 seconds before he takes the turn. Rather than just saying "yes," he starts out with a "questioning repeat" (Jefferson 1972: 299) of the question ("did i do any work for pay?", line 40) as if there were a problem with this utterance. This may very well be so, because the respondent knows that the interviewer knows he is in the military. As Sacks (1992b: 723–9) discusses, utterances are interpreted within their sequential context. When an utterance or phrase seems to be contextually irrelevant, recipients tend to have a problem comprehending the point of that talk. Next we get:

(2e)   continued
    42 I.   A:nd what was your ↑JOB last week
    43   that is what KIND of work were you doing
    44 R.   .hhh uh:: i'm a platoon leader
    45   in the::- (0.5) ARMY
              (. . .)
    46 I.   what wr::- what WERE your MOST important
    47   activities or duties on THIS jo:b
    48   (1.8)
    49 R.   uh:: this PAST week i had to lead uh:

```
50              my⌈platoon out to uh (0.2) field exercise.⌉
51    I.            ⌊..............      ((typing))...............⌋
52              ⌈.hhh oka(gh)::y⌉
53              ⌊((typing    ⌋
54              field exerci(gh)::se:
54              ⌈((typing))⌉
55    →         ⌊.hhh  ⌋↑oh kay: and do you work for
56    →         yourSELF (h)in a fa(h)mily business
57              or for someone else:?
58    R.        uh:: i WORK for the gov⌈ernment
59    I.                               ⌊#
```

In lines 55–7 the interviewer asks a question to which she knows the answer. Part of our and the interviewer's cultural knowledge is that people in the American army work for the government. Apart from the fact that this question is redundant, the first two response options are really strange. How could a military man work for himself or in a family business? This may explain the hesitant beginning of the answering turn: "uh:: i WORK for the government."[6] After some time the interview proceeds as follows:

(2f)   continued
```
60    I.        a::nd did any of thee OTHER adults in your
61              household have any ↑income from any SOURCE in
62              the past twelve months:
63              (0.8)
64    R.        uh yeah⌈the- (0.6) my roommate's: (0.2)
65    I.              ⌊#
66    R.        got the same job i have
```

The formulation of this question in line 60–1 shows some remarkable dimensions. First of all, the respondent knows that the interviewer knows only one other adult lives in this household. The phrase "any of the OTHER adults" (line 60) presupposes the possibility of more adults. Secondly, the respondent knows that the interviewer knows that Mark is in the military. The interviewer may be expected to have inferred that Mark has an income from this source. This knowledge makes the entire question redundant, unless the respondent is supposed to hear the question as "any of the other adults, but for Mark," but he has already told the interviewer that Mark is the only other person in the household.

The interviewer clearly does not take into account the information she received earlier. One could reason that the respondent might know by now that the interviewer does not recipient design her questions. But in talking about "the OTHER adults," the interviewer suggests that she knows about other adults, in addition to Mark and the respondent, living in the respondent's household. In fact, the interviewer just reads this formulation from her screen, but the respondent is not in a position to know this. From his perspective, he interacts with the interviewer. Even if he knew that this line is on the interviewer's screen, why would he expect the interviewer to read redundant lines?

This redundant question may have confused the respondent as to what answer he is expected to give. This may explain why it takes 0.8 of a second to begin his turn in line 64: "uh yeah the- (0.6) my roommate's: (0.2) got the same job I have."

The analysis of this fragment shows that the interviewer is acting in a misleading way when it comes to whether or not she is following the conversational rules. On certain occasions, and especially when providing non-scripted acknowledgments, she orients toward what the respondent told her. When she asks questions, however, she does not take into account what the respondent told her previously.

Research methodologists sometimes say that respondents know that a survey interview is not an ordinary conversation. Even if this is true, it does not necessarily mean that respondents will expect interviewers to follow a set of interactional rules entirely different from conversational rules. This analysis shows that, to some degree, the respondent expects the interviewer to follow the conversational rules, and it shows that he rightly does so. The interviewer indeed follows these rules, and engages in recipient design, if not always. When it comes to the non-scripted activity of acknowledging the respondent's answers, she demonstrates to have heard and remembered what she was told, and to be able to make inferences. When she produces questions, however, she tends not to engage in recipient design. She just reads the questionnaire.

The standardized interview will likely be a combination of two different forms of talk. When interviewers ask questions, they follow the rules for standardized interviewing for the most part. However, when they acknowledge the respondents' answers, they act conversationally. Adopting a sequential perspective, we can see that when interviewers ask questions in first-turn position, they speak for someone else. That is, they "do interview" (Schegloff 1989). When they acknowledge the answer in third-turn position, they "do conversation." This playing of both football and baseball in the same field may well confuse respondents as to what is going on in the interview.

Let me speculate on the way this respondent operates. He first tries to interpret each successive question as if the interviewer is following the conversational rules/maxims. Indeed, more often than not, the interviewer's questions do not cause the respondent to assume that the interviewer is not following the rules/maxims. But when she seems to violate these rules/maxims, the delays and hesitations that precede and accompany the respondent's answering turns may point to the respondent trying to see what the conversational implicature of the interviewer's questions is.

When he fails to see any implicature, he realizes that she is asking redundant or "funny" questions and that he wrongly assumed that she was following Grice's co-operation principle and recipient designing her talk. She therefore must be following some sort of standardized survey interviewing principle, or, the rules for standardized interviewing. These standardized interviewing rules are more like grammatical rules, in that they constitute the standardized interview. The conversational rules/maxims are, in principle, no part of this set of rules.

When the respondent answers the interviewer's questions, he does so in a conversational way. He displays that he is normatively oriented to the conversational maxim of recipient designing one's utterances. He also provides more elaborate answers than these questions formally seek. That is, he sometimes provides the sort of information that conversationalists know their conversational partners may ask for next, if one does not volunteer this information right away. However, when presented with a question that specifically asks for a number, the respondent revises his initial descriptive answer into "one." He thus revises his conversational answer into a formulation in line with the requirements of the standardized interview. In that respect, the respondent may occasionally be considered to be following the rules of standardized interviewing as well.

Therefore it may well be that question–answer sequences in standardized interviews are produced by participants who follow two sets of interactional rules, both conversational rules/maxims and standardized interviewing rules. Schematically:

T1	I:	reads scripted question	STAND. INTERVIEWING RULES
T2	R:	provides answer	CONVERSATIONAL MAXIMS
		perhaps revises answer	STAND. INTERVIEWING RULES
T3	I:	acknowledges answer	CONVERSATIONAL MAXIMS

In the next section we will see Dutch interviewers who solve the problem of the questions that seem irrelevant for a specific respondent or that have become redundant in the process of the interview. Whereas the American interviewers discussed here strictly follow the standardized interviewing rules for requesting information, the Dutch interviewers seem to combine both interviewing rules and conversational rules when asking questions.

5   Recipient design in questioning[7]

In a series of Dutch standardized survey interviews, we see that occasionally the interviewers ask a question and provide the answer themselves. In doing so, they may be seen as acting against the expectation that holds true for ordinary conversation: one does not ask one's co-participant for information that he or she has already provided. At the same time, the interviewers violate the interviewing rule that they should not answer for respondents.

Asking a question and then providing its answer is a device interviewers use to solve the interactional problems caused by their recipients' orientation toward ordinary conversation. Furthermore, I will argue that while interviewers depart from the interviewing rules, they do continue to manage their task of gathering valid information.

In this section I make use of a series of Dutch computer-assisted telephone survey interviews on adult education. The questionnaire for these interviews is designed by two sociologists who carried out the research. The interviews are conducted by trained interviewers employed by a market research company.

The respondents interviewed form a random sample of Dutch people "18 or older, who attended High School or Lower Vocational School, but who have *not* completed it," as the questionnaire states. The respondents are asked questions such as: "Have you ever heard of the adult educational institution by the name of such-and-such?" "Would you be interested in taking any courses?" "What do you consider good reasons to take any courses?" and "How much time and money would you be prepared to spend on them?" The pseudonyms of the respondents are given in the headings of the fragments.

In the first fragment the interviewer asks a question and provides the answer himself:

(3)   Adult education CATI, Christine, question 74
         1   I.   and (1.0) u:h (1.0) could you tell
         2   me your <u>age</u>, =
         3   = you've already s<u>ai</u>d that,
         4   →   s<u>e</u>venty⌈one
         5   R.   ⌊seventy one.
         6   I.   s<u>e</u>venty <u>one</u>. you said, right?
         7   I.   ((next question))

Following the interviewer's age question, the next sequentially relevant action is the respondent's answer. However, rather than allocating the turn to Christine and waiting for a response, the interviewer immediately takes the next turn and provides the requested information himself. In doing so, the interviewer may be considered to be doing a "self-repair" (Schegloff et al. 1977) with respect to the action he performed in his immediately prior turn at talk. What initially was a question he now redefines as an action that does not call for a respondent's answer, because she has "already said that," as the interviewer indicates. The status of "could you tell me your age" is retrospectively redefined by the interviewer as a case of reading a scripted line.

This redefinition changes the co-participants' institutional identities (Heritage and Greatbatch 1991) of interviewer and respondent. The normative procedure in research interviews is that the interviewer asks the questions and the respondent answers them.[8] The interviewer then fills in the answer box on the form, an activity that falls outside of the immediate scope of the interaction. Now, rather than being involved in questioning and answering, the interviewer and respondent begin to complete the form collaboratively. Christine helps the interviewer do his institutional work by repeating what she has told him previously, and the interviewer makes sure he got it right by saying, "seventy one. you said, right?" (line 6).

Before mentioning the respondent's age, the interviewer gives the basis of his knowledge by stating, "you've already said that," (cf. Pomerantz 1984c). Later on he asks Christine to confirm the correctness of his assertion: "seventy one. you said, right?" The interviewer's initial statement thus becomes a candidate answer that is confirmed by the respondent. The authorship of the information, as it will be recorded, can then be credited to the respondent (Pomerantz 1988). The interviewer has generated "accountable information," information that is taken as verifiable, objective, valid, and properly achieved (Marlaire and Maynard 1990, Maynard and Marlaire 1992, Schaeffer and Maynard 1996). In self-repairing his initial question, the interviewer prevents a possible "other-correction" (Schegloff et al. 1977) by Christine, who otherwise might have said, "I have already told you."

By generating accountable information, the interviewer manages to do both institutional work and interactional work. His phrase "you've already said that," demonstrates to his recipient that he is a competent conversationalist who listens to her and who does not request information which he has already obtained several times. The American Census Bureau calls this interviewing practice "verification" (Schaeffer and Maynard 1996). Census Bureau interviewers are allowed to verify both that they have correctly heard and remembered information already provided, and that the information is the correct answer to the question.

The fragment above comes from the last section of the interview devoted to demographic questions, one of them being the respondent's age.[9] The interviewer's situation is that the questions and the answer slots show up on the screen one by one, in a fixed order. However, merely asking this question and waiting for the answer, as the interviewer is supposed to do according to the interviewing rules, would occasion an interactional problem, because Christine has already mentioned her age voluntarily earlier in the interview. In ordinary conversation, participants take the history of the conversation into account. From that perspective, the interviewer is not expected to ask the age question, and he shows that he is oriented to this conversational principle.

The very first question of the questionnaire concerns the respondent's highest level of education. This question comes right after the interviewer makes sure that the person who has answered the telephone meets the research criteria. The question on the questionnaire is worded as follows:

> Adult education CATI, item 12
> First of all I would like to ask you,
> what is the highest level of education
> that you took in FULL-TIME daytime education.
> By full-time daytime education we mean
> any course or education that is taken
> at least three days a week.

In the following three fragments where this question is delivered to the respondents, we again find the interviewers providing the answers themselves.

(4)   Adult education CATI, Doris, question 12

```
 1  I.    first of all I'd like to ask you
 2        what is your highest level of
 3        education (.) that you took in full-
 4        time daytime education, =
 5   →    = >that was elementary school you
 6        said, right?<
 7  R.    elementary school, and then I also
 8        took a uh c- a uh a year for the
 9        store a uh (1.0) well, what's it
10        called uh (0.4) I had to get
11        this certificate. =
12  I.    = what's the name of this certificate?
13  R.    professional knowledge.
14  I.    <PRO FES SION AL KNOWL E:D GE>
15  R.    prof- eh yes because of the store I
```

```
16            had to know all this. .hh
17   I.       yes, and was this a school? =
18   R.       = that was uh (1.2) a few times a week.
19            I had to go the ⌈ re
20   I.                       ⌊AT LEAST three days a
21            week? ⌈ or
22   R.              ⌊ye:s, ye:s. three times a week.
23   I.       three times a week.¹⁰
24   R.       and in Maastrich I went for that certificate,
```

As in fragment 4, the interviewer reads the question and rather than waiting for Doris' answer, he says "that was elementary school you said, right?" (lines 5–6). Note that he explicitly refers to Doris having provided this information. Also, by adding the tag "right?" he turns his statement into a request for confirmation.

Doris' response is built as a dispreferred turn-shape (see chapter 2). She first confirms that elementary school is her highest level of education, and then adds a course she took after elementary school. In mentioning this course she implicitly denies that elementary school was her highest level of education.

This fragment also exemplifies the relevance of giving respondents the opportunity to elaborate on their answers for the validity of the answers, as Suchman and Jordan (1990a: 236) suggest. The respondents behave as ordinary conversationalists when they structure their disagreeing responses in a dispreferred turn format. The respondents' production of dispreferred turn formats is part of the conversational character of the standardized interview. Consequently, when interviewers are allowed to engage in a limited form of recipient design, for example, verification, they should be prepared for the respondents to produce an agreement token, followed by a disagreement.

When we compare the interviewer's questioning turn to the item on the questionnaire, we can see that he left out the specification "By full-time daytime education we mean any course or education that is taken at least three days a week." This is an important specification, as the everyday meaning of "full-time daytime education" is a form of education that requires attendance about five full days a week. In terms of recipient design and Grice's maxim of manner, the omission of this specification means that the question is not formulated with reference to what the respondent may be assumed to know.

After having dealt with question 12, the interviewer is supposed to ask, "Have you, or have you not completed this education, or are you still busy with it?" In fact he says:

(5)   Adult education CATI, Doris, question 13
1   I.   you've completed this education, (.)
2   and ((next question))

The interviewer transforms the question into a statement that he assumes to be correct. When Doris does not contradict this during the brief silence that follows this statement, the interviewer proceeds to the next question. In fact, it is not clear whether Doris has really gotten her certificate. Her prior talk about this in fragment 4 is rather vague: "I also took a uh c- a uh a year for the store a uh (1.0) well, what's it called uh (0.4) I had to get this certificate" and "and in Maastrich I went for that certificate." She "had to" get this certificate, and she "went for it," but she does not say she passed the examination.

As one of the designers of the questionnaire told me, by "having completed" school or a course, they meant having passed the examination. However, as becomes clear in the next fragment, this is not necessarily how respondents understand this term. Respondent Bert, for example, says in the introduction of the interview, "I am the only one ((in the family)) who completed this u::h Lower Vocational School, but I u:h did not pass the exam." When the interviewer verifies, "So you have not completed it?" Bert says, "I have not passed the carpenter's exam. no."

This instance demonstrates why questionnaire designers should pretest their questionnaires by making a detailed analysis of some interviews. This analysis would show to what extent the terms used on the questionnaire are also "members' terms" (Garfinkel and Sacks 1970). Researchers should expect that some of the notions they believe are common and generally shared, and that they use in the questionnaire, may be understood quite differently by (some part of the) respondents.

In the fragment below we see the interviewer using a similar procedure as in the prior ones:

(6)   Adult education CATI, Bert, question 12 and 13
1   I.   first of all I'd like to ask you what
2   is the highest level of education that
3   you took in full-time daytime education? =
4   →   = well, so that was l.v.s., right?
5   R.   that was l.v.s., yes.
6   I. →   and you have not completed it,
7   R.   no. I have uh, the final uh test year
8   >graduation year< I have finished only
9   uh half a year. =
10   I.   = yes.

The interviewer reads question 12 without specifying it, and immediately continues to state the requested information, adding a question tag ("right?") to it. Bert confirms the information in line 5. By saying "so" in "well, so that was l.v.s., right?" the interviewer implicitly refers to earlier talk by Bert. After this question, the interviewer is supposed to ask, "Have you, or have you not completed this education, or are you still busy with it?" However, he transforms the question into the statement "and you have not completed it," (line 6) which is confirmed by Bert.

Ordinary conversationalists usually ask questions without explicitly saying that they are about to do so. In survey interviews, however, many questions are prefaced by a "question projection" (Schegloff 1980), generally formulated on the questionnaire as "I would like to ask you." In the two previous fragments, the question projection was followed by the projected question. However, in the next fragment it is not:

(7)   Adult education CATI, Elly, question 12 and 13
1   I.   →   u:hm, first of all I'd like to ask you,
2   uh you went to the uh v.g.l.o then,
3   R.   yes,
4   ⌈ ((sound of typing)) ⌉
5   ⌊   0.9 sec.   ⌋
6   I.   and you've completed it, right?
7   R.   yes.
8   I.   yes?
9   ((1.0 second sound of typing))

Although he projects a question (u:hm, first of all I'd like to ask you), the interviewer does not produce one. He already knows the answer from the introduction of the interview, and this enables him to produce the answer to the unstated question himself by saying, "uh you went to the uh v.g.l.o then" (line 2), which is confirmed by Elly. The interviewer also knows the answer to the next question on the questionnaire, which he reformulates as a request for confirmation: "and you've completed it, right?" (line 6). Again, Elly confirms it.

In this set of interviews it is clear that the highest school levels completed by the respondents are known to the interviewers before the question appears on their screens. This pre-knowledge is due to the way in which the respondents are selected. The computer randomly selects telephone numbers, and the interviewers inquire as to whether or not the person who answered the telephone meets the criteria for the research.[11] These criteria are that the person should be over eighteen years old and should not have completed a certain level of education. By the time it has been established that a call answerer is a candidate respondent for this interview, the interviewers already know the answers to the first few questions which they must ask. The selection procedure creates an interactional problem for the interviewers. From the beginning of the interview, they are supposed to request information they already have. They solve this problem by answering the questions themselves, using the information provided earlier by the respondents.

In the fragments shown earlier, the interviewers produce the question and then provide the answer. In other instances, they give a reporting that may serve as an account for a specific answer. This happens, for example, in the following fragment, when the interviewer asks a woman if job security or promotion would be a possible motivation for her to take a course. The fragment is part of a series of questions that are concerned with whether or not something would be a reason for the respondent to take courses.

(8)   Adult education CATI, Christine, question 24
    1   I.   \<to b<u>e</u>tter secure my present job or to
    2   increase my chances for a prom<u>o</u>tion>
    3   →   .hh well (.) you >are seventy <u>o</u>ne<,
    4   R.   ye::s.

This woman has already indicated several times that she is seventy-one years old. Now the interviewer mentions her age right after having produced the question. Being seventy-one years old is indeed a plausible reason for Christine not to take any more education for job reasons. This can be inferred from what she said earlier in the interview:

(9)   Adult education CATI, Christine, question 16
    1   I.   uh for the last five years (.) you have
    2   n<u>o</u>t taken any courses or education,
    3   R.   ⌈no:
    4   I.   ⌊could you say why n<u>o</u>t?
    5   R. → we:ll, because I uh I I am too <u>o</u>ld n<u>o</u>w.
    6   (1.2)
    7   R.   I'm seventy <u>o</u>ne.
    8   I.   yes, you you are saying I'm too <u>o</u>ld.⌉
    9   °seventy one<°
   10   ⌈ \<too:: (.) o::ld (1.2) se::ve::nty:: <u>o</u>ne> ⌉
   11   ⌊ ((s o u n d o f t y p i n g)) ⌋

When a person indicates she is seventy-one, and that this is too old to take any further education, it stands to reason to assume that she will not be interested in further education for the sake of increasing her security in her present job, let alone for promotion. Apart from this, considering her age, it is most likely that Christine does not have a paid job anyway. In saying, "well (.) you're seventy one", the interviewer demonstrates not only his competence to listen but also to understand the social world in which he and his recipient live and draw inferences.

At the same time, the interviewer acts out his role as a relayer of the text when he moves on and reads question 12 as worded on the questionnaire. I will quote the first part of the fragment again:

(10)   Adult education CATI, Christine, question 24
        1   I.   <to better secure my present job> or to
        2   increase my chances for a promotion.
        3   .hh well (.) you'>re seventy one<,
        4   R.   ye::s.
        5   I.   → u:h (.) that- is that a very >important,
        6   an important or not such an important
        7   reason for you to take any course or
        8   education<, .hh or (.) <does this
        9   reason not apply to you?>
        10 R.   no:, that does not apply.

At first glance it is surprising that the interviewer reads the question after having already indicated that this specific reason to take any courses does not apply to Christine. His action makes sense when we think of fragment 4, where the same participants were collaboratively doing the organizational work of filling out the questionnaire. Seen from this perspective, here the participants are "doing the interview." The interviewer reads the question and makes it clear that he knows that this is an irrelevant question for his co-participant. Christine's "ye:s" may be seen as an agreement with this. Having "discussed" the irrelevance of the question, they go back to work and continue to do the interview. The interviewer reads what he has to read, and the respondent does her part of the interviewing work when she provides the requested information.

Note, however, the pace the interviewer uses when he continues to read the questionnaire. The first part which is irrelevant for Christine is read relatively quickly and in "text-locked voice"[12] (Goffman 1981b: 239): "u:h (.) that- is that a very >important, an important or not such an important reason for you to take any course or education<." He slows down when he reaches the last and relevant part: "or (.) <does this reason not apply to you?>" (lines 8–9), Christine responds to this last part by saying, "no:, that does not apply." (line 10). In changing his pace of reading, the interviewer is able to instruct Christine that one part of the utterance is only to be heard as his reading aloud and the other part as a question to be answered (Uhmann 1992). Christine's participant role shifts from a ratified overhearer to an addressed participant during this short episode.[13]

In the fragment below, the interviewer both answers the question and gives an account:

(11)   Adult education CATI, Doris, question 42

```
1  I.       is it important to you that there are day
2           care facilities in the place of the course?
3              (1.7)
4  I.  →  n⌈o
5  R.     ⌊day care?
6  I.  →  no::. not anymore. n⌈o.
7  R.                        ⌊no::.
8  I.  →  no, your children aren't that small anymore. =
9  R.     = no, they all have stores.
```

Rather than taking the turn and answering the question, the respondent keeps silent (line 3). The interviewer waits for 1.7 seconds and then takes the next turn himself to make an educated guess. Almost at the same time, Doris displays her surprise at the question by her questioning repeat "day care?" in line 5, after which the interviewer again gives the answer, "no::. not anymore. no."

One might wonder what is so troublesome about this question that it is met with a questioning repeat instead of an answer. Earlier Doris informed the interviewer that she is an elderly woman with grown-up children. In the everyday world this implies that one has no personal interest in day-care facilities, which consequently makes this question an irrelevant one in the context of ordinary conversation. To formulate it in terms of Grice, by asking this question the interviewer violates the maxim of relation.

With the phrase "not anymore" (line 6), the interviewer shows to Doris that, whatever obvious questions he seems to be asking, he is a competent listener and conversationalist who takes his co-participants' particulars into account. He has learned from Doris that her "children aren't that small anymore", (line 8) and he demonstrates his cultural knowledge that day-care facilities are not of personal interest for people with grown-up children.

Earlier in this interview, the interviewer indicated to Doris why he sometimes asks questions that are irrelevant for her. On several occasions, Doris displays her conviction that the questions do not make sense. At one point the interviewer says, "We ask these questions to everybody in the same way, you see," and later on, "But, as I said, we ask these questions to everybody in the same way, right." Apparently these statements did not instruct Doris about the rules of standardized interviewing, according to which she is supposed to answer whatever question the interviewer asks her. That is to say, these rules of standardized interviewing apply to the interviewer. When respondents are expected to treat an interview question as the first pair part of an adjacency pair, they, too, are expected to follow the rules of standardized interviewing, and answer every question. When research methodology designs rules for interviewers that tell them how to do the interview, it consequently designs interactional rules for respondents. However, whereas interviewers are explicitly informed on these rules, and usually about their methodological reason as well, respondents are not. They are supposed to find out all by themselves. As may have become clear, for many respondents this task seems too difficult.

6   Conclusion

According to the theory of standardized survey interviewing, interviewers should not give the answers themselves, should not lead respondents in a certain direction, and should not rephrase any questions.

However, because the questionnaires are audience designed, that is designed for a large and heterogeneous group of people, they contain questions that may be rather peculiar when delivered to a particular person. In other cases scripted questions become redundant in the process of the interaction.

When interviewers stick to their role as survey interviewers, they present themselves to their co-participants as incompetent conversationalists who do not listen to what they have been told, who are unable to deal properly with this information, who ask the same thing several times, and who have no knowledge of the social world in which they live. For the main part, these interviewers do act out their role as survey interviewers, and the respondents demonstrate on several occasions that strange things are happening indeed.

The American interviewer presented here tends to stick to the interviewing rules when it comes to asking questions and expecting the respondent to provide the information. The Dutch interviewers solve this problem by means of answering questions themselves when they have already obtained the information. At the same time, they structure their talk in such a way that respondents are invited to confirm the correctness of the interviewers' answers, or to correct them when they are wrong. In this way the interviewers follow the interviewing rule that says they should not answer for the respondent. They just use a more conversationally adequate form to generate the information that is sought. The effect of this procedure is that the interviewers are able to generate accountable survey data.

In this way the Dutch interviewers are able to meet both ends, that is, being a competent interviewer as well as a competent conversationalist. A few fragments made especially clear that this may be done by shifting participation frames. The co-participants may collaboratively shift from conversationalists, who implicitly comment on the irrelevance of a specific question, to then take up their institutional identities and do the work of asking and answering questions according to the rules of standardized interviewing.

Let me conclude this chapter by quoting Sudman, Bradburn, and Schwarz (1996: 245), who say:

> Those conducting the survey are asking questions of respondents in situations that are very similar to ordinary conversations and, as such, follow the linguistic and social rules that govern conversations. To be sure, this conversation has some special characteristics that set it apart from others, but the activity is still a conversation and needs to be understood as such.

Sudman et al. discuss the consequences of this for the way respondents interpret questions, as well as its implications for questionnaire design. In my opinion they do not accept the full consequence of their perspective on the survey interview as a form of talk that is guided by conversational maxims. In this chapter I have shown that these maxims also impact on the interviewing process. If we accept that survey interviews are guided by conversational maxims, we have to accept that this holds true for both respondents and interviewers alike. Consequently, this poses problems for standardization.

When Sudman, Bradburn and Schwarz discuss the effects of conversational maxims on respondents' possible interpretations of questions, one would expect the authors to come forward with a plea for more freedom for interviewers and respondents to discuss the intended meaning of the questions. The authors state: "The tacit assumptions that govern the conduct of conversation in daily life are key to understanding a wide range of response effects, from the impact of response alternatives to wording and order effects" (1996: 247). They might add that response effects might be reduced if interviewers were allowed to speak on behalf of the researcher rather than just relay the questions and the response options to the respondent. So, I fully agree with Sudman, Bradburn and Schwarz (1996), when they say: "Any comprehensive theory of the survey interview has to incorporate these aspects of human communication. However, such a theory would be incomplete without a consideration of the cognitive processes that individuals engage in when responding to a survey question" (250). I would like to add that, in order to make such a theory even more complete, we also need a consideration of the conversational process that individuals engage in when asking and answering survey questions.

Although Sudman et al. say it is important to consider the survey process as "fundamentally a social encounter" (1996: 245), they, in fact, keep seeing it as a cognitive process. When they use the notion of "social encounter," they seem to mean the encounter between a respondent, the question relayed to him or her by the interviewer, and the situational and conversational context that influence how the question may be interpreted. They neglect the fact that cognition is not just in the individual's mind. Cognition is established in and through interaction (Resnick 1991), for example with a survey interviewer. Or, as Schegloff (1991: 168) says:

Our understanding of the world and of one another is posed as a problem, and resolved as an achievement, in an inescapably social and interactional context – both with tools forged in the workshop of interaction and in settings in which we are answerable to our fellows. Interaction and talk-in-interaction are structured environments for action and cognition, and they shape both the constitution of the actions and utterances needing to be "cognized" and the contingencies for solving them.

When we discuss survey interviewing we have to face the fact that an interviewer is present who is a participant in the social encounter and who plays a role in how questions will be understood and answered. We should make better use of interviewers by allowing them to bring the respondents' cognitions in line with the researchers' intentions.

5   Questioning-turn structure and turn taking

1   Introduction

In survey methodology questions are primarily seen as semantic entities, that is, linguistic units that have a certain meaning. Taking a conversation analysis viewpoint, we may look at survey questions as turns-at-talk. In addition to questions being semantic units, they are also interactional units to be used in an interview. Turns have an internal organizational structure. As we will see in this chapter, many survey questions are designed in such a way that their organizational structure is unfit for adequate use in the interview. This holds especially true for closed questions that are followed by a set of response options, as well as questions that contain a term or concept that is further explained or specified. The turn-organizational character of these two types of questions makes them vulnerable to interruption by the respondent.

A speaker can perform several actions in one turn-at-talk. For example, when a speaker says, "Uh, John, can I have the sugar, please?" he first takes the turn and indicates that he is going to say something ("Uh"). Next he attracts somebody's attention ("John"), displaying that he selects John rather than Liza as his addressee. Next he requests the sugar ("can I have the sugar"), and finally he is being polite ("please"). Note that "being polite" is a separate action, and that this action can be performed by several phrases, such as "please" or "Do you mind?"

When people talk they not only produce meaningful utterances. They also construct a turn-at-talk, the vehicle that transmits the information to the intended recipient. An important part of the construction of turns deals with the organizational requirement of making clear that the turn is completed and that the recipient is expected to take the next turn or to perform the requested action.

When I speak of the organization of turns, I will use the notion of "turn format" or "turn structure." When a speaker produces a turn that does the work of requesting information, I will refer to the turn as a "questioning-turn format" or "structure." "Questioning-turn format" is different from the term "question format" as it is used in survey methodology literature. In survey methodology "question format" refers to aspects such as open versus closed questions, statements versus questions, unbalanced versus balanced questions ("Do you oppose X?" versus "Do you oppose or favor X?"), questions that do or do not contain a "don't know" response option, and the like. (See, for example, Schuman and Presser 1981.)

In this chapter I will provide a conversation analysis (CA) account of the fact that some questioning-turn formats seem especially vulnerable to not being completely read. Questions, or "items," will be analyzed here as turns-at-talk and in terms of the successive activity components that compose these turns. I will show that questionnaire questions are often structured so that they lead to violations of turn-taking rules. These violations may in turn cause interviewers to violate interviewing rules by omitting specific parts of some questions. This analysis is partly based on a Dutch survey on adult education. In the second part of this chapter, I will make use of some American survey data.

2   Turn structure of survey questions

Survey questions are designed either as single-unit turns or multi-unit turns. An example of a single-unit turn is item 80 of the Dutch questionnaire: "Were you born in the Netherlands?" The "were" in turn-initial position signals the onset of a question. The end of the utterance is then heard as the end of the question, and therefore the place where the respondent is expected to take the next turn to answer the question.

In some cases the question is prefaced by an action projection (Schegloff 1980), an utterance that defines the action that follows it, in this case as a question, such as, "Could you please tell me?" or "May I ask you?" For example:

> Adult education CATI, item 71
> First of all I would like to ask   ACTION PROJECTION
>
> how many people, including yourself,   QUESTION
> live in your household.

Note that the item starts off with the sequence marker "first of all" (Sacks 1987), indicating that this is the first in a series of actions. An action may also be marked as the next action ("next," "then"), or as the last action ("finally") of the series.

Many of the questionnaire items are built as multi-unit turns, for example:

Adult education CATI, item 29
Now we would like to talk about your possible future
plans with respect to such courses or education.

They may be either fixed plans or vague ideas
Do you have any plans for the COMING YEAR to take
any course or education?

As Heritage and Greatbatch (1991) and Heritage and Roth (1995) point out, the activity of questioning may be accomplished across multiple-turn construction units (TCUs) in what they call "question delivery structures" (Button n.d.). People not only organize the content of the turn and the allocation of turns, but also what activities are contained within a turn. A multi-unit turn may be designed so that each TCU contains a different activity.

Item 29 is built out of four TCUs, each unit containing a different activity component. The last component is the question per se. Button (n.d.) refers to such a component as the "question delivery component" (QDC). The preceding TCUs contain question-relevant activities that support the question delivery component. The turn begins with an action projection. Although the action to come is announced as something "we would like to talk about," because it is produced in the institutional setting of a survey interview, it is recognizable as a question (Greatbatch 1988, Heritage and Greatbatch 1991). The next statement announces what the question will be about: "your future plans with respect to such courses or education." Following Button, I will call this second component the "question target component" (QTC). The next TCU defines or specifies the term "plans." This TCU is the "question specification component" (QSC). This multi-unit turn is structured in the following way:

[Action Projection Component, APC]
+
[Question Target Component, QTC]
+
[Question Specification Component, QSC]
+
[Question Delivery Component, QDC]

The item is systematically organized as a coherent multi-unit turn of which the first components work towards the question delivery component in final-turn position. This turn structure is designed to instruct respondents when to take their turn to answer the question. This turn structure also informs respondents exactly what the question is about and what type of answer is expected.

Now that it is clear how a conversationally adequate questionnaire item may be designed, we can turn to items that are structured differently and see what the consequences may be for the interaction in the interview and, subsequently, for the information the interviewers gather:

> Adult education CATI, item 12
> First of all I would like to ask you
> what is the highest level of education that
> you took in FULL-TIME daytime education.
> By full-time daytime education we mean a course or
> education that is taken at least three days a week.

The turn is composed of (1) the action projection, (2) the question as such, and (3) the specification of what is meant by "FULL-TIME daytime education," which is a technical term with a different meaning from what non-experts in the field would expect and therefore needs to be specified. So, item 12 is designed as follows:

[Action Projection Component]
First of all I would like to ask you

[Question Delivery Component]
what is the highest level of education that
you took in FULL-TIME daytime education.

[Question Specification Component]
By full-time daytime education we mean
a course or education that is taken at least
three days a week.

This way of designing a questioning turn is general practice in questionnaires. However, once such a question format is used in interaction it is vulnerable to conversational problems, as the fragments below will make clear.[1]

In the first fragment, the interviewer starts to read the question as worded in the questionnaire, but upon completion of the question delivery component, the respondent takes a turn to provide the answer:

(1)   Adult education CATI, Christine, item 12
1   I.   .hh uh first of all I'd like to ask
2   you what is the highest level of
3   education that you took in full-time
4   daytime education?
5   R.   in full-time day- a uh basic knowledge course.
6   I.   no, I⌈mean the high⌈est-
7   R.   ⌊( )   ⌊the school.

8	I.	right, ⌈ the sch<u>oo</u>l,
9	R.	⌊ the school.
10	I.	right, d<u>aytime</u> school right. =
11	R.	= n<u>o</u>, s<u>e</u>ven years of elementary school.
12	I.	that's- that's it?
13	R.	y<u>e</u>s.

According to the rules for conversational turn taking, Christine answers the question upon its completion in line 5. The consequence is that she has not been informed about its idiosyncratic meaning. Considering the answer she gives, it seems as if her course lasted all day and met over an extended period of time. However, this type of course is generally taken for only a few hours a week and meets for a limited number of weeks. Christine's answer, therefore, is very likely to be incorrect.

Having noticed this possible problem, the interviewer produces a third-position repair in line 6: "n<u>o</u>, I mean the h<u>i</u>ghest-." This utterance is completed by Christine with "the sch<u>oo</u>l" (line 7). Although "school" is not the only thing the researchers refer to when they so carefully talk about "courses or education,"[2] the interviewer agrees on this term in line 8, "right, the sch<u>oo</u>l," and in line 10 "right, d<u>aytime</u> school right." Not only is standardization at stake now, but also, the original survey question is interactively transformed into a question with a different meaning. Furthermore, Christine provides an answer that is appropriate, though not necessarily correct, in terms of what the researchers meant to ask. It is appropriate because "s<u>e</u>ven years of elementary school" matches the category of "courses that are taken at least three days a week." But because the respondent has not been informed of the idiosyncratic meaning of the technical terms in the question, she may very well have given an incorrect and therefore invalid answer.[3]

When we look at item 14 we see the same problem. This multi-unit turn is made up of (1) a question delivery component, (2) a question specification component explaining an important notion that is mentioned in the question, and (3) another question specification component that further specifies the question.

Adult education CATI, item 14
Have you, for the last five years, during or   QDC
after this education you just mentioned,
taken any courses or education in so-called
adult education?

You may think of part-time education, such as   QSC 1
daytime, night or weekend education, service

training, courses at the School for Adult Classes,
adult centres, creativity centres, et cetera.

Also courses that you have not completed,   QSC 2
are to be counted.

When this item is presented to the respondents, various kinds of problems may arise:

(2)   Adult education CATI, Bert, item 14
1   I.   have you <for the last five years> (.)   QDC
2   during or after this education you
3   just mentioned (0.7) uh taken any
4   courses or education in so-called
5   adult education? =
6   R.   ⌈ = n o . ⌉   ANSWER
7   I.   ⌊ = .hh you- ⌋ you >may think of part-time   QSC 1
8   education, such as daytime, night or
9   weekend education<, service training,
10   courses at the school for adult classes,
11   adult centres, creativity centres,
12   et cetera.
13 R.   no:, I haven't taken any of these. =   ANSWER
14 I.   = okay.

Again, immediately upon completion of the question, respondent Bert takes a turn to provide the answer. At the same time the interviewer holds the turn by taking an inbreath (".hh", line 7). He begins to read the specification, to the effect that both speakers talk at the same time. The interviewer drops out, and as soon as Bert has completed his answer, the interviewer restarts, reading the specification. When this specification is completed, and before the interviewer has started the third component of the question turn (the second specification), Bert again answers the question: "no:, I haven't taken any of these." (line 13). Note that he now also refers to the examples of courses and education that followed the question. In this way he shows that his answer is a "next-positioned new answer" (Jefferson 1981b) that responds to the now-specified question.

Whereas Bert's first answer was left unacknowledged by the interviewer, the second one is acknowledged in line 14 by means of the third-turn receipt "Okay." With this receipt, the interviewer also terminates the question–answer sequence. This means that Bert has not been informed that the courses and forms of education mentioned in the question also count when they have not been completed. It is important to mention this explicitly because only completed forms of education counted in the previous question.

The same question is delivered to Ann in the following way:

(3)   Adult education CATI, Ann, item 14

```
 1  I.    u:h have you, for the last five years,        QDC
 2         during or after this education you
 3         just mentioned, taken any courses or
 4         education in so-called adult education?
 5         .hh you may think of >part-time            QSC 1
 6         education, such as daytime, night or
 7         weekend education<,⌈sERvice training,
 8  R.                     ⌊u:h                       ANSWER
 9  I     courses at the school for adult             QSC 1
10        classes, adult centres, creativity
11        centres, e::t⌈cetera.
12  R.              ⌊u:h ((laughs)) no,               ANSWER
13        no,⌈no.
14  I.      ⌊no, y(h)ou ha(h)ven't.    ACKNOWLEDGMENT
15  R.    no.
```

After the interviewer has completed the question, he takes an audible inbreath in line 5 and produces the first specification. Halfway through this specification (the intonation indicates that the interviewer has not yet finished), Ann decides that the utterance is "completed-for-response" (Schegloff 1980: 150), and she begins to speak: "U:h" (line 8). As Oksenberg, Cannell, and Kalton (1991: 355) suggest, "Respondents probably often think that the question has been completed before the interviewer has finished reading it, or they feel that they have heard enough to answer it."

But the interviewer continues and holds Ann off by increasing the volume for a short while ("sERvice"). This specification is completed in line 11 with "e::t cetera," as stated in the questionnaire. Since "et cetera" is a common last element of a list, a "generalized list completor" (Jefferson 1990: 66), it is not surprising that Ann begins to talk again in line 12 ("u:h") in overlap with this possible turn-final "e::t cetera." The interviewer acknowledges the answer ("no, y(h)ou ha(h)ven't", line 14), and, shortly after, proceeds to the next item. Therefore, the second specification ("Also courses that you have not completed, are to be counted") is omitted. If Ann ever took courses she did not complete, her present answer is invalid from the point of view of the researchers.

The possible invalidity of the anwers given by Ann and Bert is due to a questioning turn that is structured so that it projects two completion points not intended as such by the questionnaire designer. When the respondent "legitimately" takes the turn at such a point, she finds the floor still occupied by the interviewer who acts out his institutional identity as an interviewer as instructed. From a conversational perspective, his institutional identity forces the interviewer to interrupt the respondent twice.

The next fragment shows a fierce competition for the floor. Although the respondent answers the question twice, the interviewer continues to read the question to her:

```
(4)     Adult education CATI, Christine, item 14
        1   I.    have you for the last five years during        QDC
        2             or after this education (.) during this
        3             elementary school taken any courses or
        4             education in so-called adult education?
        5   R     no:.                                            ANSWER
        6   I.    you may thi⌈nk-                                 QSC 1
        7   R             ⌊no, not for the last the               ANSWER
        8             last five years, because u⌈h
        9   I.                                  ⌊ >you may        QSC 1
        10            think of part-time education, such as day-
        11            night or weekend education<, or service
        12            training, or courses at the school for
        13            ⌈adult classes,
        14  R.    ⌊no, no, not a⌈t all.                           ANSWER
        15  I.              ⌊.hh not,⌈no.    ACKNOWLEDGMENT
        16  R.                       ⌊no.
```

Christine provides a "no:" (line 5) right after the first TCU that is built as a yes–no question. When the interviewer continues to read the first question specification, Christine interrupts him to repeat her answer in lines 7–8 ("no, not for the last the last five years") and to account for her answer: "because uh." She may be heard as repeating her initial answer in a more elaborate way, indicating that she understood the question very well, and that there is no need for further explanation of the question. The interviewer interrupts the account and speedily continues to produce the specification. Before this is completed, the respondent interrupts him again in line 14, and gives a new answer that is formulated more strongly than the first one: "no, no, not at all." The interviewer stops reading the specification, and acknowledges the receipt of the answer.

For the research on behalf of which these interviews are conducted, the omission of the second specification in both of the aforementioned fragments is rather problematic. This specification, indicating that incompleted courses are also to be counted, is very important. In the next excerpt, the interviewer leaves out the specifications altogether when the respondent provides the answer right after the question:

(5)   Adult education CATI, Ernst, item 14

```
 1  I.    have you (.) after (.) or during (.)          QDC
 2         this education,
 3  R.    ye⌈:s?
 4  I.        ⌊uh >so this v.g.l.o. school right<,
 5         .hh for the the last (.) five years
 6         taken any courses or education in (.)
 7         so-called adult education?
 8  R.    no.                                      ANSWER
 9  I.    no.                              ACKNOWLEDGMENT
10         ((typing))⁴
```

Having analyzed what happens in these interviews when a [Question] + [Specification] format is used in interaction, it is clear that respondents tend to behave like ordinary conversationalists. They treat the first possible completion point of the question as a turn-transition relevance place. When the interviewer continues to produce a specification, thus treating the prior answer as a premature one, the respondent may look for the next possible completion point of the meanwhile-specified question.

Furthermore, conversationalists do not necessarily await the end of an utterance when it seems clear how the rest of the utterance will turn out. They may begin to respond as soon as the prior utterance seems complete enough to them (Suchman and Jordan 1990a). This makes the first specification of item 14 vulnerable to interruption.⁵ When the interviewer has mentioned a few types of courses given as examples of what is meant by adult education, the utterance may be heard as complete enough to respond to again. In the perspective of the original research, however, it is important that the respondents hear the entire list. The category of "types of courses that constitute adult education" is larger than non-experts in the field of adult education research would expect.

When the respondent has answered the question near or around the completion point of the first specification, the interviewer still has a second specification to read. This means that he or she would define the respondent's sequentially proper answer as misplaced for a third time. It is therefore not surprising that this second specification is omitted in all interviews studied.

The analysis makes clear that specifications following the question they specify have a good chance of being omitted by the interviewers. The [Question] + [Specification] format is fundamentally contrary to the principles of turn taking and turn construction in ordinary conversation.

When a question needs to be specified, the specification should precede
any utterance that could possibly be heard as the end of a question turn
(cf. Oksenberg, Cannell, and Kalton 1989; Schaeffer 1991a). A good
example of this is found in an American CATI interview, where the
respondent is first presented with a specification "and taking into account
any extra hours worked or time taken off last week," before the question
proper, "How many hours did you actually work at your job?"

(6)   USA CATI, Schaeffer, Maynard, and Cradock 1993: 4
        1   I   and taking into account any extra hours
        2   worked or time taken off last week =
        3   = how many hours did you actually work
        4   at your job?

Below I will briefly outline how an unconversational questioning-turn
format in the introduction to the interview may lead to problematic sampling procedures.

3   Questioning-turn structure and sampling procedures

This unhappy turn structure can also be found in the introduction to
standardized survey interviews. A methodologically important aspect of
the introduction phase of the interview is the selection of the respondent
who meets the research criteria. The following question from the introduction to a Dutch CATI interview is meant to select the proper respondent. Notice that the question is followed by two specifications:

> Dutch CATI Survey, van Gerven. Item 7
> In order to determine whom I should ask the questions,
> I would like to know how many people live in your
> family or household,
> for at least 4 days a week.   SPECIFICATION 1
> This, of course, includes yourself. SPECIFICATION 2

The following fragment shows what may happen to post-question
specifications. The fragment will be presented in three parts.

  First, we see that the respondent takes the turn immediately upon completion of the unspecified question:

(7a)   Dutch CATI Survey, van Gerven, item 7
        1   I.   and in order to determine whom I should
        2   ask the questions, I'd like to know how
        3   many persons live in this family?
        4   R.   four.
        5   I.   four persons.

After the reception of the answer, the interviewer produces a follow-up question, adding the second specification "yours_e_lf included" (line 8):

(7b)   (continued)

     6   I.   a:nd how many of those four persons
     7   are thirteen o_r older?
     8   yours_e_lf included?
     9   R.   well, two_ persons.
   10   I.   two persons.

It is next established who these two persons over thirteen years old are:

(7c)   (continued)

   11   I.   a:nd who a_re these two persons?
   12   R.   my hu_sband and m_e. ((laughs))
   13   I.   ye:s. so ma_le head of the family,
   14   f_emale head of the family.
   15   R.   ⌈right.
   16   I.   ⌊is the family situation.
   17   then we would like to have the
   18   interview with yo_u.

By the time the interviewer informs his recipient that she is the selected respondent for this interview, he has failed to present the first specification "for at least 4 days a week." It is most likely that the recipient and her husband are the parents of the two persons under thirteen (cf. Sacks 1972a, 1972b).[6] This makes it quite likely that the two persons over thirteen will live in the household for at least four days a week. However plausible this may be, the interviewer is instructed to establish this possible fact by presenting the specification.

In the next fragment we find the same interactional structuring of the talk. The recipient answers the questions right after their completion points, and, again, the interviewer omits the second specification:

(8)   Dutch CATI Survey, van Gerven

    1   I.   .hh bu::t in order to determine who_m
    2   I should ask the questions, first of all
    3   I'd like to know how many persons l_ive
    4   in your household.
    5   R.   f_ive.
    6   I.   that's five persons.
    7   R.   ye:s. =
    8   I.   = and how many of these five persons
    9   are o_ver thirteen.

```
10   R.    u:h two.
11   I.    two persons?
12   R.    yes.
13   I.    and could you please tell me who
14         these two persons are? =
15         = you yourself sound like the female head
16         of the family?
17   R.    tha:t's correct yes.
18   I.    and then there ⌈ 's
19   R.                  ⌊ this little man ((laughs))
20   I.    ( ) head of the family ((laughs))
21         u:h then I'd like to have the interview
22         with the male head of the family.
```

In both fragments, there is no indication in the candidate respondents' talk that all members of the two households actually live there at least four days a week. As a consequence, it is unclear whether the interviewer has selected the proper respondent. When the specifications are omitted, the person interviewed may be the wrong one. The respondent in excerpt (8), for instance, may be producing an answer that does not take the qualification "for at least four days a week" into account. If so, then she may also be giving a wrong number, which then alters the selection of the person to be interviewed.

These two fragments show what may happen to survey interviews, and to the eventual research data, when questionnaire questions are followed by specifications. It puts interviewers in a difficult interactional position, and it often results in interviewers following an ad hoc interactional procedure that may threaten the validity of the research data.

4   [Question] + [Response Options] turn structure

The majority of questions in standardized surveys are closed questions, consisting of a question, followed by a set of response options. The interviewing rules say that the interviewer should read both the question and the response options. Studies that made use of behavior coding, however, show that interviewers often do not act according to these rules of standardized interviewing. Oksenberg, Cannell, and Kalton (1991), who tested several question formats, found that the interviewers' reading of questions was sometimes interrupted by the respondents. This happened especially often to a question followed by two instructions for answering the question and to a question followed by response options. Studies by Loosveldt (1995) and by Van der Zouwen and Dijkstra (1995) also suggest that when scripted questions are followed by response options, interviewers often fail to read the entire scripted text.

The list of response options to a closed question is often structurally separated from the question, resulting in a multi-unit turn that is formatted as a [Question] + [Response Options] turn. For example:

> USA CATI, item 6
> How much have you heard or read about   QUESTION
> the issue of federal agencies sharing
> information about individuals?
>
> A great deal, some, not very much or   RESPONSE OPTIONS
> nothing at all?

As in the case of the [Question] + [Specification] format discussed previously, this turn format is misleading when it comes to turn allocation. The end of the question constitutes the place where the respondent is implicitly instructed to start his response turn. There are no indications in the formulation of the question that a list of response options will follow the question. An utterance that starts out with "how much" is legitimately heard as an open question. It is therefore not surprising that a respondent may provide the answer before the options have been read. In chapter 2 we saw an example of this:

(9)   USA CATI, Wisc onsin AW-1
     1   I.   an how much have you heard or REA(GH)D
     2   about the issue: of federal agencies
     3   sharing information about individuals?
     4   .hh a gr⌈eat DEAL some not very much or
     5   R.   ⌊none
     6   I.   nothing at all?
     7   R.   none
     8   I.   nothing at all?
     9   (1.0) ((typing??))
    10   would that be nothing at all?
    11   R.   YES
    12   I.   oh(gh) kay(gh)

Immediately after the respondent says "none" (line 5), the interviewer could have stopped reading the response options, especially since "none" seems clear enough to be coded as "nothing at all," but the interviewer sticks to the rules and reads the set of options.

This list of response options is formatted such that it nicely projects the completion point of this turn. As the last component of the list is

preceded by the connective "or," the respondent knows that after completion of the element that follows "or," the turn is hers. She takes the
response turn and, rather than selecting one of the options presented to
her, she repeats her prior answer in line 7: "none." When the interviewer
next asks the obvious question, whether the respondent means "nothing
at all" when she says "none," the respondent confirms this with a remarkably loud voice in line 11: "YES."

In the fragment below the same respondent again starts up her
response turn before the response options are read. Note again that the
formulation of the question does not contain any indication that response
options follow.

```
(10)    USA CATI, Wisconsin AW-1
     1   I.     .hh how would ↑YOU feel: about a national
     2          health system. providing information about
     3          YOU to the CENsus bureau for use in
     4          the POPulation census. .h⌈hh
     5   R.                             ⌊good idea
     6   I.     (h)ok(h)ay(h)
     7          would you (.) favor it STRONGly
     8          (.)
     9          favor it somewhat
    10          (.)
    11          oppose⌈it somewhat
    12   R.           ⌊stro:ngly
    13   I.     or oppose it stro:ngly
    14   R.     strong⌈ly
    15   I.           ⌊#
    16          °okay°. FAVOR it strongly.
    17   R.     mm hmm
```

The respondent's "good idea" (line 5) does not clearly match one of the
response options that the interviewer has in front of her: "favor it strongly,
favor it somewhat." The interviewer proceeds with reading her response
list, and before she has finished, the respondent interrupts and says
"strongly" (line 12).

Note that the interrruption is not placed right after "favor it somewhat," but after "oppose." This can be explained by the structure of the
list. The first two elements are not connected by a connective, which displays that there are more elements to come. It is only when the respondent, who "favored the idea," hears that the third element is an "oppose"
option, that she decides the list is complete enough for her response.
She now revises her initial "good idea" into "stro:ngly" (line 12), but the

interviewer continues to read the list. When she has completed it, indicated by the fact that the last element is preceded by "or," the respondent takes the turn again in line 14 and repeats her "strongly."

Considering the preference for contiguity (see chapter 2), one would hear this last "strongly" as "oppose it strongly." However, though the interviewer kept on reading and thus acted as if the respondent had not yet answered the question, it now becomes clear that the interviewer correctly heard "strongly" as being related to "favor."

When I looked at a set of ninety-eight Dutch interviews[7] in which the reading of a certain question was to be followed by five response options, it turned out that in thirteen cases the respondents answered the question before the interviewers had the chance to begin to read the options. In fourteen cases the interviewers were interrupted by the respondents providing an answer when the interviewers were only halfway through the list of options. Therefore, more than 25 percent of these [question] + [response options] structures were interrupted.

As Van der Zouwen and Dijkstra (1995) have shown, one solution to this problem of closed questions being vulnerable to interrruption is to present the respondents with showcards that contain the response categories. However, this procedure is more or less limited to face-to-face interviews. For telephone interviews there is another way of presenting the options without the risk of being interrupted. This will be discussed below.

5   The response instruction component

In the two previous fragments, the formulation of the question did not display that more was to follow after completion of the question as such. Below we find an example of how the list of response options can be presented without the risk of being cut off by the respondent:

> Culture P&P Survey, item 18
> The following questions are about music.
> I will mention different types of music.
>
> Next to the given choices, please indicate whether
> you like to listen to the particular type of music
> not at all, a little or much.

This preface to a set of related questions contains a number of action components. First we see the action projection component that says that a number of questions about different types of music will follow. Then we see what we may call the "response instruction component" (RIC), which states that each question has three response options: "not at all, a little or much." This way of introducing a question or a series of questions provides for the interviewer being able to present the response options without the risk of being interrupted.

The projected set of questions and the response options are given on the questionnaire as follows:

```
                        | not at all | a little | favorite music |
                        |     1      |    2     |       3        |
   pop music
   hardrock, punk, house etc.
   easy listening music
   light opera
```

Since the response options have already been mentioned in the preface to the question series, mentioning them again after each subsequent item seems redundant and may lead to interruptions. Looking at the interviews, the interviewers are never interrupted when they present this series of related questions. In this respect such a turn structure seems to work well.

There is a negative effect to the fact that the response options are not repeated next to each subsequent question, however. The first few questions are usually answered with one of the pre-coded response options. After a while, though, the respondents tend to break away from these formulations. They often answer by either "yes" or "no." The "no" answers are generally coded by the interviewer as "not at all." When the respondents say "yes," the interviewers may probe for a more precise answer, as follows:

(11)   Culture P&P Survey 12b
   1   I.   f<u>o</u>lk mus↑ic
   2   (1.4)
   3   from other c<u>u</u>ltures for example.
   4   (0.6)
   5   R.   u::h uh y<u>e</u>s.
   6   I.   a- a l↑ittle or: m<u>u</u>ch.
   7   R.   m↓uch.

(12)   Culture P&P Survey 48a
   1   I.   jazz or bl↑<u>ue</u>s
   2   R.   u:hm <u>ye:s</u>
   3   I.   m<u>u</u>ch? or: (.) a ⌈l↑ittle
   4   R.   ⌊uhm (0.5) yes
   5   let's say much

Note that these two respondents hesitate before they say "yes." It turns out that if the respondents provide a "yes" immediately after the question, and without any hesitation marker, the interviewers do not probe. This tendency on behalf of the interviewers may well mean that they interpret a quickly produced and short "yes" as "very much," whereas the interviewer is not sure what a hesitantly produced "yes" refers to. When respondents say "u::h uh y<u>e</u>s" or "u:hm y<u>e:s</u>," they may indicate either that they are making up their minds or that they like this type of music a little. When we analyze how respondents produce a yes-answer to these questions and when interviewers do and do not probe for a more precise answer, it becomes clear that the interviewers listen very carefully to how the yes-answers are being produced.

Not repeating the response options after each successive question also has the potential danger that after some time respondents may forget the options. In the following fragment the respondent asks, "What was the largest possibility again?" Immediately after this question he decides it must be "very much." This answer is incorrect as the "largest" option is actually "much."

(13)   Culture P&P Survey 32a
    1 I.   orchestral m↑usic
    2 R.   what was the largest possibility again,
    3   positively, very much with pleasure yes.
    4 I.   and serious music by m<u>o</u>dern compos↑ers

Announcing the response options of a set of related questions without repeating these options each time seems like a good solution to the problem of the respondents interrupting the ongoing turn by the interviewer. However, it has the disadvantage that the respondents may forget the response options, leading to the interviewers having difficulty in correctly coding the answers.

6   Building the response options into the question

I have shown that questions followed by response options are vulnerable to interruption. One solution to this problem is to introduce the question or the set of related questions. This makes it possible to use a response instruction component before any questions have been produced. In other cases, the response options can be built into the question proper such that they are presented before the completion point of the question delivery component. In a paper by Cradock, Maynard, and Schaeffer (1993) we find two examples of such a questioning turn structure:

(14)   USA CATI, Cradock, Maynard, and Schaeffer 1993: 10
1   I.   generally speaking, do you usually think
2   of yourself as a republican, a democrat,
3   an independent or something else?

(15)   USA CATI, Cradock, Maynard, and Schaeffer 1993: 11
1   I.   mkay .hh .hh and then during the next twelve
2   months do you think prices in general will
3   go up? go down? or stay where they are now?

Structurally speaking, this is a conversationally felicitous questioning-turn format, as it does not project a turn-completion point that was not intended by the researcher. The utterances contain a list of which the last element is projected by the connective "or." This last element not only projects the completion point of the list, but the completion point of the questioning turn as well. Right after the production of "or something else," the floor goes to the respondent, who can answer the question.

In the examples above, the response options are built into the questioning turn by means of a list. These lists are structured such that they project the completion point as intended by the researcher. That is, the last element of the list is projected by the connective "or." With this in mind, we may say that the following question is ill-structured. The structure is misleading when it comes to instructing the respondent as to what is the end of the turn.

(16)   USA CATI, Cradock, Maynard, and Schaeffer 1993, 6
1   I.   do you think that during the next twelve
2   months it will be larger or smaller than
3   during the past twelve months:? or about
4   the same

The questioning turn contains three response options. First we get two options which are connected by "or": "it will be larger or smaller than during the past twelve months:?" After the possible completion point, when the respondent is implicitly informed that he or she can take the turn to answer the question, the interviewer goes on and presents a third response option: "or about the same." What initially is presented as a question with two response alternatives is transformed into a question with three alternatives. A more conversationally adequate way of structuring this question would be:

> Do you think that during the next twelve months it will be larger or smaller than or about the same as during the past twelve months?

We need research based on a quasi-experimental design to find out to what extent such a way of structuring and formulating closed questions makes a difference when it comes to interviewer–respondent interaction in standardized survey interviews. Conversation analysis studies can only give the theoretical basis for the formulation of a hypothesis.

7   Conclusion

When a question needs to be specified, the specification should precede any utterance that could possibly be heard as the end of a question turn. This may prevent respondents from answering prematurely and interviewers from omitting specifications and being forced to interrupt respondents. As a consequence, standardization may be increased, as well as the validity of the research instrument.

It is difficult to prove that a question followed by one or more specifications is likely to generate invalid answers as long as respondents do not say anything that contradicts earlier answers or answers yet to be provided. However, as I have argued, answers generated in this way cannot always be trusted at face value.

Apart from challenging the validity of the answers, there is no doubt that this structure has a negative influence on standardization. It may tempt interviewers to omit the specifications. When a respondent begins to answer right after the completion of the actual question, one way for an interviewer to produce the specification is by interrupting the respondent. The other way is to continue reading the response options after a respondent's "premature" answer, and thus to ignore the answer. Both possibilities are unhappy interactional devices in that respondents may be offended and lose their motivation to co-operate fully and seriously.

6 Generating recordable answers to field-coded questions

1   Introduction

Field-coded questions are open questions from the respondents' point of view. While closed questions consist of both the question and the response options, field-coded questions consist of the question only. From the perspective of the interviewers, however, a field-coded question consists of more than just the question. The interviewers have a set of response options in front of them, and they must record the respondents' answers by checking the corresponding box. As Fowler and Mangione point out (1990: 88), field-coded questions require interviewers to be coders, because they have to classify the respondents' answers in order to be able to check one of the answer boxes.

Because the respondents are not informed of the responses they can choose from, their answers are often unformatted, that is, they do not match the response categories. Unformatted answers occur not only in response to field-coded questions. We also find them when the response options have been read to respondents. When answers are not fit for recording, in whatever context they are produced, interviewers are faced with the task of probing for a recordable answer. How do they do this? What conversational devices do interviewers employ to probe for a recordable answer?

Textbooks on survey interviewing do not offer much information on how to probe for answers, except to say that the interviewer should not probe in a directive manner. When interviewers have a set of response options in front of them, they should present the entire set of options. If they present only part of the options, they may influence the respondent's answer. Suppose a respondent answers the question "How often do you do X? Very often, pretty often, or not too often" with "often." According to the rules of standardized survey interviewing, in such a situation the interviewer should re-read all three options, rather than saying, "Would that be very often or pretty often?"

In this chapter I will show that interviewers who present only part of the response options in response to the production of an unrecordable answer cannot necessarily be seen as behaving directively. They may use a conversational device that makes it possible to present a selected number of the response options in a non-directive manner (section 2). I will also show how interviewers sometimes present only one of the set of response options if the respondent's answer is not formulated for recording. When the interviewers do so, they usually base this selection on the information the respondent has provided earlier, as well as on their everyday knowledge of the world.

In section 3, I will briefly mention some reasons why respondents provide unrecordable answers to field-coded questions. Analysis of answers to field-coded questions, which are open questions from the respondents' perspective, provides us with some insights into just how answerable certain questions are. Section 4 is devoted to how interviewers reformulate unformatted answers in order to be able to record them.

The analysis in this chapter is based on nine Dutch interviews that were carried out on behalf of a sociological study on cultural education and participation. They are referred to in the fragments as "Culture P&P Survey." The interviews take about half an hour. The respondents are twenty to forty years old, and live in Amsterdam.

The interviews are paper-and-pencil interviews, and are carried out by telephone from the interviewers' homes in Rotterdam. The interviewers were paid for completed interviews only. The way the interviewers were paid, and the fact that they were not monitored during the interviews, may account for the fact that the interviewers seem to aim for smooth and time-effective interviews. Another possible reason for them to complete the interviews as quickly as possible is that they have to pay the bills for these long-distance calls.

The interviewers have been instructed to always read the questions. The questions are printed on the questionnaire in capitals. A question sometimes contains a clarifying element, which is not printed in capitals. It is left to the interviewer to decide whether or not to read these clarifying elements. For example, question 5 of the questionnaire reads:

> HOW OFTEN IN THE PREVIOUS YEAR (since March last year) HAVE YOU BEEN TO A MUSEUM?

The response categories are meant for the interviewer only, which make these questions field-coded questions.

2   Generating recordable answers

The main question in this chapter is "What interactional devices do interviewers use to generate a recordable answer, if such an answer does not follow the question?" I make a conceptual and terminological distinction between "answers" and "responses." As discussed in chapter 3, this distinction coincides with a distinction between the level of the interaction on the one hand and the level of the written document on the other. The term "response option" or "response category" refers to the categories as they are written on the questionnaire. The term "answer" is used for the talk the respondents provide in response to the questions.

2.1   Providing candidate answers

When a respondent provides an answer that does not match one of the pre-coded response categories, or when a respondent states that he or she is not able to answer the question, the interviewer may present one or more of the response options that are sitting in front of her. Rather than just reading these options, the interviewer presents them in a conversational way. That is, though the interviewers present the scripted response options, they sound as if they are creating them on the spot. For instance:

(1)   Culture P&P Survey 23, question 35
    1 I.   and the:n some background questions,
    2   what is currently your main activity?
    3   (1.7)
    4 R.   what what do you mean?
    5 I.   uh do you have a paid ↑job
    6   do you attend some form of educat↑ion
    7   are you unempl↑oyed
    8 R.   well no. well, I just work.

The question about someone's "main activity" in research interviews is a notoriously difficult question. "Main activity" is a research-theoretical concept that is not clear to everyone. Formulated in ethnomethodological terms, "main activity" is not a "member's term." It is unlikely that people will consider being unemployed as an "activity."

After the respondent requests a clarification of the term, the interviewer provides a selection of the response options. They are presented with a rising intonation (marked as ↑) as if the interviewer improvises then and there. These options sound like they are random examples of the concept "main activity." It is quite easy to extend these options as presented by thinking "or that sort of thing." Apparently the presentation of this series of answer options has the desired effect, since the respondent then says, "Well I just work."

Research shows that this way of presenting possible answers is not unique to research interviews (Schuman and Presser 1981; Schuman and

Scott 1987). An analysis of interviews in different types of institutional settings (Houtkoop-Steenstra 1990) shows that interviewers sometimes must ask questions that do not make clear what sort of answer is expected. In this situation, interviewers sometimes add candidate answers to the question that specify the type of answer that is being sought (Pomerantz 1988). By adding candidate answers, the speaker offers his or her co-participant a "searching instruction": go and find an answer that is not only correct, but also fits into the categories of which the candidate answers are examples. (See, for example, Sacks (1972a), Jayyusi (1984), and Mazeland (1994) on devices people use for descriptive practices.) These candidate answers are produced in such a way that they are just examples and that other answers are possible as well.

The following five structures are described in Houtkoop-Steenstra 1990:

Type 1: [X or what]

(2)   Pomerantz (1988) school attendant–absent pupil interaction
       1 I.   When was the first day that you were out ill.
       2 R.   I don't know.
       3 I.   Well you know how long it's been,
       4   **couple of weeks? or what?**
       5 R.   Yeh.

Type 2: [X or Y]

(3)   Dutch radio interview
       1 I   How did you get the idea.
       2   **Did it arise suddenly or was there an occasion**.
       3 R   We:ll no: >it took us a long time, really (..)

Type 3: [X or uh]

(4)   Mishler (1986) doctor–patient interaction
       1 D.   And how did- how did the ulcers present.
       2   What uh- What happened? **Just pain or uh**
       3 P.   It's a- Wel:l. Ye:ah. Pa- lot- lots of pain
       4   sour stomach

Type 4: [X, or Y, or]

(5)   Dutch courtrooom
       1 J.   I don't know, what's the limit for
       2   you before you say "I won't u:h I
       3   won't u:h drive anymore".
       4   (1.2)

5   **Is that <u>eight</u> beers, or-or-or tw<u>o</u> beers, or:**
6   D.   We:ll, that depends.

Type 5: [X, Y,]

(6)   Dutch radio interview
       1   I.   Well, then you start doing b<u>u</u>siness a:nd how
       2   do you proc<u>ee</u>d? **Do you take initiatives**
       3   **your↑selves, do you w<u>ai</u>t till somebody**
       4   **comes a↑long** =
       5   R.   = Well (0.4) in the beginning uh we didn't. (..)

All five types of lists of candidate answers are produced in such a way that
the recipient is instructed that the candidate answers are not to be treated
as a set of fixed-choice answers. The "Is it X or what?" format invites the
recipient to provide an answer, which may not be the one mentioned. In
an American survey interview, an interviewer uses such an "X, Y or
what?" format. When the respondent asks what she means by "or what?"
the interviewer says, "It's whatever you wanna say." This is the interviewer's mundane formulation of the third response option that sits in
front of her: "other <specify>."
      The other list formats invite the recipient to complete the incomplete
list. Apart from the first type, all lists are produced as recognizably incomplete utterances that invite the co-participant to complete them. Some are
marked as incomplete by virtue of the marked intonation at the end of the
utterance, for example, "Is it X or Y?" Others are incomplete syntactic
structures. For example, type 5 "Is it X, Y" lacks the list-final "or Z"
element. Type 4, "Is it X or Y or" contains the connective "or" but lacks
the list-final element. In type 3, the candidate answer is followed by "or
uh."
      In the next fragments the interviewers, again, take a selection from the
response categories and present them in a conversational way as the candidate answers.

(7)   Culture P&P Survey 12, question 29
       1   I.   with whom did you <u>go</u> to your first concert
       2   (2.3)
       3   R.   >I don't rem<u>e</u>mber<
       4   I.   uhm fr↑iends, sch↑ool,
       5   R.   just fr<u>ie</u>nds. (yes.)
       6   I.   °hmhm.°

The respondent may have assumed that he was expected to mention the
name of the person with whom he went to his first concert. When the

interviewer presents some examples that demonstrate the type of answer that is expected, the respondent answers "just friends. (yes)."

In the next fragment the interviewer waits only briefly for the respondent to answer the question and then proceeds to illustrate the requested type of answer by providing a few examples taken from the set of response options:

(8)   Culture P&P Survey 48, question 28
1 I.   and do you remember which genre of classical
2   music it was?
3   (.)
4   was it orchestra mus↑ic or chamber mus↑ic
5 R.   no, it was orchestra music.
6 I.   °orchestra music.°
7   ((next question))

Sometimes the interviewers present candidate answers immediately after the completion of the question. They are more likely to do this with questions that frequently cause problems for the respondents. For example, the formulation of question 11 does not instruct respondents that museums are supposed to come in two kinds, that is, "art museums" and "no art museums," as the pre-coded response options show the interviewers:

(9)   Culture P&P Survey 81, question 11
1 I.   a:nd what kind of museums were visited? =
2   = was it↑art
3   or all kinds of th↑ings
4 R.   we:::ll, not a:rt.
5 I.   not art.
6 R.   no, toy muse↑um
7 I.   whatever kind of museum there happens to be.

There is another problem with question 11. Question 2, which also deals with "kinds of museums," presents the respondents with several kinds of museums: open-air museums, maritime museums, antiquity rooms, and a few more. By explicitly mentioning these kinds of museums, the interviewer demonstrates the meaning of the concept "kinds of museums" to the respondents. When presented with question 11, the respondents have no reason to understand the concept "kinds of museums" differently, unless the interviewer explicitly states the difference, as in the fragment above.

In some cases the question, as worded in the questionnaire, is immediately replaced by the interviewer with a question formulation that incorporates (part of) the response categories. This happens in the fragment

below. The question to be read is number 8, "WITH WHOM DID YOU GO
TO A MUSEUM FOR THE FIRST TIME?" Immediately prior to this, the
respondent has answered question 7, "HOW OLD WERE YOU WHEN
YOU VISITED A MUSEUM FOR THE FIRST TIME?"

(10)   Culture P&P Survey 71, question 8
1   I.   was this with your par↑ents,
2   or with your sch↑ool, or something?
3   R.   n:o, I think it was w:ith a friend of mine,
4   we then were in Leiden.
5   I.   °with friends.°

Rather than asking the question as scripted, the interviewer asks, "Was
this with your par↑ents, or with your sch↑ool, or something?" In doing so,
she includes some of the response options in her initial presentation of the
question and indicates the type of answer that is expected. The respondent then states that it was "with a friend of his." When the interviewer
acknowledges her receipt of the answer, she more or less repeats it.
However, rather than repeating "a friend," she uses the formulation of the
corresponding response option: "°with friends,°" which the respondent
does not offer to change or correct.

By reformulating the scripted question, the interviewer transforms the
written style of the questionnaire into a style that is more appropriate for
speech and interaction. Questionnaires often contain redundant phrases
and other characteristics typical of written texts (Chafe 1982). These
style features are easily changed by interviewers (Houtkoop-Steenstra
1990). For instance, in the previous example the phrase, "did you go to a
museum for the first time," is replaced by "this," making the interview
more conversational. These examples, and others not shown here, make
clear that interviewers quickly learn which questions constitute problems
for respondents. They change the scripted wording to clarify the type of
answer that is expected.

These actions can be considered corrections of the potentially troublesome scripted questions. Elaborating on the work by Schegloff, Jefferson,
and Sacks (1977) on repair in conversation, we can refer to such changes
as "interviewer-initiated questionnaire repair." The interviewers thus
attempt to avoid the possible problems of respondents providing unrecordable answers or indicating that they do not understand the purpose
of the question.

2.2   Proposing a specific answer

Rather than presenting a portion of the response options, interviewers
may present only one of the options. For example:

(11)   Culture P&P Survey 26, question 19
    1 I.   do you yourself have records, tapes, cds?
    2 R.   well, if I'm supposed to mention all of them,
    3   it will surely take a few uh hours.
    4 I.   they are more than a hundred in total?
    5 R.   ye:s, most certainly.

The interviewer was supposed to read "DO YOU HAVE RECORDS, TAPES OR CDS, AND, IF SO, HOW MANY IN TOTAL?" Note that this formulation contains two questions, first a yes–no question, and then, "if so, how many?" This formulation may be adequate for a written questionnaire, but it is not adequate for a text that is to be used in an interview. It is, therefore, not surprising that the interviewer splits up the two questions. She begins with the first question, "Do you yourself have records, tapes, cds?" The respondent displays, in his answer to this question, that he anticipates the follow-up question. When a person owns so many records, tapes and cds that it would take a few hours to count them all, in a manner of speaking, he or she owns "many." (See Sacks, 1988/89, on "members' measurement systems.") The interviewer infers from this that the respondent may own over a hundred tapes and records.

When we look at the questionnaire, we see that the interviewer's follow-up question refers to option 5. The field-coded response options are: (1) none, (2) 1–10, (3) 11–50, (4) 50–100, (5) more than 100. Option 5 is presented by the interviewer as a yes–no question. Although this yes–no question is directive, as the declarative syntactic structure of the utterance indicates that the interviewer expects a yes–answer (Abbenbroek 1993), the answer "ye:s, most certainly" sounds convincing.

The next fragment shows how two successive questions, numbers 7 and 8, are dealt with by the interviewer proposing a specific answer. Let me first give the questions and field-coded response options, as they are written on the questionnaire:

Question 7
HOW OLD WERE YOU WHEN YOU VISITED A MUSEUM FOR THE FIRST TIME? about — years.

Question 8
WITH WHOM DID YOU GO TO A MUSEUM FOR THE FIRST TIME?
    1 with primary school
    2 with secondary school
    3 with parents
    4 with brothers and/or sisters and other family members

    5 with friends and acquaintances
    6 by myself

These two questions are dealt with in the following way:

(12)   Culture P&P Survey 67A, questions 7 and 8

1	I.	uh how o̲ld were you when you visited a
2		museum for the fi̲rst time?
3	R.	.hh that was with ↑scho̲ol
4		(.)
5		about (.) ↑te̲n, tw↑e̲lve
6	I.	yes.
7		(.)
8		we̲nt with primary school, then. =
9	R.	= yes. =
10	I.	= °yes.°

When the respondent, in his answer to question 7, states that he first visited a museum with his school, the interviewer knows that response options 3 through 6 for question 8 do not apply to this respondent. Also, under normal circumstances, Dutch children enter some form of secondary school when they are about twelve years old. Thus, if the respondent was around ten to twelve years old when he went to a museum for the first time, he was most likely in primary school. Based on her knowledge of the Dutch educational system, and based on the respondent's prior information, the interviewer can make an educated guess, "we̲nt with primary school, then," which is confirmed by the respondent.

The same procedure is followed in other instances when the interviewers are to ask questions 7 and 8. When one respondent indicates that she went to a museum for the first time when she was fourteen years old, the interviewer says, "uh -s >with secondary school.<," which is confirmed by the respondent. Another respondent says that he was about eleven when he went to a museum for the first time, and that this was with a "school o̲uting." Again, the interviewer suggests "pri̲mary school, then," which is confirmed by the respondent.

However, when respondents do not provide any information in response to question 7 from which the interviewers can infer the answer to question 8, the interviewers do ask the question, rather than suggest an answer:

(13)   Culture P&P Survey 32a, question 7

1	I.	.pt and about how old were you when you
2		first vi̲sited a museum?
3		(0.5)

4   R.   °well about° t↑en
5   I.   °about ten.°
6   → and with whom uh did you go?
7   R.   with my p<u>a</u>rents

In many cases, however, interviewers do not read question 8, but instead suggest an answer to this question. From a formal point of view, these interviewers engage in leading interviewing behavior. When we study the sequential context in which they suggest an answer, however, it is clear that these suggestions are based on the information provided by the respondents, and it is therefore not surprising that these suggestions are confirmed by the respondents. Rather than viewing the response that is recorded as the possible product of the interviewer's leading behavior, we may well see it as a response that is established by the joint efforts of interaction participants, and therefore an accountable answer. Rather than claiming that these interviewers ask leading questions, we may say they are asking "recipient-designed questions." As the examples above make clear, asking a recipient-designed question may mean that one skips the question altogether and merely suggests the answer to this question.

3   The degree to which questions can be answered

The analysis of this set of interviews provides some understanding of what may cause respondents to deal with questions in ways that were not intended by the researcher.

3.1   Wrong instructions

An important problem for interviewers is that questionnaire items may be formulated such that they request a type of answer that differs from the pre-coded response categories. For example, item 29, "WITH WHOM DID YOU GO TO YOUR FIRST CONCERT?" suggests that the name of a person is being requested. The response options show, however, that the answer should be put in categorical terms (primary school, secondary school, parents, friends, etc.). In the case of closed questions, the response options function as an instruction for the respondent as to what type of answer is being requested. Field-coded questions lack this instruction, which results in an extra burden on the formulation of the questions. Because some of the questions in this questionnaire do not instruct respondents about the type of answer they should provide, the interviewers bring the response options into play as candidate answers.

3.2   Lack of knowledge

Respondents occasionally lack the information that is required in order to provide an adequate response to a question that is posed to them. For example, item 55 of the questionnaire reads: "DID YOUR PARENTS GO TO MUSEUMS WHEN YOU WERE 10–12 YEARS OLD?" The respondents tend to provide a qualified yes–no answer, as people do in ordinary conversation (Churchill 1978). Rather than giving an exact number that would match the pre-coded response options, they provide vague numbers such as "not very often." One might say that respondents should not be expected to know exactly how many times a year their parents went to museums when they (the respondents) were about ten years old, but this is just one example of such a difficult question. Respondents are also often asked, and often cannot produce responses to, questions about the highest level of schooling completed by their parents and siblings, and whether or not their siblings engage in certain activities.

In addition, a respondent is assumed to be able to report on all sorts of things that occurred when he or she was between the ages of ten and twelve. For example, how many books, and what type of books, were in his or her house? What job did his or her father have then, and did he supervise other people, and if so, how many? Such information may be very important for a Bourdieu-like research project, but, as these interviews clearly show, one cannot simply assume that individuals have immediate access to such information.

3.3   The order of things

Another potential problem of interview questions is related to the different ways in which phenomena can be categorized (see Sacks (1972), Schegloff (1972), and Mazeland, Huisman, and Schasfoort (1995) on categorizing). Many questions in this questionnaire contain key terms that are categorical, for instance, classical concert, art, modern art, and old art. The definitions of these categories are highly disputable, and this issue is not merely theoretical. Several times during these interviews respondents display that they have problems in this respect. In one case, when a respondent states that for him "hardrock, punk, house" does not constitute a single category of music, the interviewer explicitly says, "There is a lot of discussion about this category."

Professionals working in specific institutional settings often use categorizations that do not match the experience and the "everyday reasoning" of their co-participants outside the institution. For example, Mazeland, Huisman, and Schasfoort (1995) show that in the world of travel agencies, the notion of "child" can have a different meaning from the one used in the mundane world. As one agent says, "Fifteen years old is an adult with us," while everyday reasoning might argue that an individual is not considered an adult until the age of eighteen. Also, the notion of what age groups "count" as children may differ from one institutional setting/situation to another.

Questionnaires usually contain a number of notions that are prototypical for social research, for example, "household," "family," "income," "profession," "job," and "main activity." Respondents often do not know that they are supposed to interpret such notions as research-technical concepts with a specialized meaning. For example, in mundane reasoning, being unemployed is not an activity, let alone a "main activity." One respondent who was only employed for a few hours a week indicated that he did not have a job. This response suggests that in the social world outside the research interview, one of the constituting features of the concept "job" may be that it requires a minimal number of hours per week. In another example, after doing some cognitive interviews, the Dutch Census Bureau realized that respondents often interpreted the notion of "income" as "the money you earn from having a job." Whereas the Census Bureau included scholarships, welfare, old age pensions and the like in its definition of income, the respondents did not necessarily do so (Snijkers and Conen 1995).

Research methodologists are, to some degree, aware that technical terms like the ones just mentioned may pose a problem for respondents. That questionnaire designers belong to a specific socio-cultural sub-group, which differs from the majority of the respondents, seems to be less acknowledged, however (Briggs 1986). Therefore, a questionnaire designer who uses the concept "completed course" may not realize that some respondents may feel they have completed a course, even though they never took an examination, as another analysis of standardized interviews shows.[1] Careful analysis of survey interviews is needed to detect these sub-culture-specific meanings. Sometimes just one respondent can display that a term may be interpreted in ways that vary greatly from the assumed meaning. As Suchman and Jordan (1990a) point out, as long as respondents are not allowed to discuss the questions, it will never become apparent that they may understand a term in a way that differs from the researcher's understanding or intention.

3.4   Preference for instances over categories

The analysis of factual interviews leads to another observation. When a question is formatted such that it clearly requests an answer in terms of some category, respondents often mention a particular instance rather than the category of which the instance is a member. For example, when asked "what kinds of museums" they have ever been to, respondents usually mention the names of specific museums, such as the Stedelijk Museum or the Rijksmuseum. When they are asked "what genre of concert" they have been to, respondents may say "to Whitney Houston" or "the Stones."

Such answers raise the possibility that individuals do not think of their experiences in terms of categories. If this is so, questions that seek categorical answers may be vulnerable to receiving unrecordable answers, resulting in interviewers needing to probe for different responses. Because research methodology favors standardization of the interviewing process, designing questions that may lead to the need for probing, such as questions requiring categorical responses, should be avoided.

3.5   Lack of knowledge of classification

Although the designers of this questionnaire may have assumed that the interviewers would be able to categorize the Stedelijk Museum as a museum of modern art and the Rijksmuseum as a museum of old art, the interviews make clear that the classification of museums places heavy demands on the interviewers' knowledge of the Dutch cultural landscape. The interviewers make mistakes in this regard several times. Here is one example:

(14)   Culture P&P Survey 48b, question 3
```
1   I.      .hh and the last time you went to a museum,
2           what ki- what kind of museum was that.
3   R.      uh that was an ethnography museum
4   I.      °ethnography.°
5           (.)
6           so nature museum, is where I put it, right?
7   R.      uhm, we:ll not in the sense of nature museum,
8           but it's uh it's not about u:h about nature.
9           if that's what you mean.
```

The tape recordings make clear that respondents also make mistakes here. They sometimes display that they do not know in which category a specific museum belongs. This confusion even holds for museums that they (claim to) have visited. When asked if they ever went to a museum of modern art or a natural history museum, for example, respondents may say "yes" and then mention the particular museum they have been to. These elaborations sometimes show that they categorize the museum incorrectly; that is, differently than the experts classify it. The interviews suggest that some people do not really know what type of museum they have been to, especially when they did not go there by their own choice. They may have once been to "the museum on the big square," or to "the museum with the old dolls," for instance.

These interviews also show that the same confusion manifests itself when respondents categorize music. When respondents are asked about the "genre" of classical music performance they first attended, we find all sorts of answers: "classical guitar," "an orchestral uh school concert,"[1] "light classical music, like the bolero," "a symphony orchestra," "something like uh Slavic uh dance. singing an:d something else like that. with these wooden instruments." The field-coded response options, however, are:

> (1) classical orchestral music
> (2) classical chamber music
> (3) opera
> (4) light opera
> (5) other, —

Most of the performances mentioned by the respondents belong to the category "other." Since there is no indication that the interviewers are copying down these answers in the category "other" after they receive these descriptive answers, they may have categorized these answers as classical orchestral music or as classical chamber music.

These interviewers are also required to do calculations in order to arrive at recordable responses. There are several questions that require an answer about "how long ago" something happened. It appears that respondents tend to answer such questions by providing a specific year. Let me give one example:

> (15)   Culture P&P Survey 48b, question 6
> ((how long has it been since the respondent went to))
> 1   I.   the Allard Pierson Museum.
> 2   R.   that is u:hm let me see: (...)
> 3   → that's been (.) in nineteen ninety.
> 4   I.   so: three years ago.

Such "how long ago" questions sometimes force the interviewer to do calculations. According to the rules of standardized interviewing, they should leave this to the respondent, but in a case like the fragment above, it would undermine the interviewer's credibility if she were to ask, "So, that's how many years ago?" She would appear to not be able to do a simple calculation. In fact, this interviewer makes a mistake here. The interview was carried out in 1992, which means that the correct answer would be "two years ago."

Fowler and Mangione (1990) claim that interviewers should not be left with the coding of the interview data. However, when it comes to field-coded questions, interviewers are supposed to code the respondents' answers. The analysis of this set of interviews shows that coding requires that interviewers be quite knowledgeable about the domain of the questions. These data also show that respondents should not be responsible for the coding either, as they do not necessarily know how to categorize their experiences (Hak forthcoming).

Textbooks on research methodology pay much attention to question formulation. However, question formulation seems to be concerned primarily with problems of ambiguity, referentiality, and presupposition. In some cases Gricean maxims are also addressed, for example, by Sudman, Bradburn, and Schwarz (1996) and Schwarz (1996). There is little discussion, however, about the fact that the formulation of the question should make clear to the respondents what type of answer they are expected to provide (Briggs 1986). This may be because there is no tradition of doing detailed studies of interview transcripts. Detailed analyses of survey interviews illustrate why respondents fail to do what they are supposed to do; a question that seems to be adequate initially may turn out to be inadequately or infelicitously formulated when studied in its interactional context.

4   Reformulating unformatted answers

When generating recordable answers to field-coded questions, interviewers have a double task. They must generate valid answers to the questions, and they must generate answers that match the pre-coded response categories. As we saw in section 1, a respondent may provide an answer that is formulated in a way that cannot be recorded. When this happens, the interviewer sometimes reformulates the answer so that it matches one of the response options. In most cases the initial answer will not be distorted in the process. However, this reformulation procedure can easily lead to invalid research data. For instance, in the fragment that was discussed earlier:

(16)   Culture P&P Survey 23, question 35
         1   I.   and the:n some background questions,
         2   what is currently your main activity?
         3   (1.7)
         4   R.   what what do you mean?
         5   I.   uh do you have a paid j↑ob
         6   do you attend some form of educat↑ion
         7   are you unemp↑loyed

```
 8  R.     well no
 9         well I just work.
10  I.     a- a paid job.
11  R.     °yah°.
```

The answer "well I just work" does not match the response categories, as they distinguish between "a paid job" and "unpaid work." The interviewer reformulates the answer "well I just work" as "a- a paid job" (line 10). We do not know if this response is correct, but the respondent does not contradict it. Based on the conversation analysis research on the preference organization of responses as discussed in chapter 2, we may doubt whether the "yes" or "yah" that follows a reformulation is always an acceptance of this reformulation.

A reformulation, as discussed in this chapter, corresponds to the notion of "formulation" used by Heritage and Watson (1979). A reformulation is the first pair-part of a "reformulation-decision sequence." The decision has two alternatives: a confirmation or a rejection of the reformulation. Heritage and Watson show that a preference exists for the acceptance of a reformulation, and like other dispreferred responses, the rejection of a reformulation tends to be formatted differently than the preferred response. Dispreferred responses are prefaced by delays, hesitations, and token agreements, pushing the rejection further back into the response turn. Below, the respondent's rejection is prefaced by "uh (.) yeah":

```
(17)   Culture P&P Survey 48, question 6
       1   I.    .hh and the Amsterdam Historical Museum? =
       2         = have you ever been ⌈there?
       3   R.                         ⌊tha- that's been a
       4         few years ago.
       5         (.)
       6   I.    about three?
       7   R.    uh (.) yeah >longer<
```

This example is rather exceptional for standardized survey interviews. The standardized survey interview is typically a social interaction in which the respondents readily agree with the interviewers' statements, even though they may not be (quite) correct. For example:

```
(18)   Culture P&P Survey 32, question 25
       1   I.    I will now mention a number of halls in eh
       2         Amsterd↑am, and you can indicate if you
       3         have ever been th↑ere (0.6) for a music
       4         performance that ↑is, and uh how long ago
       5         was the last t↓ime.
       6   R.    °hm mm°. =
```

```
 7   I.      = music theatre?
             (. . .)
 8   R.      u:h no yes I have been there. once.
 9           and u:h (2.0) °°when was this?°°
10           (2.0)
11           it had just been opened. then.
12           (1.0)
13   I.      °until° about three years ago or so? =
14   R.      = yes °something like that°.
15   I.      °yes.°
```

The respondent may not remember, but the Music Theatre opened in September 1986. This interview took place in the early summer of 1992. Thus, that the respondent was in the Music Theatre "about three years ago or so?" (line 13) is improbable, but he nevertheless accepts the proposed response.

The next respondent is presented with a statement about modern art. In this fragment, as well as the following ones, the participants frequently use the ambiguous Dutch word *ja*, which I translate as "yah."

```
(19)     Culture P&P Survey 42, question 17
 1   I.      u:h I'll present four statements on modern art.
 2           could you indicate for each of these
 3           statements, if you agree with it, disagree,
 4           or maybe that you have no opinion here.
 5           (1.1)
 6   R.      y↑a:h
 7   I.      here you go. art is very important as a means
 8           to encourage people to start thinking.
 9   R.      what? PARdon me?
10   I.      art is very important as a means to encourage
11           people to start thinking.
12   R.      very important (.) as a means (.) to thinking?
13   I.      yah? (.) to encourage start thinking
14   R.      uhm, bit philo(h)sophical. ((laughs))
15   I.      ((laughs))
16   R.      uh an important means to thinking
17           (0.5)
18   I.      should I show you a work of art?
19           who knows it will help?
20   R.      yah. uhm (1.2) rather a difficult question.
21           just got to think about it.
22           u:::::h repeat it will you. "cause then⌐
23   I.                                          ⌊art
```

```
24          is very important as a means to encourage
25          start thinking.
26    R.    y::ah
27    I.    yah. you agree with that.
28          I"m not interested in modern art because (...)
```

Although the respondent's "y::ah" in line 26 may have been an introduction to some action other than an agreement with the statement, the interviewer concludes that the respondent agrees, and the respondent does not contradict this. Notice that after saying, "Yah. you agree with that," the interviewer immediately moves on to the next statement. She does not provide the respondent with the possibility to display that his "y::ah" was perhaps the beginning of a non-agreement.

The Dutch *ja* (yah) is highly ambiguous.[2] This is especially true when it is used in turn-initial position. The interactional function of *ja* becomes clearer when the speaker continues. A *ja* may be used as an acknowledgment token or as an agreement with the prior speaker's talk. It may also be used as the beginning of a non-agreeing action, much like the English "well." The consequence of the ambiguity of *ja* for the survey interview is that interviewers should be careful not to immediately treat a respondent's turn-initial *ja* as an agreement or a confirmation.

The interview data discussed here contain several instances in which respondents seem to agree with disputable reformulations. This apparent contrast may be caused by the interviewer, who does not await further talk by the respondent. The next fragment shows another example:

```
(20)   Culture P&P Survey 23, question 6
       1    I.    a:nd I mention a list of museums in Amsterdam,
       2          please indicate which ones you have ever
       3          been to.
                  (...)
       4          d- Tropical Muse↑um
       5          (1.0)
       6    R.    yah, that was primary school uh
       7          (1.2)
       8          ya:h yah sixth grade or something (    )
       9    I.    abou:t ten years, say.
      10    R.    ⌈yah
      11    I.    ⌊.hh and u:h that was with your primary school?
```

The interviewer implies that the respondent was in the sixth grade of primary school when he was "abou:t ten years, say." In the old Dutch school system, a pupil was approximately twelve years old in the sixth grade.[3]

The interviewer does not await the respondent's evaluation of this reformulation and proceeds to the next question. Simultaneously, the respondent says "yah." Although this may be a confirmation of the reformulation, the rising intonation suggests that the "yah," is the beginning of a longer turn. It is likely that the respondent is about to produce a disagreeing response but stops his turn upon hearing the interviewer take the floor.

In these interviews respondents frequently provide answers that are marked for uncertainty and/or estimation (Schaeffer, Maynard, and Cradock 1993). These approximations are directly related to the nature of the information respondents are asked to provide. Especially when dealing with autobiographical questions, respondents have difficulty providing responses that are not vague. The problem for these interviewers, however, is that they frequently have to code these responses as exact numbers nevertheless. In order to perform this interview task, they have to transform respondents' vague answers into precise responses. Heritage and Watson show that, in formulating a summarizing interpretation of the preceding utterances, parts of the talk are deleted. When survey interviewers reformulate imprecise answers, they leave out the uncertainty and preserve the portion of the response that they can use for recording.[4]

There are numerous examples in these interviews of interviewers reformulating imprecise answers as precise answers, for example:

(21)   Culture P&P Survey 42, question 10
        1   I.   how often have you been to a museum with your
        2   class in primary school? =
        3   R.   = we::ll (1.8) I think about once, twice,
        4   yah (2.1) twice perh↑aps three t↑i:mes =
        5   I.   = °tw↓ice°
        6   R.   ya:h.

This fragment contains a number of linguistic devices respondents employ to mark their statement for uncertainty. The respondent first indicates that the answer to come is a subjective answer: "I think." Next she indicates that the number of times she is about to mention is an approximation: "about." When she mentions the number of times, she also indicates that this is an estimation by using rising intonation: "once, twice, yah (2.1) twice perh↑aps. three t↑i:mes." The uncertain character of the answer is further indicated by the hedge "perh↑aps." In other interviews we find similarly formulated answers:

• "and I th:ink it was four or six times, but (.) I couldn't swear to it."
• "pff, I think about (1.4) <two, three> years, say."
• "say li::ke we::ll fifteen, or ↓so."

- "well about t↑en"
- "well, I guess (.) s<u>i</u>x. six years. ab↓out."
- "Jewish Historic museum I was there u:h about three years ag↑o. °two three years ag↑o°

Fragment 21 is one of many examples that suggests respondents in survey interviews follow Grice's maxim of quality, which states that one should not say things that one does not believe to be true. Although the respondent clearly indicates that her answer is an approximation, it is reformulated by the interviewer as "°tw↑ice°." The respondent's carefully stated approximation now becomes a fact: the respondent has been to the museum twice.

Jönsson and Linell (1991) describe a similar procedure in police interrogations. The vagueness of the defendant's spoken narrative is transformed to precision in the written police reports (see also Zimmerman 1969). In a similar fashion, patients' reformulated talk ends up in their medical files (Heath 1982, Treichler et al. 1984, Beckman and Frankel 1984). It is quite likely that this process of reformulation for precision occurs in all situations in which spoken talk is transformed to meet the requirements of forms and other organizational documents.[5]

Such documents usually do not constitute the end of the encounter between the organization's representative and his or her client. The "social facts," as they become in these documents, form the basis of further professional actions or decisions, such as an individual's referral to a hospital or some form of psychotherapy, or an individual's conviction by a judge, for example. In survey interviews, however, the survey is almost always the end of any contact between the interviewer and the respondent.

In the case of survey interviews, respondents' approximate answers are transformed into precise responses that match the pre-coded options. One could even say that the validity of the respondents' answers is invalidated by the requirements of the questionnaire. Looking at it from a Gricean perspective, one might conclude that such survey questions do not take as their primary activity the search for valid answers (Lynch forthcoming), which seems to contradict research methodology's stated quest for response validity.

5   Conclusion

Literature on interviewing in social research tacitly assumes that questions are formulated such that they result in answers that are easily coded. However, this is clearly not always the case. Interviewers use a number of interactional devices to generate answers that can be coded, but these devices are violations of the rules of standardized interviewing as presented in textbooks.

A wide range of research (Brenner 1982, Dijkstra, van der Veen, and van der Zouwen 1985) indicates that these violations are considered by survey methodologists to be very serious, for two primary reasons: they endanger the standardization of the research instrument, and they are considered to be directive in nature, which destroys the validity of the final answer. As the present research shows, however, interviewers may depart from the standardization because a respondent does not provide an adequate answer, which may be caused by an inadequacy in the questionnaire.

What can we learn from the research on the half-open standardized research interview, as presented in this chapter? We can see that the preference organization of responses, which can cause respondents to agree with incorrect reformulations, results in research data with doubtful validity.

7 Establishing rapport

1 Introduction

Respondents are social and emotional beings who cannot be forced to provide the information that is sought by the interviewer. The interviewer therefore needs to establish a relationship with the respondent that may improve the his or her willingness and ability to co-operate. Fowler and Mangione (1990) state, "We want a warm, professional relationship, one in which the interviewer is respected and trusted, but nonetheless the kind of professional who is accepting and nonjudgmental" (64).

In the literature on survey methodology, two types of interview styles tend to be distinguished: the task-oriented, or formal style, and the person-oriented, or socio-emotional style (Hyman 1954, Dijkstra 1983 and 1987). However, the literature does not make clear how a person-oriented interview style is achieved. The person-oriented interviewer is generally described in evaluative terms, such as "personal," "warm," and "friendly," or as "the sort of person to whom one might tell personal information that would be more difficult to tell to a stranger" (Fowler and Mangione 1990: 64). Such qualifications do not clarify what an interviewer is supposed to do in order to be perceived as personal or warm.

The literature on the effects of these two types of interview styles occasionally includes examples of interviewers' utterances that are supposed to reflect a personal style. For example, Dijkstra (1983: 44) states that he instructed his interviewers, who were to use a personal style:

to respond in a personal, understanding way, especially when the respondents express their feelings, or talk about personal experiences[. . .]. For example, with utterances such as "I understand what it must have meant to you when you got this house," and "How troublesome for you, all these problems with your neighbors."

Although examples of interviewers' responsive actions give us some idea of what such an interview style may look like, we do not know what person-oriented interviewers actually do. How do they act out their role, both in their questioning and in their responsive behavior?

One way of gaining knowledge about this topic is to study tape record-ings of research interviews carried out in a style that can easily be recog-nized as warm, friendly, and personal, in order to identify what makes the interviews so pleasant and what devices the interviewers use when con-structing a personal interview style. This chapter provides an analysis of eight Dutch social science research interviews and examines the devices through which the interviewers construct an interview style that may be seen as warm, friendly, person-oriented, or briefly, as a personal interview style. The respondents are Dutch adults who attend a basic literacy program. They are interviewed about their daily problems with basic literacy skills and about the courses they take to improve their skills. The interviews are carried out in the context of a research project on reading, writing and mathematics skills. The interviewers are graduate social science students who are trained in the methods of standardized survey interviewing. Each interview lasts approximately ninety minutes and is conducted in the respondent's home. Because only audio recordings of these face-to-face interviews were made, the analysis is necessarily restricted to acoustic aspects.

The interviewers use a written questionnaire that consists of three parts. Part 1 is a short list of closed demographic questions. Part 2 is titled "Context, Problems and Educational Needs (Open Part)," and is intended to generate information for an eventual description of what it means to be semi-literate. It contains open questions and possible probes. For example, item 15:

Do you ever come across things that you would really like to do better, or things that you find difficult?
If so, what are these things? (Probe if necessary):
- Problems with reading (writing, speaking, listening, doing sums): do you find that difficult?
- Standing up for yourself, having the courage to have your say: do you ever find that difficult?

The questions and probes in part 2 are primarily designed as a schedule or agenda for the interviewers, who are relatively free to formulate the questions and to choose the order of presentation.

Part 3 of the questionnaire is intended to generate statistical informa-tion on the level of literacy and the educational needs of the sample popu-lation. It contains sixty-four topic questions, each of which is followed by a series of three related closed questions, and all of these questions are supposed to be read aloud verbatim. After the topic of the question is stated, the interviewers should read from the script:

1   Do you ever do this? Or: do you ever come across this? (yes/no)
2   How well do you know this (or: can you do this)? (well/reasonably
    well/badly)
3   How important is it for you to learn more about this in a course? (very
    important/not that important/not important)

In this chapter, the heading of each fragment indicates whether it comes
from the open or the closed part of the questionnaire.

The reason I selected these interviews for an analysis of personal interview style is that the interviewers strike me as particularly friendly and
warm. It almost seems as if these are the interviewers Fowler and
Mangione have in mind when they refer to "the type of persons to whom
one might tell personal information that would be more difficult to tell to
strangers." The respondents seem at ease with the interviewers and do
indeed provide rather delicate information.

In section 2, interviewers' reactions to respondents' answers are discussed. This analysis is inspired by the survey methodological literature,
which suggests that the interactional features that constitute a personal
interview style are to be found in the interviewers' reactions to the
respondents' answers. While analyzing the data, however, it became clear
that the interviewers also display a person-oriented style in the ways that
they change the script, neutrally reformulating the closed questions in
part 3 of the questionnaire. This discovery is discussed in section 3.

2   Interviewers' reactions to respondents' talk

When recipients respond to speakers' talk, they may use an acknowledgment or an assessment. Acknowledgments are neutral and merely provide
an indication that the speaker has heard and/or understood the previous
talk. Assessments provide an evaluation of the persons and events
described within the talk (Goodwin and Goodwin 1987).[1] Assessments
usually contain contrast terms, such as good/bad, right/wrong, and the
like. For example, in the fragment below:

(1)   Conversation, Pomerantz 1984a: 57
        1   J.   Let's feel the water. Oh, it ...
        2   R. →   It's wonderful. It's just right. It's like
        3   bathtub water.

Assessments are not limited to the lexical and syntactic levels of the conversation. They may also be performed non-verbally (M. H. Goodwin
1980) or prosodically (Goodwin and Goodwin 1987, 1992). For
example:

(2)   Conversation, Goodwin and Goodwin 1992: 157
        1   E.   An this beautiful, (0.2) Irish Setter.
        2   D. → Ah:::,
        3   E.   Came tearin up on ta the first gree(h)n
        4   an tried ta steal Pau(h)l's go(h)lf ball.

Research on standardized survey interviews shows that interviewers tend
to refrain from assessing respondents' answers. In doing so, interviewers
display that they are neutral towards what they are being told; they just
"collect" the requested answers. Interviewers in standardized survey
interviews restrict themselves to acknowledgments, generally an "okay," a
"yes," or a repetition of the answer (Houtkoop-Steenstra 1994; Schaeffer,
Maynard, and Cradock 1993).

A noticeable feature of the research interviews examined here is that
the interviewers frequently do produce assessments following the respondent's talk. In fragment 3 below, the interviewer provides an assessment
of the respondent's report that he is now working on writing without
making errors:[2]

(3)   Literacy Survey (Dirk, closed part)
        1   I.   ah you you have already-
        2   reading and writing you've managed, right?
        3   R.   jawe:l ((we:ll, yes))
        4   (0.3)
        5   except u::h that's what I'm doing now,
        6   writing without making errors. ↑you know. =
        7   I.   = yes.
        8   't's difficult, isn't it.   ASSESSMENT

Below, the interviewer produces an acknowledgment followed by an
assessment, after the respondent informs him that she will soon move on
to "MAVO," a higher educational level.

(4)   Literacy Survey (Cora, closed part)
        1   R.   we'll get it soon in uh-
        2   August we'll start at mavo level.
        3   I.   yes.   ACKNOWLEDGMENT
        4   (.)
        5   °oh that's very good!°   ASSESSMENT
        6   R.   yes.

In order to gain knowledge about what constitutes a personal interview
style, I will discuss how the interviewers react to the respondents' assessable statements. By "assessable statements," I refer to statements that

have an assessment as a possible response. (See Goodwin and Goodwin (1992) on "assessables".) We will first focus on utterances in which the respondent makes a statement of some fact that in Dutch society tends to be valued positively, such as doing well in class or passing to a higher educational level. I then look at utterances in which the respondent refers to his or her lack of literacy skills. I refer to these utterances as "positive" and "negative" statements, respectively.

2.1   Interviewers' praise actions

In the interviews discussed here, the interviewer often provides an assessment that can be viewed as a "praise assessment" after the respondent says something that is considered positive. The "°oh that's very good!°" in fragment 4 is an example of a praise assessment produced in reaction to the respondent's report that she is making progress.

In the next example the respondent explains how she deals with her everyday writing problems:

(5)   Literacy Survey (Mary, open part)
```
 1  R.    like mi:lk, .h well I know how to write that,
 2         but sugar is difficult, (.) .h well then I'll
 3         check (.) if there's a supply of sugar left,
 4         and I copy it from that. =
 5  I.    = ye:s.
 6         (.)
 7         oh how smart. ye:s.        PRAISE ASSESSMENT
 8  R.    yes.
 9  I.    yeah that ( )
10  R.    and there is not a soul who's checking.
11         and not a soul who knows anything about it.
12  I.    I see.
```

The interviewer evaluates the respondent's solution as smart, and the respondent in her turn seems to agree with this evaluation when she adds a favorable aspect of her solution: "and there is not a soul who's checking. and not a soul who knows anything about it."[3]

Instead of responding with a praise assessment utterance like "°oh that's very good!°" or "oh how smart," interviewers may also perform their praise actions by means of a "praise assessment token," which is a receipt token performed with an intonation that marks it as praise. The interviewer below produces her receipt tokens with a lengthened sound and fall-rise intonation.

(6)   Literacy Survey (Dirk, open part)
  1 I.   wh<u>a</u>t kind of job do you have?
          (. . .)
  2 R.   I'm r<u>i</u>ght under a f<u>o</u>reman.
          (. . .)
  3 I.   and you also have a team <u>u</u>nder ↑you.
  4   people <u>u</u>nder ↑you⌈that you:.
  5 R.   ⌊j<u>a</u>:ja. ((I see))
  6 I. → s↓<u>o</u>:↑::.   PRAISE ASSESSMENT TOKEN
          (. . .)
  7 R.   t<u>e</u>n people we have °<u>u</u>nder us°.
  8 I.   ↓o:↑:h.   PRAISE ASSESSMENT TOKEN
  9   (0.8)
 10   <u>a</u>nd uh which sch<u>oo</u>l education have you had?

The interviewer performs her receipt tokens in such a way that they may be heard as "Well, that's impressive!"

In the next fragment the praise assessment token is followed by commentary that also orients toward the positive nature of the respondent's activities:

(7)   Literacy Survey (Dirk, open part)
  1 I.   how- h<u>o</u>w many years is it you're doing this
          ((= this course))
  2   (.)
  3   three y<u>ea</u>rs?
  4 R.   N<u>OHO</u>, I've been on this more than u:hm (.)
  5   <u>ei</u>ght years I guess.
  6   (2.2)
  7 I. → ↓o:↑:h.
  8   (1.1)
  9   quite so:me t<u>i</u>me you've been at it then. =
 10 R.   = yes.
 11   (1.7)
 13 I.   °hold out°.

Before this utterance is produced, the respondent indicates that he can write and is now learning to write without errors. He attends the Dutch course two hours a week. Furthermore, he shows the interviewer his homework. As for his reading, he says, "I can I can a l<u>e</u>tter I can r<u>ea</u>d. Especially when I'm by mys<u>e</u>lf, then uh I m<u>a</u>nage." From this information, the interviewer proposes that the respondent has been taking this course for three years. This proposal is strongly rejected, and subsequently corrected, by the respondent, who says in lines 4–5, "I've been on this more than u:hm (.) eight years I guess."

One might expect the interviewer to be surprised when she learns that it took the respondent more than eight years to reach this level of reading Dutch. This may explain the 2.2 second pause before she reacts to the respondent's talk with a praise assessment. After the praise assessment, she indicates her admiration of the respondent for going to class for more than eight years, and she offers encouragement when she advises him to "hold out" in line 12.

In conclusion, these interviewers provide praise when a respondent makes a statement that can be heard as positive. Some of the statements that precede praise actions could also be evaluated negatively. For example, in fragment 7, we could also hear the respondent as saying that even after eight years of training he is still not able to read properly. However, the respondents do not, in one way or another, orient toward these facts as though they are problematic or troublesome. The respondent in this example hurries to correct the interviewer's wrong assumption, and the respondent in fragment 5 does not display any embarrassment when she says that she copies the word "sugar" from a sugar bag. Following the respondent's lead, the interviewers also orient toward these statements as though they are positive and, by praising the respondents, they offer support and encouragement.

2.2   Interviewers' reactions to reported competence problems

The respondents discussed in this chapter are being interviewed because of their literacy problems, so it is not surprising that they frequently mention various sorts of difficulties. When they report lack of knowledge or skill in some field, the interviewers tend to minimize the importance of this lack. They do so in the various ways discussed below.

2.2.1   Shifting the referent of the problem

When one has difficulty understanding a text, this difficulty is usually caused by one of two things: either the reader/listener has a deficiency, or the text is too difficult. When a respondent reports on some personal literacy problem, the interviewer may re-characterize the problem as one resulting from the task and not the respondent. The procedure is similar to a response to compliments that is described by Pomerantz (1978: 101):
1.   A praises B
2.   B praises other-than-self
For example:

(8)   Conversation, Pomerantz 1978: 102
         R.   You're a good rower, Honey.
         J.   These are very easy to row. Very light.

In our data a similar process occurs, though the roles are reversed.
The person who is the target of the assessment does not perform the
referent-shifting in the data discussed here, perhaps because blame is
being assigned rather than praise. A blames self, and then B blames
other-than-A. In other words, the interviewer shifts the referent of
this of anti-compliment from the respondent to someone or something other than the respondent, which can be schematized as
follows:

         R.   states or suggests that he/she has a problem
         I.   shifts the cause of the problem

The respondent below states that she often has difficulty understanding
what is being said on certain television programs. The interviewer then
volunteers an account for the respondent's lack of understanding by
declaring that the people responsible for this problem are the producers
of the programs:

(9)   Literacy Survey (Kea, closed part)
         1   I.   and tho:se programs on uh t.v.,
         2   on politics, and and ta:lk shows,
         3   and the social items,
         4   (.)
         5   .hh do you ever watch those?
         6   those programs?
         7   R.   I do watch now and again,
         8   but I'm not always able to follow it.
         9   (1.0)
        10   I.   °hm mm.°
        11   R.   and because I can't follow it, then I-
        12   there's this moment when I start doing this
        13   and then I completely lose interest. =
        14   I.   = yes.
        15   (0.8)
        16   So in fact it just is- it's uh the
        17   language that they use, ⌈and
        18   R.   ⌊yes.
        19   (0.9)
        20   I.   the information they give is so limited,

```
21              ⌈ and that one that one can't ⌈ follow it.
22   R.         ⌊ yes. that's what I think.    ⌊ it is just that
23              I ⌈ myself find it hard to follow.
24   I.          ⌊ yes.
25   R.         ⌈ and    p o l i t i c s as    well. ⌉
26   I.         ⌊ and do you find it important? ⌋
```

When the respondent says that she is not always able to follow certain television programs and therefore loses interest in lines 7–13, the interviewer
volunteers an explanation of the respondent's answer by saying, "So in fact
it just is- it's uh the language that they use, and the information they give is
so limited" (lines 16–20). The respondent agrees with this assertion, and
the interviewer continues her turn, overlapping the respondent's agreement such that the problematic talk and the limited information are determined to be the reasons "that one that one can't follow it."

Note that, according to the interviewer, not only can the respondent
not follow the problematic talk, but it is a general problem; most people
cannot follow it. While the respondent agrees with the assertion that the
"information they give is so limited," she implicitly contradicts the
general character of the statement that "one" cannot follow these shows
when she shifts the referent from "one" to herself by saying, "It is just that
I myself find it hard to follow" (lines 22–3).

When the respondent below reports that he thinks writing Dutch correctly is difficult, the interviewer states that writing correctly "is" difficult,
"especially in Dutch" (lines 8 and 10):

(10)   Literacy Survey (Dirk, closed part)
```
 1   I.       ah you you have already-
 2            reading and writing goes all right?
 3   R.       jawe:l ((we:ll yes))
 4            (0.3)
 5            except u::h that's what I'm doing now,
 6            writing without making errors. ↑you know. =
 7   I.       = yes.
 8            't's difficult, isn't it.
 9   R.       ⌈ yes. well look, it is it is a uh
             ⌊ ((R shows what he is currently doing at
               the course))
10   I.       especially in Dutch.
11            (1.9)
12   R.       °especially° t and dt and d =
13   I.       = yes.
```

Thus the cause of the difficulty is not the respondent's lack of knowledge, but rather the inherently problematic nature of writing correctly, especially writing in Dutch.

When a person claims that something is difficult, he or she claims knowledge of what is being assessed (Pomerantz 1984a, 1988). The interviewer, through assessing, is claiming knowledge of the task of writing Dutch. This puts the interviewer and the respondent in a somewhat similar position, at least in regard to understanding what this task is like. In claiming knowledge about the difficulty of the task confronting the respondent, the interviewer offers to identify with the respondent. Note that the assessment that writing is difficult is followed by "isn't it" in line 8, by which the interviewer offers affiliation and empathy with the respondent who faces this difficult task.[4]

2.2.2 Normalizing respondents' problems

When interviewers minimize the importance of some negative or problematic aspect of (the lives of) respondents, they claim that this is a normal and common condition. The respondents' problems are re-characterized as "normal" and "common" problems. For example, we find the following fragment after the interviewer asks whether or not the respondent will continue to attend the course:

(11)   Literacy Survey (Dirk, open part)
    1   R.   reading is all right, but (1.0) .hh I'm afraid
    2   people watch me closely what I'm doing,
    3   you ↑know. =
    4   I.   = yes °uh(h)° =
    5   R.   = yes. =
    6   I.   °that ha(h)ppens often yes.° =
    7   R.   = °but that comes often- is no big problem.°

The interviewer offers the respondent support and encouragement when she claims that people's reading skills "often" decrease when they are watched by others; this is not a problem that is specific to the respondent. The respondent seems to accept this offer when he says that it is "no big problem," and (not shown here) that he may soon move to a higher course level. The interviewer and respondent collaboratively define this potential problem as "no problem."

The topic of the following fragment is arithmetic. The respondent has been asked if she ever works with ratios. When she states that she does not know what this term refers to, the interviewer explains. The conversation proceeds as follows:

(12)   Literacy Survey (Kea, closed part)
```
1  R.     yes no that doesn't mean a thing to me.
2         ⌈that.
3  I.     ⌊not a thing, right?
4  R.     no.
5         (0.5)
6  I.     very f- very few people (0.6)
7         ⌈do °that uh at primary school.°
8  R.     ⌊doesn't mean anything to me
```

The interviewer accounts for the respondent's lack of knowledge by stating that it is normal considering her situation. The respondent did not receive any education past the primary school level, and ratios are not usually taught during primary school. The interviewer replies to the respondent's answer that ratios do not mean a thing to her by saying, "Not a thing, right?" (line 3). In producing this tag, the interviewer may be seen as implying that she expected this answer. The interviewer also, when claiming that very few people do ratios in primary school, cuts off her "very f-" in line 6 in order to stress the "very" in her reiteration "very few people," further marking the normalcy of the respondent's lack of knowledge regarding ratios.

Another interviewer also points out the consequences of a respondent's having not been taught a certain subject:

(13)   Literacy Survey (Dien, closed part)
```
1  R.     writing without errors, I'm just not able to. =
2  I.     = no, (.) well if you haven't learnt that,
3         well, listen, if you didn't learn how to
4         ride a bicycle you can't bike, right?
5  R.     no, ex(h)actl(h)y.
6         ⌈hah hah⌉
7  I.     ⌊hah hah⌋
8         .hh ea(h)sy a(h)s th(h)at.
```

The interviewer normalizes the respondent's lack of knowledge by saying, "Well, listen, if you didn't learn how to ride a bicycle you can't bike right?" (lines 3–4). This statement can be applied to anyone who has not been taught a specific skill, and thus the respondent's lack of knowledge is characterized as normal.

The respondent in the following fragment indicates that she is still confronted with "plenty of difficult things" when it comes to reading and writing Dutch:

(14)   Literacy Survey (Cora, closed part)
     1 I.   cause Dutch itself is doing all right in fact.
     2   reading and ⌈writing and doing⌉ sums
     3 R.   ⌊t i l l   n o w.   ⌋
     4 I.   and ⌈so on is no problem at all.
     5 R.   ⌊yes, I have no problem with that.
     6   we:ll, we've just started with this Dutch,
     7   and well, if you st<u>a</u>rt,
     8   well, there's plenty of ⌈difficult things then
     9 I.   ⌊j<u>a</u>:. ((intonation like
            'Sure. Of course.'))
    10 R.   like putting c<u>o</u>mma's, putting full st<u>o</u>ps,
    11   ⌈when uh composing a letter, ⌈and all that,
    12 I.   ⌊yes.   ⌊yes.
    13 R.   yah ((well)) g<u>o</u>sh uh (0.5)
    14 I.   but you'll always keep that ((these difficulties)).
    15 R.   you'll always keep tha- we ⌈:ll
    16 I.   ⌊d and t's,
    17   things like that. =
    18 R.   = yes. =
    19 I.   = these are things where you:: ⌈
    20 R.   ⌊I find that
    21   terribly d<u>i</u>fficult. =
    22 I.   = yes.
    23   (1.0)
    24   kn<u>o</u>w what you mean. anyway:
    25   ((next question))

When the respondent says that she is confronted with "plenty of difficult
things" (line 8), the interviewer produces her "ja:" in line 9 just before the
respondent's "difficult things" has been produced.

Partly due to its early placement, this _ja:_ appears to be functioning as a
disagreement, with the possible implication that the respondent's statement indicates that she might have a deficiency. The respondent therefore
elaborates on what these difficult things are in lines 10–11. The interviewer then normalizes these difficulties when she proposes that these are
the type of writing problems that one will never really overcome: "but
you'll always keep that."

Dutch _je_ (you), as used in "but you'll always keep that," is an ambiguous
personal pronoun, as is "you" in English. It may be used both as an informal address term and as a generic personal pronoun that stands for "one,"
"everyone," or "anyone."[5] Since these respondents are addressed with the

formal Dutch pronoun *U*, the interviewers' use of *je* should be heard as the generic pronoun "one." When the interviewer says, "but you'll always keep that," the respondent treats the pronoun as a generic "you." Had she understood "you" as exclusively referring to herself, meaning that the interviewer had shifted from the formal to the informal address term, she would have used "I" when repeating the interviewer's assertion. However, she retains the "you/one" form by saying, "You'll always keep tha-."

In repeating the interviewer's assertion, the respondent seems to agree with it. But just before the possible end of her utterance in line 15, she suddenly halts and restarts with a "we:ll," projecting a possible disagreement (see section 3). At that moment the interviewer interrupts the respondent's restarted utterance and mentions another difficult aspect of the Dutch language: "d and t's, things like that." In mentioning this particular difficulty in the Dutch writing system, the interviewer chooses one of the most notorious spelling problems: when to end a verb form with "d," "t," or "dt?" When she continues with "these are things where you::," in line 18, this may project an utterance such as "you/one will always keep making errors."

Rather than waiting for the end of this utterance, however, the respondent interrupts and indicates that she herself finds this aspect of the Dutch spelling system "terribly difficult." By shifting from the generic "you" to "I," she separates herself from the assertion that this problem is everyone's problem. (See also Watson 1987: 269.) Whereas the "d and t's, things like that" may be difficult for everyone, the respondent finds it "terribly" difficult. She seems to be downgrading the interviewer's proposal that these difficulties are everyone's difficulties, and therefore normal. Rather than making another normalizing proposal (for example, claiming that everybody finds this "terribly" difficult), the interviewer claims "know what you mean," in line 23, and hence offers to identify with the respondent by offering affiliation and encouragement.[6]

When respondents claim to lack particular knowledge or skills, the interviewers try to invalidate the potentially problematic and self-deprecating character of the respondents' information.[7] The potentially problematic issue is (re)characterized by the interviewer as normal and ordinary. This (re)characterization can be achieved either by depicting the problematic issue as something that is common to the respondent's group, for example, people with only a primary education, or as a general problem for everyone.

2.2.3   Sharing the respondents' problems

Interviewers may suggest that a respondent's problem is a common problem, perhaps by suggesting that they themselves face it as well. Sometimes they explicitly state that they also have similar literacy prob-

lems. Because the respondents know that the interviewers are highly educated, these remarks may strengthen the suggestion that the reported
problem is a common one.

In the following fragments the interviewers offer identification with the respondents by explicitly stating that they share the respondents' lack of skills:

(15)   Literacy Survey (Wolf, closed part)
        1   I.   so you're doing very poorly here
                    ((= working on the word processor))
        2   (0.6)
        3   just like me.

(16)   Literacy Survey (Kea, closed part)
        1   I.   and do you ever use the memory of a
        2   pocket calculator?
        3   (.)
        4   you don't use a p̲ocket calculator⌈no.
        5   R.   ⌊I never
        6   use one.
        7   (.)
        8   I.   would you be a̲ble to?
        9   (1.4)
       10   °neither could I̲, by the w(h)ay.° =
       11   R.   = no:.

The interviewers present themselves as less clever and competent than
the respondents may expect them to be. In doing so, the interviewers
propose that the problems the respondents report are more common and
less delicate than the respondents might think. By presenting themselves
in this way, the interviewers suggest that even highly educated people
have such problems. The respondents are offered affiliation, support, and
encouragement.

In the fragments above the interviewers claim that they share a problem
with the respondents. The interviewer below is more convincing in that
he not only claims to share the problem, but also demonstrates how the
problem manifests itself in his life. (See Sacks (1992a: 146–7) on "claiming versus demonstrating".) After the question on whether or not there
are many occasions when the respondent needs to write, the interview
proceeds as follows:

(17)   Literacy Survey (Mary, open part)
        1   I.   well, doing one's shopping is of course every
        2   day day u:h⌈happens to be, right?
        3   R.   ⌊ye:s. that's why:.

```
 4  I      that (        ), yes.
 5         (0.8)
 6         u:h do you otherwise forget? =
 7         = if you can't u:h can't make a note of it?
 8         (0.8)
 9  R.     yes.
10  I.     I s(h)ee. I see. right.
11         you come home and ⌈u:h
12  R.                       ⌊I'll have forgotten it
13         and then I'll have to go out again. =
14  I.     = J(h)A hahaha.
15         I(h)'m havi(h)ng the sa(h)me thing, y'kno(h)w,
16         tha(h)t's terrible. yes.
17         (1.3)
18         °yes.°
19         (2.3)
20         °ok↑ay.°
21         (2.6)
22         ((next question))
```

Rather than just responding to the reported problem with a "me too," the interviewer displays in lines 6–7 that he knows from experience what may happen if one goes shopping without a shopping list: "u:h do you otherwise forget? = if you can't u:h can't make a note of it?" When the respondent confirms the suggestion, the interviewer further displays that he is familiar with the problem. After he laughingly produces acknowledgment of the confirmation, he begins to describe what happens in such a situation: "you come home and." The respondent interrupts the turn in progress and completes the utterance by saying, "I'll have forgotten it and then I'll have to go out again." The interviewer then produces a "me too" in line 15: "J(h)A hahaha. I(h)'m havi(h)ng the sa(h)me thing, y'kno(h)w." He knows from experience that "tha(h)t's terrible. yes."

The interviewer may be seen as attempting to establish a shared world in which people go shopping and run into problems if they do not have a shopping list. However, there is reason to believe that the interviewer does not fully understand the scope of the respondent's problem. Whereas the interviewer produces his troubles-talk laughingly, the respondent does not. Jefferson (1984b) discusses laughter in talk about troubles and finds that "a troubles-teller can, and perhaps should, laugh in the course of a troubles-telling, and thus exhibit that he or she is in the position to take it lightly, that is, exhibit that he is troubles-resistive"

(367). The respondent neither joins in with the interviewer's laughter, nor does she laugh at her own trouble. (See Glenn (1995) on "laughing with" versus "laughing at".) This lack of laughter on the respondent's part may mean that, although both the interviewer and the respondent share the problem of forgetting certain shopping items if they do not have a shopping list, the respondent takes this less lightly than the interviewer does. They are indeed different in one crucial respect: the respondent has no shopping list because she is not able to write, whereas the interviewer merely forgets to bring one.

Above we have seen examples of interviewers claiming to be as incompetent in a particular field as the respondents. Sometimes interviewers suggest that they are even less competent in certain fields than the respondents, as in the following fragment:

```
(18)    Literacy Survey (Cora, open part)
        1   I.    .hh and did you uh after primary school
        2             take a uh (.) other training courses?
        3   R.    u:h no.
        4             I once got my uh typing certificate. =
                      but nothing more.
        5             ((2.6 sec. sound of writing))
        6   I.    °also touch-typing?°
        7             (0.8)
        8             °°I I can't type.°°
        9   R.    well I would probably no longer be able to do
        10            it, but in those days it went fairly u:h well.
```

After the respondent says that she has a typing certificate, the interviewer states in line 8 that she cannot type. The interviewer enlarges this difference between herself and the respondent to the extreme, suggesting in line 6 that the respondent may even have a touch-typing certificate.

The respondent below reports that her friend sometimes helps her with her homework for the English class. The interviewer then volunteers a story:

```
(19)    Literacy Survey (Cora, open part)
        1   I.    I recently went to the parents' evening
        2             of my (.) little daughter ((her school)).
        3             (0.7)
        4             and she was talking about finite forms.
        5             (1.7)
        6             I hadn't got a clue what the child was
        7             on about.
```

```
 8          (1.3)
 9          I still haven't, by the way(h).
10  R.      hah hah hah.
11  I.      h(h). but then I always think well you had
12          primary school in the old days- all these terms
13          have changed⌈and and (0.3) so much has changed
14  R.             ⌊yes.
15  I.      in⌈that field. y'know.
16  R.        ⌊yes.
```

The gist of this story is that certain things are now taught differently in primary school then they used to be, and therefore one's knowledge may be out of date. If this holds true for the interviewer, it also holds true for the respondent. Therefore, if the interviewer knows less than her young daughter and the respondent knows less than her friend, this is only because things have changed since they left primary school. The respondent could point out that the interviewer has also attended high school and a university, while she has not. However, because the respondent does not point out this difference between herself and the interviewer, she may be seen as accepting the interviewer's offer to identify.

This section shows that interviewers may try to minimize the gravity of the respondents' literacy problems by suggesting that the respondents' problems are common ones, shared by other people, including the interviewers themselves. Whenever possible, they praise the respondents for their achievements. In producing these friendly and personal assessments and commentaries in response to the respondents' talk, the interviewers may be seen as offering affiliation, support, and encouragement.

3   Reformulating scripted questions as no-problem questions

Section 2 covers the personal and positive ways in which interviewers react to respondents' assessable statements. However, the interviewers' positive orientation is not restricted to their reactions. As will be discussed in this section, interviewers also display a positive approach by rephrasing neutrally formulated questions.

The third and closed part of the questionnaire consists of questions intended to establish the respondents' degree of competence with respect to specific activities. There are sixty-nine topic questions. Each topic question is followed by an example, such as, "Do you ever calculate ratios? For example, you wish to calculate how much foreign money you will get for your Dutch guilder." These topic questions are then followed by three recurring questions and their response options:

1 Do you ever do this? Or: have you ever come across this? (yes/no)
2 How well do you know (or can you do) this? (well/reasonably well/badly)
3 How important is it for you to learn more about this in a course? (very important/not so important/not important)

The interviewers are instructed to "read the questions and answer options aloud for each item, or allow respondent to read the text if possible." In spite of this instruction, the interviewers almost always change the wording of the questions. While the first question is often read out as scripted, questions 2 and 3 are usually revised into yes–no questions, and the formulation "How well can you do this/do you know this?" hardly ever occurs in these interviews.

In their reformulations of the "how-well-can-you-do-this" question, the interviewers present an optimistic view of the respondents' skills, as in fragment 20 below. The question "and you manage well?" is a revision of the scripted question "How well can you do this?"

(20)   Literacy Survey (Kea, closed part)
1   I.   do you ever do on paper additions
2   or subtractions?
3   R.   yes I do.
4   (1.5)
5   I.   and you manage we̲ll?
5   R.   ja:we:l. ((weak agreement)).

A similar reformulation happens below in line 3:

(21)   Literacy Survey (Dirk, closed part)
1   I.   BU̲T your your learning to read and write
2   you've do̲:ne.
3   that uh learning how to ↑spe̲:ll,
4   = and and ⌈reading just goes all right.
5   R.   ⌊ja. =
6   (0.4)
7   R.   mhhm we:ll, it's not so bad.
8   we:ll, I can a le̲tter I can re̲ad.
9   particularly when I'm alo̲ne,
10   then uh it's all ri̲ght. =
11   I.   = yes. =
12   = when other people are around,

13		then it becomes more difficult, right. =
14	I.	= then it becomes more difficult.
15	R.	filling in forms and things like that.
16	I.	yes.

The following analysis of one example will show how such formulations transform the question into a leading one. Though the respondent below displays that she may not manage writing personal letters very well, the interviewer suggests "and that goes a(h)ll right too?" in line 9:

(22)   Literacy Survey (Kea, closed part)

1	I.	ne:xt, do you ever write a personal
2		note to someone?
3		(.)
4		that you know?
5	R.	I sometimes do. ya:h ((a bit sighingly)).
6		but not so often. hah hah.
7		(0.3)
8		⌈°hah hah°
9	I.	⌊and that goes a(h)ll right too?
10	R.	yes.

The interviewer revises the scripted question "How well can you do this? well, reasonably well, badly" into "and that goes a(h)ll right too?" (line 9). She displays an optimistic view of the respondent's skills in writing personal notes, and she achieves this display in a number of ways that would be considered leading by standardized survey interviewing protocols.

First, the question is reformatted as a yes–no question. Although a yes–no question does not necessarily force the respondent to say either "yes" or "no," it may be easier for the respondent to choose one of these two options rather than to provide a scaled or qualified answer. This reformulation could therefore be considered leading and may produce an answer that the researchers would not consider valid.

Second, the question is reformulated into a "no-problem question." According to Heritage and Sorjonen (1984), a no-problem question is a question that anticipates a "no-problem" answer. In the above fragment, the use of the positive phrase "going all right" transforms the question into a no-problem question. The question displays a preference for a no-problem response over other responses and could therefore be considered by survey methodologists to be a leading question.

Third, the question is prefaced by "and." In their examination of the forms that health visitors must fill out during their first visits with new mothers, Heritage and Sorjonen (1994) discover that "agenda-based questions" on the form are routinely *and*-prefaced. They are produced in the sequential context of an expected "no-problem" response to the previous question. When the response to the previous question is expressive of some problem, the health visitor's next question is usually not *and*-prefaced. A report of a problem or difficulty is much more likely to be followed by a "contingent question" that "elaborates or sustains a topical focus on the prior answer" and therefore "treats the prior response as problematic, something to be followed up" (8). Heritage and Sorjonen argue that, in some cases, *and*-prefacing is strategically used to normalize some difficulty or delicacy associated with a question. *And*-prefacing implies that there is nothing problematic about the immediately prior response.

The respondent in fragment 22 alludes to a possibly problematic state of affairs when she says, "I sometimes do. ya:h ((a bit sighingly)). but not so often. hah hah. (0.3) °hah hah°," in lines 5–6. Rather than following up on this by asking a contingent question, the interviewer produces the *and*-prefaced "and that goes a(h)ll right too?" in line 9. With the production of this *and*-prefaced question, the interviewer treats the prior response as no-problem talk.[8]

Finally, the question has a declarative syntactic structure rather than an interrogative structure. Abbenbroek (1993) has shown that when speakers formulate a question using declarative syntax, they already have, or believe they have, the requested information.[9] In this respect declarative questions (like other requests-for-confirmation) are not neutral, and therefore can be considered leading, because the "default" response is a confirmation.[10]

Formulations such as "and that goes a(h)ll right?" and "and you manage well?" display a preference for agreement in the sense that they are built to occasion an agreeing response, in this case a "yes." Conversation analysis shows that when a question is formatted so that it exhibits a preference for a certain answer, the answerer will tend to pick that choice. To put it more generally, the answer will tend to be designed in reference to and agreement with that preference.

As discussed in chapter 2, an agreeing response tends to be produced quickly and without delay. If a response is not in agreement, the response turn contains token agreements and delays, and may be accompanied by accounts. As Sacks (1987) says: "There is an apparent interaction between the preference for contiguity and the preference for agreement, such that, if an agreeing answer occurs, it pretty darn well occurs contiguously, whereas if a disagreeing answer occurs, it may well be pushed deep into the turn that it occupies" (p. 58). The two examples below show a question followed by a preferred response turn (fragment 23) and a question followed by a dispreferred response turn (fragment 24):

(23)   Literacy Survey (Cora, closed part)
    1   R.   well at last she did apply after all.
    2   I.   °oh that's nice ⌈yes°
    3   R.   ⌊yes.
    4   I.   here in Dr⌈ente? ((a Dutch province))
    5   R.   ⌊here in Drente yes.

(24)   Literacy Survey (Greet, closed part)
    1   I.   you can also stand up well for yourself,
    2   you can also uh have your say well.
    3   (1.3)
    4   R.   no, not quite.

The agreeing answer in fragment 23, "here in Drente yes," is produced at the earliest possible point, whereas the disagreeing answer in fragment 24, "No, not quite," is prefaced by a 1.3 second pause.

Because a disagreeing response is often delayed, the questioner can see lack of agreement in the process. He or she can then rephrase the question so that it will match the anticipated answer. In Sacks' (1987) words:

A sort of thing you get is: the person asks the question exhibiting a preference, and there is a pause, no answer, and they then revise that question to exhibit the reverse preference, and then (with no further delay) they get an answer in accord with it. . . So there is one sort of way that a questioner can be seen to be orienting to getting agreement, i.e. they try to end up with a form that can be agreed with. (64)

For example, when the respondent below does not answer the question immediately, the interviewer transforms his initial assumption that doing sums "is going all right" into "reasonable." When this reformulation is still too optimistic, as the respondent's "mwah" displays, the interviewer concludes, "oh not uh a:wfully good."[11]

(25)   Literacy Survey (Mary, closed part)
    1   I.   doing sums is going all right.
    2   (0.5)
    3   reasonable.
    4   (0.4)
    5   R.   mwah.
    6   I.   oh not uh a:wfully good.
    7   R.   not ve:ry. but I find uh reading and writing
    8   I find more important.

The same process occurs below, where the interviewer suggests that the respondent has said that she has "no trouble" with reading. When there is

no response after 1.1 seconds, the interviewer revises his no-problem
question into a question anticipating a problem answer:

(26)   Literacy Survey (Mary, closed part)
    1 I.   and w- u::h with reading you said you have
    2   no trouble with that? didn't you?
    3   (1.1)
    4   or no- or or you have indeed a bit? =
    5   = with reading certain things.
    6   (0.2)
    7 R.   °mm a bit.°
    8   well I read all sorts of stories to them aloud.
               ((to her children))
    9   I'm able⌈u::h ⌉able uh to rea:d,
   10 I.   ⌊oh ja.⌋
   11 R.   but no difficult words.

In these excerpts the interviewers start with a no-problem question. In
terms of the pre-coded response options (well, reasonable, bad), they opt
for the most positive one. When the respondents do not answer immediately, the interviewers take the next turn and revise the question. Notice
that rather than changing the no-problem question into a question that
displays a preference for a problem answer, such as "doing badly," they
come up with a revision that anticipates a minor problem.

In fragment 25, "going all right" in line 1 is revised into "reasonable" in
line 3. The interviewer in fragment 26 redesigns the question so that it
anticipates a partial reading problem. She shifts from "no trouble" (with
reading certain things) in line 2 to "a bit?" in lines 4–5. As the eventual
answers show, the interviewers correctly analyze the post-question silence
as an upcoming disagreement with the projected no-problem answer. By
subsequently presenting the respondents with a question that may be
more in line with what the respondents have to report, the eventual
answer is more in agreement with what is anticipated in the question.

Although these respondents are selected because they have literacy
problems, the interviewers treat them as if they have no substantial literacy problems. There is a strong tendency among the interviewers to
revise their questions in anticipation of a favorable, socially desirable
answer. They present positive descriptions, such as "doing well" and
"having no problems," *and*-preface their questions, and format them in a
declarative syntactic structure. When this seems too optimistic to the
respondents, the interviewers then revise their questions such that they
display a less positive, but still rather optimistic, view of the respondents'
skills.

There are a few instances where the interviewers format the "how-well-can-you-do-this" questions so that they display a preference for a problem answer. This preference display only occurs in a specific context, which is after the respondent has already indicated or implied that he or she would perhaps not be able to perform the action mentioned in the first question. For example, in line 15 below, the interviewer proposes that the respondent does not deal well with reading plans only after the respondent has indicated several times that she finds such literacy tasks difficult.

In the following fragments such indications or implications are marked by *.

(27)   Literacy Survey (Kea, closed part)
```
     1  I.      do you ever read a building plan?
     2          or a pattern? like for sewing or so?
     3  R.  *   we:ll, I do read it,
     4          but I do ⌈find it difficult.     ⌉
     5  I.              ⌊l o o k    h e r e⌋
     6          here is a pla- such a
     7          p⌈lan.
     8  R.  *    ⌊well, I just find that
     9          difficult, really.
    10          (1.6)
    11      *   it does not mean ⌈much to me.
    12  I.                       ⌊you don't deal with
    13          it, much.
    14  R.      ⌈no.
    15  I.      ⌊and don't handle it so well.
    16  R.      I don't handle it eas- so well.
```

In fragment 28 below when the respondent talks about speaking to officials, she adds, "but I don't like it at all. (1.0) I can tell you that. hah hah" (lines 10–12). This expressed dislike for talking to officials may imply that she handles such situations badly, and the interviewer designs her next question to take this implication into account:

(28)   Literacy Survey (Kea, closed part
```
     1  I.      if you have to talk to someone
     2          who works with the authorities, right?
     3          for the city council,
     4          or uh teachers also often work
     5          with the authorities.
     6          (1.3)
```

7		.hh u:h are you ever engaged in such
8		a conversation?
9	R.	I did, only recently.
10	*	but, I don't like it at all.
11		(1.0)
12		I can tell you that. hah hah.
13	I.	doe(h)sn't i(h)t work tha(h)t well,
14		or does it?
15	R.	well one m(h)ana(h)ges,
16		but⌈
17	I.	⌊they are very formal, aren't they.
18	R.	yes.

The interviewer adds the counter question "or does it?" (line 14) after asking "doe(h)sn't i(h)t work tha(h)t well" (line 13). Following the preference for contiguity (Sacks 1987), the respondent first answers the second question, the "or does it?" The answer has a dispreferred turn format; the initial token agreement, "well one m(h)ana(h)ges" in line 14, is followed by "but."

Before the respondent can complete her turn and explicitly state a problem, however, the interviewer interrupts the turn and presents an account for the unstated possible problem by saying, "They are very formal, aren't they." (See section 2.2.1 on shifting the referent.) The interviewer has heard enough to know that response option 1 ("doing well") does not apply. Rather than forcing the respondent to explain whether she is doing "reasonably well" (option 2) or "badly" (option 3), the interviewer leaves it at that.

4   Conclusion

The analysis of these literacy survey interviews shows that interviewers may be seen as "doing being personal" on two turn-sequential levels: (1) the reactions to the respondents' assessable statements and (2) the reformulation of neutrally formatted scripted questions. In their reactions to the respondents' talk, interviewers praise the respondents for their accomplishments. Even when the respondents report on their incompetence, the interviewers provide socially acceptable accounts: they minimize the severity of the problem, and they suggest that it is a common one or that they themselves have similar problems.

With respect to question formulation, interviewers present the respondents with questions formulated to display an optimistic view of the respondents' competence. Rather than reading out the questions and the three response options from the questionnaire, the interviewers rephrase the questions to project no-problem answers. In other words, they ask leading questions. From a survey methodology perspective, the interviewers make serious interviewer errors. However, these respondents do not necessarily adopt the interviewers' suggestions. There are many instances in which the respondents report that they do have problems. The research methodologists should keep in mind that the "how-well-can-you-do-X" questions in the questionnaire discussed here are preceded by a series of open questions in part 2, and it is primarily during the open part of the interview that the interviewers establish a non-threatening interactional climate by downgrading the (socially) problematic character of the respondents' literacy problems.

Research methodologists should also keep in mind that it is possible that the interviewers' respectful and positive attitude makes it easier for the respondents to provide delicate information that perhaps would not be reported if the formal rules of standardized survey interviewing were strictly followed. The interviewers' friendly reactions to the respondents' talk may be seen as "face-saving practices" (Goffman 1955). In terms of Brown and Levinson (1987), the interviewers employ "positive politeness," that is, they orient toward the positive self-image that the respondents may want to claim for themselves.

The interviewers may also be seen as employing "negative politeness" when they rephrase the scripted "how-well-can-you-do-X" questions as no-problem questions. Brown and Levinson state that the function of negative politeness is to minimize the necessary imposition of face-threatening acts. Asking an adult whether he or she performs certain tasks "well," "reasonably well," or "badly" is a delicate and face-threatening act, particularly when both participants know that most adults (and sometimes even young children) perform these tasks well.

The face-threatening character of not mastering these tasks well is expressed by the respondents themselves during the interviews. The respondent in fragment 5 expresses her happiness that "there's not a soul who's checking. And not a soul who knows anything about it" when she copies the word "sugar" from the sugar bag. She also expresses that she experiences embarrassment when her children, ages five and eight, ask her to write something down. Another respondent says she feels embarrassed every time her young son has a new school teacher. She is supposed to write a weekly note to his teacher, and with every new teacher she is forced to inform her or him that she has writing problems.

It is clear that a personal interview style applies not only to giving feedback on the respondents' answers but also to the way questions are formulated. In revising the "how-well-can-you-do-X" questions into questions that anticipate a no-problem answer, the interviewers display their orientation toward the delicate and face-threatening character of the scripted formulation. Survey methodologists place interviewers in a double-bind whey they expect interviewers to read out formulated questions non-directively at the same time that they are expected to behave in a personal and friendly way. Interviewers may attempt to solve this problem by rephrasing the scripted questions.

Furthermore the friendly way in which the interviewers address the respondents may itself be a reaction to the fact that the respondents are revealing potentially delicate and self-deprecating information. The interviewers, in their response to this talk, behave like the ordinary conversationalists Pomerantz (1984a) describes when discussing the preference for disagreement with self-deprecations. The interviewers downgrade the problematic character of the talk by "normalizing" the reported literacy problems, by shifting the referent of the problem, and by claiming to have similar problems. Both the respondents' talk about their incompetence and the interviewers' positive attitudes toward the respondents and their literacy skills can thus be seen as a collaborative, interactional achievement.

8   Quality of Life assessment interviews

1   Introduction

In spontaneous mundane talk, yes–no questions tend to be formulated in optimistic, rather than negative, terms. Rather than asking people if they are "dissatisfied" or "unhappy," one is much more likely to ask if they are "satisfied" or "happy." Below are some contrasting examples. Whereas the A-versions are the unmarked, or default, formulations, the B-versions are marked versions that may elicit the return question "What makes you think so?"

(1)   A. Did you sleep well?
        B. Did you not sleep well?

(2)   A. Is everything all right?
        B. Is anything wrong?

(3)   A. Did you have a nice holiday?
        B. Did you have a bad holiday?

These examples illustrate that an unmarked yes–no question in mundane conversation displays a preference for a no-problem response. If survey interviewers revise questions that originally have three or more response options into unmarked yes–no questions, these questions are also being transformed into no-problem questions. In this chapter we will study a number of Quality of Life assessment interviews with mildly learning-disabled persons in order to see how the interviewers deal with the scripted questions.

The data in this chapter come from the administration of ten face-to-face Quality of Life interviews that took place in the respondents' homes. These interviews were conducted as part of the psychological services audit for a supported-housing network in northern England. The interviewers are clinical or assistant clinical psychologists. The respondents all have an IQ score under 70. They have been institutionalized for between ten and forty years. Though they first lived in mental institutions, they now live in sheltered homes. Each interview lasted approximately an hour. The interview instrument used is the Schalock and Keith (1993) Quality of Life questionnaire, which Schalock and Keith developed for the sake of the assessment of "improved services and outcomes from (re)habilitation" for the developmentally retarded.

The crucial difference between these interviews and the literacy interviews mentioned in chapter 7 is the motive behind the question revision. While the interviewers for the literacy survey are primarily responding to the face-keeping concerns of their respondents when they revise questions, the interviewers for the Quality of Life survey revise questions because their respondents display that they have problems understanding the scripted versions. My discussion of these difficulties is not merely a criticism of the particular instrument used in these surveys. Rather, I am hoping to illustrate some important aspects of interviews that need to be considered in any survey.

The focus in this chapter is on the ways the interviewers revise and repair scripted questions. I will show that the interviewers produce responses that are (at least) questionable in terms of validity. I will also show that the questionnaire that is used in these interviews does not suit the respondents of the survey. It fails because it creates interactional problems, and the interviewers' attempts to compensate for these problems lead to systematic biasing of the results.

First I will discuss how the interviewers reformulate and simplify their questions after the respondent has demonstrated what might be seen as difficulty in understanding the initial question. In section 4 I will show how the interviewers reformulate respondents' post-question talk in terms of codable answers. In section 5, I will show how the interviewers reformulate and simplify the scripted question from the very beginning of the question–answer sequence. Finally I will turn to the ways in which interviewers deal with inconsistent answers.

2   Psychometrically valid questions

In the Quality of Life questionnaire under consideration, each item of the script consists of a question and three (sometimes four) response options from which the respondent is to choose the answer that matches his or her condition or situation. The format of the pen-and-paper questionnaire (held by the interviewer) looks like this:

| Questions | Answer alternatives | | record here |
	3 points	2 points	1 point
1 Overall, would you say that life	Brings out the best in you?	Treats you like everybody else?	Doesn't give you a chance? –
2 How much fun and enjoyment do you get out of life?	Lots	Some	Not much –
–			
–			
–			
40			

Each question is followed by response options, and the interviewer is supposed to read out the entire text. Note that the first option is always the most positive one; that is to say, it accumulates three points towards an end score, and a higher end score indicates higher quality of life.

The explicit instructions for the interviewer printed on the cover sheet of the questionnaire are "When reading the items, pay close attention to the exact wording." The questionnaire does attempt to be responsive to its target group, however, and acknowledges that cognitive difficulties may present themselves, which would require interviewers to paraphrase the question and to repeat it "to ensure the respondent's understanding of the item content." However, no instructions are given on how to do so. We shall see how this allowable paraphrasis and repetition comes out in practice.

3   Third-turn repair: presenting the scripted text as an optimistic yes–no question

Many of these respondents display that they do not understand the purpose of the question. When an interviewer reads out the scripted text, a respondent is expected to select one of the response options being presented to him or her. However, these respondents rarely follow this implicit response instruction.

How do the interviewers deal with this lack of understanding? In the example below, when the respondent does not select one of the options presented to him, the interviewer explicitly tells him what to do: "gi'me one of them." However, rather than "giving one of them," the respondent says "↑yeh" in line 11, and the interviewer then prompts "↑which ↓one." When the respondent still does not make a selection, the interviewer rephrases the question in line 14: ">↑d'you think you do< ↑better at things than the (public)." This version of the question is more successful, as the respondent gives an answer in line 16: "↑better (0.8) better ↓now." Before showing the fragment, I will first give the scripted question and its response options:

> How successful do you think you are, compared to others?
> Probably more successful than the average person.
> About as successful as the average person.
> Less successful than the average person.

(4)   Quality of Life interview
```
 1  I.   ↑how successful (0.2) d'you think you are (0.2)
 2       compared to other ↓people (0.2) ↑yeh?
 3       (0.5)
 4  R.   ↑m
 5  I.   ↑more successful than average (0.2) a↑bout as
 6       successful as average (0.2) or ↓less successful
 7       (0.5)
 8  R.   °(     )°.
 9       (0.5)
10  I.   gi'me one of them
11  R.   ↑yeh
12  I.   ↑which ↓one
13       (0.8)
14  I.   >↑d'you think you do< ↑better at things
15       than the⌈(public) (      )
16  R.         ⌊↑better (0.8) better ↓now
17  I.   ↑yeh?
18       (0.2)
19  R.   yes
20       (2.0)
21  I.   ((Next question))
```

When we look closely at the answer in line 16 "↑better (0.8) better ↓now," it clearly does not match the question as presented by the interviewer, "Are you doing better than the public?" I will not address this right now, however. What I want to point out is that the scripted question is repaired as a question that projects a positive response.

When the interviewers see that the respondents are experiencing difficulty in answering a question that is followed by three response alternatives, they often initiate third-turn repair and reword the initial question (the trouble source) into a yes–no question. As discussed in chapter 2, Schegloff (1992) describes four forms that a "repair proper" can take: (1) repeating the turn more clearly, (2) using a repair marker, for example

"I mean," followed by a contrast with the understanding of the first turn, (3) reformulating the trouble source in different words, and (4) specifying the first turn. What we find the interviewers doing here is a variant of (3); they reformulate the initial question, but in a different question format (yes–no) rather than merely in different words.

Notice two things about the new yes–no question format. For one thing, by simplifying and shortening the question, it makes the respondents' task easier. Rather than making them understand and remember three alternatives, from which they have to choose and repeat one, they are presented with a question to which a "yes" or "no" is an adequate response. What is even more interesting, however, is that in formulating these yes–no questions, the interviewers make use of the most positive response option from the script.

To turn to other examples in the data, when reformulating the initial question, "Would you say life brings out the best in you, treats you the same as everyone else, or doesn't give you a chance?" the interviewers may say, "Does life bring out the best in you?" rather than "Would you say life doesn't give you a chance?" or "Would you say life treats you the same as everyone else?" In choosing the most positive option for their reformulation, the interviewers present an optimistic view of the quality of respondents' lives.

This most positive option also has the highest score of the three responses. We might therefore say that, on these occasions at least, the interviewers lead the respondents in the direction of the highest score. I discussed a similar procedure in chapter 7. In the Dutch literacy interviews, however, the apparently leading questions frequently did not produce confirmations. The respondents of these Quality of Life interviews, however, almost always confirm the yes–no questions.

In the fragment below we find a similar situation, in which the initial [question] + [three response options] is met with some non-appropriate material from the respondent. The interviewer then revises the original question into a yes–no question in which the "yes" option is the most positive alternative:

Question 30
Overall, would you say that your life is:
Free?
Somewhat planned for you?
Cannot usually do what you want?

(5)   Quality of Life interview
    1   I.   right (0.2) ↑o:k (0.2) (w'd) ↑you ↓say that
    2   your ↑li:fe is (0.5) ↑free
    3   (0.8)

```
4          or do the ↑sta:ff sometimes ↓plan things for ↑you
5          (0.8)
6          or you ↑can't do what you want to d↓::o.
7          (0.8)
8    R.    (sometimes I) (0.2) I ↑shout an' (0.2)
9          (      start screaming)
10   I.    ↓o::hh ↑dea::r ↑do ↑you >↑hehh hehh<
11         ↓hehh (0.5) hh
12         (0.8)
13   R.    (ch- ch-) ↑come he↓::re (.) ⌈(      )
14   I.                                ⌊↑oh is that ↑y'r cat
15         (0.5)
16         y'r ↑cat's come ↑ho↓me
17         (0.5)
18         ↑so can you usually ↑do what you ↓want to do
19         Ei-Eileen?
20   R.    ↑ye:s (I can) ↑ye:s (      )
```

The interviewer delivers the scripted question and its response options in
lines 1–6. Rather than choosing one of the three options, the respondent
produces talk that does not explicitly choose among the alternatives. After
both the interviewer and the respondent talk about the cat in lines 10–14,
the interviewer re-asks the initial question and response options as a
yes–no question: "↑so can you usually ↑do what you ↓want to do Ei-
Eileen?" in line 18–19. Again, the interviewer chooses the optimistic
version when rephrasing the question, which is then confirmed by the
respondent: "↑ye:s (I can) ↑ye:s (   )." The interviewer then moves on
to the next question.

A final example of repair in third position:

Question 12
Do you feel your job or other daily activity is worthwhile and relevant to either
yourself or others?
Yes, definitely.
Probably; I'm not sure.
Definitely not.

```
(6)   Quality of Life interview
1    I.    .hh do you ↑think what you ↓do during the
2          ↓day ↑Clare (0.2) helps other ↓people
3    R.    °mm°
4    I.    d'you think it ↑helps them a ↑lot (0.8)
5          some (0.2) or a li- (0.2) >or not at ↓all<
6          (2.0)
7          d'you think you ↑help other ↓people?
```

        8   R.   yeah
        9   I.   °right o:kay°

In this example, the interviewer delivers a full question and three answer alternatives. When the respondent does not take the turn after two seconds, the interviewer offers a rephrased question in the yes–no format. Note again that the reformulated question strongly projects a (general) positive response: that the respondent helps other people.

    In summary, third-turn repair is an example of a shift toward a positive-favoring yes–no question occasioned by an emergent, interactional feature of the talk. What has emerged is the respondent's display of some sort of problem (hearable as not understanding the question). What we see is that when respondents display some sort of problem, the interviewers may initiate third-turn repair and reformulate the initial question. They revise the question in such a way that it is less complex. The [question] + [three response options] is repaired as a yes–no question. What is particularly interesting is that the interviewer does not pick a negative alternative for confirmation; rather, he or she picks the optimistic option.

4   Interviewers reformulating unclear talk

In the previous section we saw how emergent trouble-with-understanding-the-question occasioned a reworking of the scripted question into one that favored a positive response. In this section the focus is on a different solution to the interactional problems of the survey. Rather than rephrasing the initial question, an interviewer may "formulate" (see chapter 2) the respondent's answer in such a way that it matches one of the pre-coded response options. Heritage (1985) discusses three types of formulations, one of which is a formulation with which the speaker provides the gist of and draws a conclusion from the previous talk. This (re)formulation is another method these interviewers use to compensate for the interactional problems caused by the questionnaire.

    Interviewers use this method in instances where the respondent's post-question talk cannot be interpreted as an appropriate answer to the prior question. This method is also used when the respondent's answer does not clearly match one of the pre-coded response options. I refer to both types of talk as "unclear talk" or "non-answers," and they will be marked in the fragments with an asterisk. Here is an example:

(7)   Quality of Life interview   .
        1   I.   .hh ↑what about >↑when you go to ↓bed and
        2   have your< ↑me↓als (0.2) Clare
        3   (0.5)

```
4              do ↑you say when you ↓want them?
5              (0.5)
6              or do ↑sta:ff ↓say
7              (3.0)
8    R.*       (we- we 'ave it-) (0.5) we're having it
9              ↓ea:rly to night =
10   I.        = yeh =
11   R.*       = because (I'm) going ↑out to↓night
```

Rather than saying who decides when it is dinner time, the respondent states that dinner will be early tonight. The response is topically related to the question without being an appropriate answer to it.

In the example below the respondent seems to misunderstand who or what is helping whom:

(8)   Quality of Life interview
```
1    I.        .h the ↑things that you do↓::: during the
2              ↓da::y >Arthur do you think that they ↑help
3              other ↑pe↓ople<
4              (0.8)
5              or they help people a ↑little bit
6    R.*       they 'elp me a ↓little bit
```

In the next fragment, when the respondent is asked how he decides what he does, he answers instead with what he does:

(9)   Quality of Life interview
```
1    I.        How do you (0.2) decide to ↓do what (0.2)
2              you >do at the moment< (0.2) °↑yeh?°
3    R.*       (well) clean ↑up.
```

In this section, then, we will be looking closely at the ways in which interviewers deal with non-answers/unclear talk. Recalling the theme of the argument so far, we will also show how these sequences finally result in the interviewers recording the highest scores possible.

These interviewers systematically formulate respondent's talk as if (1) it were an appropriate answer to the question, and (2) it matched the most positive or optimistic option. In some cases, this formulation is marked by the interviewer as a conclusion, which begins with "so" (Mazeland 1992: 303) and is structured in a declarative format, as in line 23 below:

Question 22
Who decides how you spend your money?
I do.
I do, with assistance from others.
Someone else decides.

(10)   Quality of Life interview
```
 1  I.    who decides how you spend your ↓money?
 2        (2.0)
 3  R.    °well° =
 4  I.    = d'you make your ↓own mind up?
 5        (d') ↑staff help you or
 6        (0.2)
 7  R.    if I go out?
 8  I.    yeh (0.8) (ts-)
 9  R.★   (     ) to Mc↑Donald's to: (     )
10        cup of tea an' that =
11  I.    = mhm
12  R.★   and e:r (0.2) ham↑burger
13  I.    yea:h
14  R.★   an' ↓chips
15  I.    m↑hm
16        (0.8)
17  R.★   and (     ) (↑they) comes out with (0.2)
18        (     ) with a (saucepan)
19        (0.2)
20  I.    r(h)ight
21  R.★   (y'see) see (     ) for ↓tea
22        he said ↑right yes you can ↑'ave one
23  I.    ↑right (0.2) so ↑you decide how you spend
24        your money =
25  R.    = yes
26  I.    yeh?
27        (2.0)
28  I.    °o↑k.°
```
In response to the question in line 1, "Who decides how you spend your ↓money?" when going out, the respondent reports going to McDonald's and having tea, a hamburger and chips. The interviewer treats this talk as if the gist of it would make an appropriate answer to the question: "↑right (0.2) so ↑you decide how you spend your money" in line 23. This is confirmed by the respondent.

Note, as mentioned above, that the answer receipt in line 23 begins with a "so," which marks the utterance as a conclusion, and that the utterance is structured using declarative syntax. As discussed in chapter 7, declarative questions are treated by recipients as requests for confirmation and tend to be confirmed rather than disconfirmed.

Questions are structured in a declarative syntax when the speaker has good reason to believe the proposition is a fact. Therefore, the most likely response to a declarative question is an agreement/confirmation, as the question is built to occasion an agreeing response. In the rare case that a recipient disagrees with a declarative question, we might expect to find the disagreement put in a dispreferred turn format. In this set of data, however, the respondents never disagreed with a declarative question. When we look at declarative questions from a survey interview standpoint, we can say that they have the quality of being leading/directive questions.

We also see that interviewers proffer conclusions that are not marked as such. In line 4 of the fragment below the respondent answers the question in such a way that it is not clear what he means. His "to do it" in line 4 may be a shortened version of option three: "cos you ↓want to do it." He may be heard as merely echoing the last three words of the interviewer. However, the interviewer's answer receipt, "↓cos ↑you want to do things," can be heard as a formulation of what the respondent meant to say, according to the interviewer.

Question 21
How did you decide to do the job or other daily activities you do now?
I chose it because of pay, benefits, or interests.
Only thing available or that I could find.
Someone else decided for me.

(11)   Quality of Life interview
      1   I.   d'y (0.2) d'y do what you do bec'z (0.8) you
      2   ↓have to: (0.2) or because you're ↓told
      3   to (0.2) or cos you ↓want to do it.
      4   R.*   to do it.
      5   I.   hah?
      6   R.   ↓yeh.
      7   I.   ↑cos ↑you want to do things
      8   R.   yes.
      9   I.   °yeh?°
     10   (2.0)
     11   I.   ((Next question))

Even though it is unclear what the respondent refers to, the interviewer treats the respondent's talk as though it matches the third and last presented option, "cos you ↓want to do it." The interviewer's formulation of the respondent's "to do it" in line 4 as "↓cos ↑you want to do things" in line 7 is confirmed by the respondent.

Note that the option used in the above reformulation is also the most positive option. The same process occurs in fragment 8, where the interviewer formulates the respondent's unclear talk as matching the most positive option: "right (0.2) so ↑you decide how you spend your money." In both cases, the most positive option carries the most point-value, and each respondent is awarded three points for his answer.

5   First-turn repair: presenting the scripted question as an optimistic yes–no question

Interviewers who are to read aloud a standardized questionnaire often revise the scripted questions to take into account what they have come to learn about a specific respondent. This action is seen as "interviewer-initiated questionnaire repair" and, consequently, as first-turn repair. The respondents in our data have a learning disability, and, as we have seen above, their contributions to the interview are at least sometimes hearable as evidence of problems in understanding what is expected of them. In this regard, it is interesting that the interviewers almost always deliver the very first question on the schedule with no revision, and that repairs seem to occur only after an "obvious" instance of misunderstanding.

Let us look at how the interviewers treat the scripted questions as a potential trouble source and repair the potentially troublesome questions in first-turn position. Item 12 of the questionnaire reads as follows:

Question 12
Do you feel your job or other daily activity is worthwhile and relevant to either yourself or others?
Yes, definitely.
Probably, I'm not sure.
Definitely not.

The respondent below has already shown evidence of not understanding a previous question. Therefore, when presenting question 12 to him, the interviewer says:

(12)   Quality of Life interview
   1   I.   d'y think what you ↓<u>do</u>: (0.5) is (0.2) er
   2   ↑worth ↑while?
   3   (0.5)
   4   >what you do< (0.2) >(of a) ↑day<
   5   R.   ⌈yeh
   6   I.   ⌊yeh?
   7   yeh?
   8   (3.0)
   9   ((Next question))

In his initial posing of the question, the interview revises the scripted question in three respects. First, the revised version is much shorter and less complex. Having learned earlier that this respondent does not have a job, the interviewer rephrases the scripted "your job or other daily activities" as "what you ↓do:." Also, the question of whether this activity is "worthwhile and relevant to either yourself or others" becomes simply "↑worth ↑while."

Secondly, the question format has been revised in that the response options are not read out. The scripted question initially is a yes–no question that is redefined as a fixed choice question by virtue of the response options to be presented. The options "yes, definitely," "probably, I'm not sure," or "definitely not" make clear that the question seeks a qualified answer. Therefore, one could also say that the options redefine the initial yes–no question into the question "How relevant and worthwhile do you think ... ?" By not reading out the response options, the interviewer turns the scripted [question] + [options] format into a simple yes–no question.

Thirdly, the respondent is only presented with an alternative worth three points (yes) and an implicit alternative worth one point (no). In addition, a question like "d'y think what you ↓do: (0.5) is (0.2) er ↑worth ↑while?" displays a preference for a yes–answer, rather than for a no–answer. In that respect, the revised version projects an optimistic/positive answer; it asks whether the things the respondent does are worthwhile, rather than the opposite ("not worthwhile"), and therefore leads the respondent in the direction of the answer with the highest point-value.

The same revising procedure in first-turn position is visible in the fragment below:

Question 12
Do you feel your job or other daily activity is worthwhile and relevant to either yourself or others?
Yes, definitely.
Probably; I'm not sure.
Definitely not.

(13)   Quality of Life interview
   1   I.   ↑o↓kay (1.0) ↑thinking about (0.5) what
   2   you ↓do (0.5) during the day↑time (0.2)
   3   Bob y'know your (0.2) ↓pottery and
   4   your (0.2) ↑cookery (0.2) yeah (0.5)
   5   ⌈↓do ↓ye ↑think that's er:m (0.5)
   6   R.   ⌊↑yeah
   7   I.   worth↓whil::e an' (0.2) an' ↓relevant to
   8   what you ↓need
   9   R.   ye- y⌈eah
  10   I.   ⌊↑yeah (0.5) do you ↑think- (0.5)
  11   ↑yeah (0.2) ↑very ↓definitely
  12   (4.0)

Again, the interviewer revises the original question in three ways. First, the question is less complex. The somewhat abstract topic of the scripted question, "your job or other daily activities," is revised into the more concrete and recipient-designed "your (0.2) ↓pottery and your (0.2) ↑cookery." Secondly, the scripted [question] + [response options] format is turned into a yes–no question. Thirdly, the "yes" alternative presented for confirmation is the most positive one. When the respondent confirms it, the interviewer rates his job as "↑very ↓definitely" worthwhile and relevant.

Below is another example from the same section of questions. This time the official script runs:

Question 14
How do people treat you on your job?
The same as all other employees.
Somewhat differently than other employees.
Very differently.

(14)   Quality of Life interview
    1   I.   ↑how a↓bout (0.2) getting ↑on with other
    2   ↓people at work (0.2) is tha' (0.5)
    3   is that ↑go͟o͟d
    4   R.   y͟e͟s:
    5   I.   yeah?
    6   R.   ↓yes
    7   I.   o↓kay (0.5) °>two for ↑that<°

The scripted question seeks to ask how respondents are treated by their colleagues. The response options make clear that this "how" is to be heard as "compared to all other employees." This comparison is not to be made in evaluative terms (better/same/worse), but in terms of same/different. This is quite different from what the interviewer makes of it, when he asks, "↑how a↓bout (0.2) getting ↑on with other ↓people at work (0.2) is tha' (0.5) is that ↑go͟o͟d." Note that again, the interviewer proposes that the state of affairs is good, which is confirmed by the respondent.

6   Dealing with inconsistent answers

As we have seen, the scripted questions have three possible answers that should be read aloud by the interviewer. As is now familiar, the scripted response options proceed from a positive one (3 points) over a middle one (2 points) to a negative one (1 point). In order to provide the respondents with the all the options from which they are to choose, the interviewers should present all three options in one stretch of talk. It turns out however, that the interviewers hardly ever produce the entire [question] + [answer options] structure in this way. They usually deliver the three options in a staged way. That is, a TRP, "transition relevance place," occurs after the first (and most optimistic) option. If there is no response, the second option is delivered, and then the third. For example, in the following two fragments:

Question 30
Overall, would you say that your life is:
Free.
Somewhat planned for you.
Cannot usually do what you want.

(15)   Quality of Life interview
    1 I.   (w'd) ↑you ↓say that your ↑li:fe is (0.5)
    2   ↑free
    3   (0.8)   TRP
    4   or do the ↑sta:ff sometimes ↓plan
    5   things for ↑you
    6   (0.5)   TRP
    7   or you ↑can't do what you want to ↑d::o
    8   (0.8)   TRP
    9 R.   (sometimes I) (0.2) I -shout an'(0.5)

Question 1
Overall, would you say that life:
Brings out the best in you?
Treats you like everybody else?
Doesn't give you a chance?

(16)   Quality of Life interview
    1 I.   ↑wo͟uld you ↓say (0.2) ↑life brings out
    2   ↑best in you
    3   (0.5)   TRP
    4   treats you the same as everyone else
    5   (0.5)   TRP
    6   or doesn't give you a chance   TRP
    7 R.   ↑doesn't give (me) a ↓chance
    8 I.   ↓righ↑t (0.2) o↑k: .hh
    9   ((Next question))

As the completion of the first-response option constitutes a TRP, the respondent may take the turn and answer the question at this point:

Question 12
Do you feel your job or other daily activity is worthwhile and relevant to either yourself or others?
Yes, definitely.
Probably; I'm not sure.
Definitely not.

(17)   Quality of Life interview
    1 I.   do ye fee:l what you do: (0.5) during the day
    2   is (0.2) worth whi:le an' (0.5) ⌈(↑rele↓vant)
    3 R.   ⌊↑yeah
    4 I.   yeah
    5 R.   >↓yeah it's ↑worth↓while< (0.2) ↑yeah

The interviewer may accept this answer and credit it three points. But interviewers don't always do so. At times they still (following the interviewing rules) present the next option, and then perhaps the third one. This, however, may lead to the problem of the interviewer proposing a series of yes–no questions and receiving an agreement to each one. In the example below the inconsistent answers are marked with an asterisk:

Question 1
Overall, would you say that life:
Brings out the best in you?
Treats you like everybody else?
Doesn't give you a chance?

(18)   Quality of Life interview
    1 I.   overall would you say ↑that ↓life brings
    2   ↑out (0.2) the ↓best in you
    3 R.★   ↑yes
    4 I.   treats you like everybody ↓else =
    5 R.★   = ↑yes:
    6 I.   or doesn't give a chance
    7 R.   eh:?

How do interviewers deal with the problem of receiving inconsistent answers? They generally proceed in the way described in fragment 17 above, that is, they take the most optimistic answer and offer it to the respondent for confirmation. In the example below the interviewer first requests confirmation of the answer to the first option. When the respondent does indeed confirm it, the interviewer nevertheless presents the second option. When this meets with a confirmation as well, the interviewer takes the turn again and requests confirmation of the first and most optimistic answer:

Question 16
Are you learning skills that will help you get a different or better job? What are these skills?
Yes, definitely (one or more skills mentioned).
Am not sure, maybe (vague, general skills mentioned)
No, job provides no opportunity for learning new skills.

(19)   Quality of Life interview
   1   I.   >↑are you ↓learning ↓s<u>o</u>me things< when you're
   2   at ↓Fresh⌈fields?
   3   R.   ⌊yeah
   4   I.   you are ↑learning some ↓things⌈are you
   5   R.   ⌊yeah
   6   I.   or ↑not ↓really
   7   R.   ↑not rea:l↓↓ly
   8   (0.5)
   9   I.   or just (0.2) <u>er::rm</u>
 10   (2.0)
 11   ↑>so d'you ↑think ↓you're you ↑<u>are</u>
 12   ↓learning anything⌈(   )
 13 R.   ⌊yeah
 14   (0.5)
 15 I.   °right ↑then (0.2) ((next question))

Why do interviewers choose the most positive answer in a situation in which it is unclear which answer the respondent really meant to give? It seems that the interviewers follow a procedural rule that says: select the most optimistic answer unless there are clear indications in the respondent's talk that another answer is more in accord with what the respondent means to report. The example below shows what happens in the rare case that the interviewer treats the talk as having such evidence:

Question 1
Overall, would you say that life:
Brings out the best in you?
Treats you like everybody else?
Doesn't give you a chance?

(20)   Quality of Life interview
   1   I.   overall would you say ↑that ↓life brings
   2   ↑out (0.2) the ↓best in you
   3   R.   ↑yes
   4   I.   treats you like everybody ↓else =
   5   R.   = ↑yes:
   6   I.   or doesn't give a chance
   7   R.   eh:?
   8   (1.0)
   9   I.   what >do you think ↓that< (0.2) life (0.2)
 10   brings out the best in ↑you
 11   (0.5)

```
12            ⌈or (    )
13    R.      ⌊yeah the ↑best yeah yeah
14    I.      right (0.5) so that's ↓your (0.2) your
15            answer ↑yeah⌈life >br< life brings
16    R.                 ⌊↑yes yes
17    I.      out the best in you does it?
18            ((some lines omitted))
19    I.      okay (0.2) so of those ↑three (0.2) you think
20            ↓life brings out the best it doesn't (0.2)
21            treat ↓you like everyone ↓else an ↑it (0.2)
22            it ↓doesn't (0.2) not give you a chance
23    R.      (hhh) =
24    I.      = yeah?
25            (2.0)
26    R.      °°(doesn't) give me a ↑chance°° .h⌈hh ((sniff))
27    I.                                        ⌊okay
28            (1.0)
29            al↑right (0.5) next ↑one
```

The interviewer's pursuit of the response past the point at which the respondent has given a technically satisfactory response ("Yeah the ↑best yeah yeah") in line 13 eventually leads to a wholly contradictory response in line 26: "°°(doesn't)°° give me a ↑chance." Which of these two answers is more genuine is, of course, not up to me to say, but what I want to point out is that the initial one (with which the interviewer would normally be satisfied) occurs in response to a projected no-problem question.

7   Frequency of answers generated by yes–no questions

After studying how these interviewers deal with the scripted questions, I attempted to discover the extent to which the respondents' final responses were generated by the leading nature of the interviewers' (re)formulations. However, it was impossible to come up with an accurate count. Many of the question–answer sequences discussed here proceed in such a way that it is impossible to say whether or not the final answer is the product of leading interviewer behavior. Here is one example of such a problematic sequence:

Question 21
How did you decide to do the job or other daily activities you do now?
I chose it because of pay, benefits, or interests.
Only thing available or that I could find.
Someone else decided for me.

(21)   Quality of Life interview
     1   I.   how did you decide to do (0.2) the job
     2   or (0.8) erm ⌈the things you do
     3   R.   ⌊I clean ↓u:p.
     4   I.   ↑ho̲w did you ↓choose (0.2) ↑ho̲w did you de↓cide
     5   to do̲ that
     6   R.   I clean up with the mop an- ↑bu̲↓cket.
     7   I.   yeah?
     8   R.   moppin' the ↑ki̲tchen ↓out
     9   I.   °can I put this (0.2) just ↓here°
    10   R.   yes (0.2) don't do it in me ↑ju̲m↓per
    11   ((some lines omitted))
    12   I.   ↑how did you de↓cide to do (0.2) the things
    13   you do (0.2) at the ↓moment (0.2) because
    14   of (0.5) you were ↑interested in it (0.2)
    15   or (0.2) it was (0.2) ↑good ↓money (0.5)
    16   because it was anything you could ⌈(   )
    17   R.   ⌊↑yes it
    18   ↓wa̲s good
    19   I.   yeah?
    20   R.   yes ⌈it was
    21   I.   ⌊or does someone else (0.2) does ↑someone
    22   else de↓cide ⌈what you do
    23   R.   ⌊I ↑do̲ ↓cleaning up and mo̲pping
    24   I.   yeah (0.2) is that cos (0.2) yo̲u decide to
    25   do that
    26   R.   YES
    27   I.   yeah?
    28   (2.0)
    29   R.   I ↓↑do̲:
    30   I.   ((next question))

Even though this sequence results in the optimistic yes–no question, "Is
that cos (0.2) yo̲u decide to do that?" in lines 25–6, which the respondent
confirms, it does not seem adequate to say that the interviewer has achieved
a positive answer in a leading fashion. In fact, we do not even know if the
interviewer has recorded a score here. He may well have decided to give up
and to treat this question as not having been answered, or he may have
given the respondent a score that is unrelated to her confirmation of the
final yes–no question. The interviewers sometimes know what the rules
and regulations of the respondents' homes are, and it may be that they use
this information for giving a score in cases such as above.

Rather than providing the reader with quantitative information with regard to how often certain interactional procedures occur in this set of interviews and how they affect the final answer, I restrict myself to describing the procedures as such. I believe that I do not need numerical figures to say, as I do in the following discussion, that this questionnaire is not an adequate instrument for validly assessing the quality of life of people with a learning disability.

8   Conclusion

I discussed in this chapter how these interviewers reformulate the cognitively complex scripted [question] + [response options] structure into an optimistic question. There are four environments in which this revision occurs. One is in third-turn position, after the respondent has demonstrated difficulty in dealing with the initial version. Interviewers also revise these questions at the beginning of the sequence, in first-turn position, when the respondent has indicated earlier in the interview that he or she has problems understanding the scripted question format. In addition, when the interviewers receive unclear talk in response to a question, they tend to formulate that talk as an appropriate and positive answer. Also, when respondents give two or more inconsistent answers, interviewers use this material to opt for the most positive answer. All four of these procedures result in disputable test scores (Marlaire and Maynard 1990; Maynard and Marlaire 1992).

In other words, when the scripted Quality of Life questionnaire has to face up to the actual practices of its interviewers and its learning disabled respondents, it undergoes systematic transformation. The basic principle of this transformation is for the interviewer to change the complex [question] + [three response options] format into a more basic yes–no question format. In producing the yes–no question, the interviewer uses the default, or the unmarked, formulation for the state of affairs about which they are enquiring. In general the unmarked formulation of yes–no questions is such that speakers typically propose an optimistic state of affairs, such as "Are you all right?" "Did you sleep well?" and "Do you think your life is worthwhile?"

When respondents give unclear or inconsistent answers, I propose that the interviewers follow a procedural rule that says: select the most optimistic answer unless there are clear indications in the respondent's talk that another answer is more in accord with what the respondent means to report. This most optimistic answer coincides with the state of affairs that is proposed in the unmarked formulation of yes–no questions. Face-work issues are involved in the unmarked formulation of questions and in the interpretation of unclear answers. That is, speakers follow a face-work convention that says: assume the positive and the optimistic as long as nothing speaks against this.

In the beginning of the chapter I pointed out that these assessors are free to reformulate the questions when the respondents have difficulty understanding them. Apart from the fact that this allowance does away with the standardized pretension of the questionnaire, it also leads to other problems in practice. If the project of assessing people's quality of life is worth doing by a standardized questionnaire (though see Antaki and Rapley (1996) for a contrary view), then, rather than giving the assessors so much freedom in reformulating difficult questions, it might be better to revise the scripted questionnaire to the level of the linguistic and pragmatic competence of the respondents.

This reworking of the original scripted questionnaire to match the competencies of respondents better may or may not be possible. In any case, this suggestion speaks only to the cognitive framing of the questions. As it stands, however, the evidence in this chapter shows that, when delivering an ostensibly neutral and non-leading script, questions can be redesigned to project culturally positive answers. This reformatting is a matter of recipient design, which moves away from the cognitive and into the social, interactional sphere.

9   Implications for survey methodology

1   Introduction

I would like to begin this concluding chapter by quoting De Sola Pool. Although this quote is from 1957, it could well serve as a general conclusion for the present study. In his paper De Sola Pool criticizes the assumption that we can:

> get rid of interpersonal effects so as to get at the truth which would be there if the interpersonal character of the interview didn't interfere. [...] The social milieu in which the communication takes place modifies not only what a person dares to say but even what he thinks he chooses to say. And these variations in expressions cannot be viewed as mere deviations from some underlying "true" opinion, for there is no neutral, non-social, uninfluenced situation to provide that baseline. (191–2)

In this chapter I draw conclusions from the analyses of the "interpersonal character" of the interviews I have presented in this book. The first three sections briefly point out what I believe are the benefits of a CA approach to the study of standardized interviews. Section 4 presents some possible research questions based upon the findings of conversation analysis. Section 5 explains why interviewers should be allowed more flexibility than is currently granted to them by the rules of standardized interviewing. In the final section it will become clear that the costs of flexible interviewing are considerable, but whether or not the price is too high is a question that cannot be answered by survey methodology.

2   Conversation analysis as a diagnostic instrument

When survey methodologists are interested in how the participants in a specific series of interviews behave, or when they wish to pre-test a specific questionnaire, they conduct behavior coding studies of tape-recorded interactions (Morton-Williams and Sykes 1984, Fowler 1989, Bolton 1991, Dijkstra 1987, Dijkstra and Van der Zouwen 1988, Bolton and Bronkhurst 1996, Fowler and Cannell 1996). The advantage of behavior-coding studies, especially when computers are used, is that they can process a large number of interviews. This capability enables them to produce data regarding the frequency with which certain phenomena and problems occur. But as Van der Zouwen (forthcoming) points out, the findings of behavior-coding studies only alert researchers to issues of interviewer and respondent behavior. They do not answer an important question: what is causing the phenomena that the behavior-coding studies find? In order to gain more insight into what interview participants actually do, we need more detailed analyses.

As the present CA studies have shown, a detailed analysis of only a small number of interviews can shed light on various types of problems that would otherwise go unnoticed. For instance, the CA analyst may notice that respondents often request clarification of a particular question. These requests for clarification may point to a problem with the formulation of the question. For example, some of the terms that are used may be unclear to the respondents.

Survey methodology recognizes that terms may be interpreted in a number of ways. As Belson has shown, even seemingly clear notions like "watching televison" are ambiguous. This information is primarily gathered through cognitive interviewing techniques. For example, after a respondent answers a question regarding the number of hours he or she watched television the week before, the respondent is then asked what he or she means by "watching television." One could therefore say that, in order to design clear and unambiguous questions, the designer should consult the literature, for example the work by Belson (1981, 1986).

However, consulting the literature will not solve all potential problems. Respondents' requests for clarification often make clear that the question under discussion is ambiguous in unexpected ways. Schober and Conrad (1997: 592) show a fragment of an American telephone survey that includes the question "How many people live in this house?" To the designers of the questionnaire the concept of "living in this house" may seem sufficiently clear, but when one respondent asks "Currently? Or," the potential ambiguity for the respondent becomes obvious. Does "living in this house" mean being registered at that address? Or does one "live in this house" when one has one's bed there? Does the son of the respondent, who goes to college elsewhere, still live there? We only need the clarification request of one respondent to demonstrate this ambiguity to us.

Requests for clarification are not the only behaviors that may point to a problem with a question. As we have seen, respondents may delay their answers, thus creating a silence after a question. These post-question silences may last only one second or less.[1] However, interviewers often treat such post-question silences as indications that the respondents do not understand the question, and they therefore volunteer clarifications (see chapter 6). Explicitly requesting clarification may be considered a face-threatening act by the potential requester because it demonstrates a lack of knowledge on his or her part. An alternative behavior to avoid loss of face, while still solving the knowledge problem, is to wait for the interviewer to offer clarification. Van der Sloot and Spanjer found several instances of this behavior (1998).

Respondents may also demonstrate that they are having difficulty with a question by repeating part of the question with a rising intonation, for example "Am I married?" Generally, these questioning repeats do not point to problems in understanding the semantic meaning of the question, nor to hearing problems. Rather, questioning repeats are most commonly used when respondents do not see the point of the question, perhaps because they have already provided the requested information.

If we want to know more about the quality of a specific questionnaire, we can also examine respondents' answers, especially answers that do not match the pre-coded response categories, as well as extended yes–no answers. As CA studies show again and again, recipients display their understanding of questions, as well as their misunderstanding, in their answers. The problem with yes–no questions is that a "yes" or "no" response merely demonstrates that the respondent has understood that the question is a yes–no question. Luckily enough, respondents frequently provide more than just a "yes" or "no" answer, and the resulting extensions inform us as to how they understood the question. For example, in a Dutch survey, an interviewer may ask a respondent whether or not he or she has ever visited an old town. A respondent may say, "Yes, in Greece." If the question was intended to ask about old towns in the Netherlands only, such an extension informs us directly that this question is ambiguous.

Examining the behavior of interviewers, too, may make the CA analyst aware of problems with a specific questionnaire. As pointed out in the preceding chapters, many of the interviewers' deviations from standardized interviewing rules can be explained by poor questionnaire design. By revising parts of the questions, interviewers demonstrate to us that written language is not always adequate for use in interaction. For example, when the question is too long and/or has a complex syntactic structure, interviewers sometimes shorten and/or simplify the wording.

When interviewers have learned from previous interviews that respondents have trouble providing the type of answer that a specific question is looking for, the interviewers often provide candidate answers, which they take from the list of response options. They may also revise complex multiple-choice questions into more basic yes–no questions when the respondents have difficulty understanding the question as it is scripted, for example in the British Quality of Life interviews with learning-disabled persons discussed earlier. Revising multiple-choice questions into yes–no questions also commonly occurred in the Dutch literacy interviews when interviewers felt that certain questions were potentially face threatening to the respondents. The interviewers would therefore reformulate these questions as no-problem questions, and therefore leading questions, that anticipated answers that reflected positively on the respondent.

Survey methodology is, generally speaking, interested in frequencies. Numerous studies inform us about the percentage of questions asked, or answered, inadequately in way X or way Y. A methodologist may want to know, for example, the percentage of respondents that requested clarification of a particular question. In my opinion, however, each "deviant" instance is of potential interest. We only need the one respondent mentioned in Schober and Conrad's survey to learn that the concept of "living" somewhere is ambiguous. Once we discover this, we realize immediately that we do not know how the other respondents interpreted this concept when they answered the question. This example also shows that we need information not only about whether or not, and how often, respondents ask for question clarification. We also urgently need to know what they are asking. Respondents may show us not only that a problem exists, but also what the nature of that problem is.

3   Detecting structural problems

CA research can also point to questionnaire design problems of a more general character than the ambiguity or syntactic complexity of specific questions. Sacks et al. (1974) describe how conversationalists allocate turns at talk, and how they construct their turns such that they indicate to the co-participants the stage of completion that a turn-in-progress is in. The study of turn taking problems in survey interviews, presented in chapter 5, makes clear that this description of turn taking is relevant for questionnaire designers.

If survey questions are followed by a set of response options, when the interviewers read the response options aloud they run the risk of being interrupted by respondents' answers. This, in turn, may lead to interviewers asking leading probes or to respondents not being presented with the entire list of options. Although the problem of questions followed by response options may not be entirely solved, we can reduce the problem in a number of different ways.

Respondents should be informed that the completion point of the question proper is not the completion point of the interviewer's intended turn, and that the interviewer will provide them with a set of response options. This information can be provided to respondents early in the interview by means of a general instruction. Interviewers would also be wise to explain the reason for this procedure to the respondents.

Apart from making explicit this survey-interview-specific rule of turn taking, closed questions should also be formulated in such a way that they implicitly instruct the respondents that more will follow after the completion of the question proper. So, rather than asking, "What is your race? Is it White, Black, Asian, American Indian, or Other?" we may integrate the response options into the questioning sentence: "Is your race White, Black, Asian, American Indian, or Other?" Though this reformulation does not guarantee that respondents will remain silent till the end of the question, it is perhaps the best we can do.

After designing a questionnaire, the designer should check that each question makes clear that response options will follow. A general rule is: in the case of closed questions, if a question can be appropriately answered before the response options have been presented, the question needs reformulation. The need for the application of this rule can be illustrated by a USA questionnaire. This questionnaire contains many questions that begin with the word "how," and that are followed by a set of response options, for example:

How much have you heard of X?
A great deal, some, not very much, nothing at all.

and:

How willing would you be to do X?
Very willing, somewhat willing, not very willing, not willing at all.

Respondents may answer these questions before the interviewer presents the response options. In order to prevent respondents from answering too early, the topic of the question should be presented first, such as "the next question is about X," or "talking about X," and only then should the response options be given.[2] This structuring may lead to question formulations such as:

Speaking about X,
have you heard a great deal, some, not very much, or nothing at all about this?

and:

With regard to X,
Would you be very willing, somewhat willing, not very willing, or not willing at all to do X?

Another cause of respondents' premature answers is that questions are sometimes followed by a specification or explanation. For example:

Do you have any income, from any source, in the past 12 months?
Be sure to include income from work, government benefits, pensions, and all other sources.

Again, questionnaire designers should ask themselves: what is the first possible place we can expect respondents to give an answer? If this place is positioned before the explanation of a concept, this explanation should be moved. In some cases it can be built into the question, in others it can precede the question. For example:

Next we have a question about your income.
By that we mean income from work, government benefits, pensions, and all other sources.
Now, do you have any income, from any source, in the past 12 months?

In conclusion, questionnaire designers should make sure that the questions are structured such that the last component is the question delivery component, which is the component that delivers the question to the respondent. All other components should precede this one. Each specific questionnaire should be submitted to this "questioning-turn structure test" before it is given to the interviewers.

We could examine interview behavior in terms of respondents' inadequate answers and interviewers' errors, and perhaps conclude that interviewers need more and better training. However, we could also try to determine why interviewers and respondents do not behave as they "should." I firmly believe that these two parties should not be held responsible for their "inadequate" behavior. Interviewers are expected to do a job that cannot always be performed correctly. They are expected to follow the rules for standardized interviewing in a highly interactional setting, where their co-participants are (at least partly) oriented toward a different set of interactional rules. The interviewers are also frequently presenting questionnaires that contain various problems. In my view, most interviewers make the very best of their situation.

Rather than considering interviewers "error-makers," and blaming them for this, we should assist them by finding ways to prevent errors. Most importantly, we should free them from the confines of standardized interviewing procedures that are not fit for the interactional setting in which they are applied. We cannot provide a painter with only a hammer and then blame him or her for a job not done properly. In section 4, I will argue that when interviewers are given more room in which to maneuver, they increase the validity of answers without decreasing reliability.

4   Generating new research questions on question formulation

CA studies of survey interviews can inform us about general and specific problems with particular questionnaires. They may also be used to generate research questions for experimental research or cognitive interviewing procedures.

As pointed out above, a respondent may ask for question clarification or answer a question in such a way that it points to a problem of some sort. Researchers may then wonder if this problem is incidental or structural. For example, when one respondent makes clear that for him "having completed a course" does not necessarily mean having received a certificate, we may want to know how other (groups of) respondents interpret this notion. Such singular incidents may therefore be issues to study with a cognitive interviewing technique.

Other observations may be applied in experimental research on questionnaire design. For example, the analysis of turn-taking and questioning-turn construction as presented in chapter 5 may be useful in experiments on question structure and its relationship to turn construction. Such experiments may elucidate the degree to which certain questioning-turn structures lead to interruptions by respondents. Similar experiments can be carried out pertaining to the relative placement of questioning-turn components and their relationship to interruptions.

5   A quest for flexible standardized interviewing

Having studied tape-recorded standardized survey interviews for some years now, I have become increasingly convinced that the quest for standardization is no longer tenable, at least if its purpose is to generate not only reliable, but also valid, research data.

5.1   Survey methodology and the conduit metaphor

The most important, and most often mentioned, concern for advocates of standardization is that all respondents be presented with the same question. According to these advocates, respondents' answers can only be compared, and their differences can only be attributed to differences between group characteristics, if the respondents are all presented with the same question. This stimulus-response model of the survey interview is problematic. However, we do not need to dispose of this model altogether, if we correct the current notion of "sameness."

The stimulus-response model is based on two incorrect and closely related assumptions. First, this model assumes that the linguistic meaning of a question coincides with the researcher's intended meaning and the purpose of the question, and second, that respondents will interpret the question as the author meant it. These two assumptions follow from the popular belief that language is a conduit for the transfer of thought (Reddy 1979): in our mind there is thought T, we wrap T in language and send this parcel to the addressee, who then unwraps it, thus putting the initial thought into his or her mind.

The most problematic part of this conduit metaphor is the relationship between the intended meaning of a question and its interpretation by respondents. Depending on respondents' personal backgrounds, knowledge, and experiences, as well as the information they have already volunteered,[3] they may interpret the meaning and/or the purpose of the question in a different way than the author intends. Therefore different respondents may end up with different interpretations.

When respondents ask interviewers what they mean by a question, the rules for standardized survey interviewing instruct interviewers to not clarify the question. They are allowed to say "whatever it means to you," which already acknowledges that a single question may have different meanings for different respondents. Interviewers may also use the conduit metaphor themselves and say "it's just what the question says." Although such replies do not make the meaning of a question much clearer, respondents will usually provide an answer to the question nevertheless.

When survey methodology expresses the desire to present all respondents with the same question, it really means that all respondents should be presented with the same meaning as intended by the researcher. In my perspective of the standardized interview, respondents should be presented with the same meaning-as-intended, rather than with the same questioning sentence. When some respondents are not able to extract the intended meaning from the question formulation, we need the interviewer to act as a spokesperson for the researcher (Suchman and Jordan 1990a: 241). This requires, of course, that interview training should not only include instruction regarding interviewing techniques, but also extensive explanation of the purpose of the research and, consequently, of the scripted questions.

On the basis of their knowledge of the research and the questionnaire, interviewers will be in the position (at least to some extent) to explain and clarify questions when needed. They may not know in detail exactly what the researcher/questionnaire designer has in mind concerning the meaning of each specific question, but they will be able to make an educated guess. So, in order to be proper spokespersons on behalf of the researcher, interviewers should become "informed interviewers/spokespersons."

5.2   *Allow interviewers to discuss questions and answers*

We should allow interviewers-as-spokespersons to discuss with respondents the intended meaning and purpose of questions, as well as the respondents' answers. This discussion may increase the validity of the research data, even though a more flexible way of interviewing may at times cause inappropriate interviewer behavior, such as presenting the respondent with leading questions. However, the overall result may well be positive. As Suchman and Jordan stated in 1990, we need empirical research to understand better how interviewer bias can be avoided and what the effects of flexible interviewing are on data quality.

Schober and Conrad (1997) take up Suchman and Jordan's research question on the quality of data generated by flexible interviewers. They conducted a laboratory experiment in which trained telephone interviewers used either standardized or flexible interviewing techniques. The flexible interviewers were trained in the definitions of the concepts used in the questions and were allowed to clarify concepts by improvising. Respondents answered questions on the basis of fictional descriptions that were given to them, so that response accuracy could be measured. The questions used in this experiment were taken from a large USA government survey concerning housing, work, and purchasing. This experiment showed there was no substantial difference in response accuracy when the concepts in the questions clearly mapped onto the fictional situations of respondents. However, when the mapping was less clear, flexible interviewing increased accuracy by almost 60 percent.

5.3   *Allow interviewers to accept unformatted answers*

Survey methodology assumes that if interviewers present the list of response options, respondents will understand that they are supposed to phrase their answers in these terms. However, respondents are usually not informed about this. Even in cases where interviewers make this clear, respondents still seem to have a hard time remembering this for the duration of the interview. When interviewers respond to an unformatted answer by re-offering the response options, thus implicitly informing the respondent how he or she should answer the questions, the transcripts show that respondents follow this rule for only a short time. A few questions later we find them providing unformatted answers again. Perhaps we should accept that we cannot discipline respondents to the extent we would like, and therefore we should give interviewers some freedom to accept unformatted answers.

5.4 Allow interviewers to draw and verify inferences

In interviews where interviewers try to follow the rules of standardized interviewing, respondents are expected to know that interviewers are not allowed to draw inferences. A respondent who mentions "my husband" should not assume that the interviewer will infer from this that the respondent is married. This expectation runs fundamentally contrary to the way individuals answer questions, both in ordinary conversation and in other types of institutional discourse. The analyses presented here show that respondents have a hard time realizing that survey interviewers are not supposed to draw inferences.

I believe we should give interviewers the freedom to draw inferences and then verify them with the respondents. If a respondent mentions "my husband," the interviewer should not ask whether the respondent is "single, married, a widow, or living together," but should be allowed to verify that the respondent is married. Since verifying can easily be done in a leading manner, verification is an important interviewing technique that interviewers should be trained in.

5.5 Explain the rules to respondents

Rather than allowing interviewers to be more flexible, we might decide to explain the interview-specific interactional rules to the respondents before the interview starts. However, there are several problems with this option. First, prospective respondents may be put off by the rigidity of the rules, which could reduce response rates. Second, respondents may not be able to follow these instructions. When we look at the highly standardized American interviews, we expect respondents to figure out after some time that the interviewers need formatted answers. At times the interviewers even explicitly refer to the restricted possibilities on their screens. But the respondents (one of whom is a survey interviewer herself) stick to their own course.

This is remarkable for two reasons. From a cognitive perspective, one would expect that it is much easier to merely repeat a line that was just presented by the interviewer than it is to formulate a different answer. Listening to mundane conversation makes clear that conversationalists often copy parts of their co-conversationalists' talk. But respondents do not seem to prefer this. Rather than just copying one of the given response options, they frequently produce their own formulations. Furthermore, one might expect respondents to be willing to please the interviewer and to make her task as easy as possible. However, when respondents do not provide the formatted answers that interviewers aim for, they may well have good reason.

5.6   Standardized interviewing rules pose problems for interviewers

The rules of standardized interviewing may also pose a serious problem for interviewers. If they follow these rules strictly, they frequently present themselves to respondents as impolite, insensitive, and unintelligent individuals. Standardized interviewers are expected to present themselves as persons who ask rather silly and redundant questions, who do not know themselves what they mean by the questions they are asking, who are not able to draw inferences from what the respondents tell them, who have no knowledge of the social world around them, and who do not consider the respondents' face and feelings when asking delicate questions. It must be rather difficult for interviewers to act in this way. For that reason we should not be surprised that they do not always stick to the rules of standardized interviewing. We should make the rules a little more flexible, allowing interviewers to maintain face while generating valid data.

6   The costs of flexible interviewing

Flexible interviewing has at least three disadvantages. First, it becomes far more difficult to evaluate interviewer behavior. In order to find out whether interviewers do their work according to the rules of flexible standardized interviewing, we would need a time-consuming method for analyzing interviews. When flexible interviewing would indeed increase the validity of research data, this may well be worthwhile. Otherwise, we may wonder how important interviewer evaluation really is. It may well be the case that this is mainly an academics' interest.

Second, flexible interviewing puts an extra burden on interview training. The researcher and the questionnaire designer would have to explain to the interviewers what the research is all about, and how each concept in the questionnaire is defined. If interviewers are expected to provide correct explanations of the questions and also discuss the answers with the respondents, they need a far more extensive training than usual.

Finally, the Schober and Conrad experiment showed that their flexible interviews took almost four times as long as the standardized interviews. Together with a more extensive interview training, this means that the high validity of flexible interviewing comes at great expense. It is up to the client of the particular research to decide if he or she thinks high validity is worth that price.

Notes

1 THE STANDARDIZED SURVEY INTERVIEW

1. I prefer the term "formatted answer" over "adequate answer", partly because the last term has a normative connotation that I would like to avoid.

2 INTERVIEWER–RESPONDENT INTERACTION

1. A discussion of conversation analysis more detailed than this section provides can be found in Zimmerman and Boden (1991), Drew and Heritage (1992), and Psathas (1995).
2. "Oh"-receipts are largely absent in news interviews (Heritage 1985). News interviewers are briefed beforehand and therefore know roughly what the respondents will say. Furthermore, news interviewers primarily elicit talk meant for an overhearing audience (Heritage 1985; Heritage and Greatbatch 1991). Also, medical doctors are seen as displaying neutrality by largely refraining from "oh"-receipts (Ten Have 1991), and this is also said to hold true for psychotherapists (Labov and Fanshel 1977), for arbitrators of Small Claims Court interactions (Atkinson 1992).

3 PARTICIPANT ROLES

1. In fact, Levinson talks about "spokesman," a term that is considered politically incorrect today.
2. Ten Have (1995) speaks of interviewers "harvesting" answers.
3. See Sacks (1988/89, 1992) on round numbers.
4. When I speak of interactive frames here, I use the term somewhat informally.
5. Publications on experiments in survey methodology usually inform the reader on the way the interviewers were trained or the number of years of experience they have. This suggests that the authors take for granted that the interviewers indeed followed the rules they were supposed to follow.

4 RECIPIENT DESIGN

1. This is not the case when the interviewer and the researcher are one and the same person.
2. Related notions are "pragmatic presuppositions" (Stalnaker 1974), "mutual knowledge" (Smith 1982, Gibbs 1987), "shared assumptions" (Sperber and Wilson 1986).

3. See Sacks and Schegloff (1979) and Levinson (1987) on the preference for minimization in mundane conversation.

4. The term "audience design" is different from the way Heritage and Greatbatch (1991) use it when talking about the "overhearing audience" of media interviews. In survey interviews the "audience" is not a collection of overhearing participants, but a collection of to-be-addressed participants (Goffmann 1979/1981a).

5. Ten Have (p.c.) points out that the interviewer was not in the position to recognize the name Mark, because it was not mentioned yet. For that reason Ten Have proposes that "Mark" is not a recognitional, but an "inferable."

6. For a detailed discussion of "something else" as a problematic category, see Schaeffer and Maynard (1996).

7. This section is a slightly revised version of Houtkoop-Steenstra 1995.

8. As Schegloff (1988/89) points out, this is the most fundamental component of what is considered an interview, for example, employment interviews (Button 1987, Komter 1991), medical interviews (Frankel 1984, Ten Have 1987), news interviews (Clayman 1988; Heritage and Greatbatch 1991) and court proceedings (Atkinson and Drew 1979).

9. Whereas the questionnaire says, "Could you please tell me how old you are?" the interviewers say, "Could you please tell me your age?" When I asked people what they felt the difference was between the two formulations, they considered the question as it appeared on the questionnaire to be less polite than the interviewers' formulation.

10 Notice that Doris confirms the interviewer's "three days a week?" and then adds "three times a week" to it. Although there is no hard evidence in the interview, it is likely that the answer is recorded as "three days a week." In that case the answer may be invalid, because it is not clear that the course Doris refers to takes place at least three full days a week.

11. The telephone conversation begins with talk about the interview and the possible respondentship of the answerer. When it has been decided that the interview will take place, the co-participants change their interactional status from caller and answerer to interviewer and respondent, and they begin the interview. When the last question has been dealt with, the interviewer markedly terminates the interview. The co-particiants may exchange some further talk that is not part of the interview and then terminate the conversation. The interview as a speech exchange system is thus embedded in an ordinary telephone conversation. Compare Mazeland (1983), Joosten (1995) and Haegeman (1996) on how school lessons, medical interviews, and business calls, respectively, tend to be preceded by conversational talk.

12. Goffman (1981b: 239) says about the "text-locked voice" of radio-announcers: "in switching from ordinary text to a strip that is *intended* to be heard as aloud reading (a news quote, author-identified program notes, etc.), the ostensible purpose being to relay the material instead of fully animating it, announcers can employ a voice suggesting that they themselves do not currently figure in any way as author or principle, merely as a voicing machine."

13. This example may make clear that the literal reading aloud of a scripted text is no guarantee that the text is relayed as intended by the researcher. It shows that standardized question wording does not necessarily imply standardized question delivery.

5 QUESTIONING-TURN STRUCTURE AND TURN TAKING

1 Especially in written forms meant to be filled out, for example tax forms or application forms, we find the [question] + [explanation/specification] structure. Research shows that many people tend to write down the answer without having read the specification or explanation (Jansen and Steehouder 1992). Current research is focusing on finding ways to redesign written forms so that the explanation or specification is more likely to be read (Steehouder and Jansen 1992).

2. In Dutch culture the notion of "education" is associated with formal schooling. This holds less true for the term "course."

3. Mazeland (1992), who studied non-standardized social research interviews, found that interviewers work more towards appropriate answers than towards correct answers.

4. Earlier I said that the interviewer can accept an answer by acknowledging it. In this excerpt it is audible from the tape that the interviewer, right after his acknowledgment, enters something into the computer, which can hardly be anything other than the respondent's answer.

5. Although this would be a case of overlap (Sacks, Schegloff, and Jefferson 1974), I speak of an interruption here because this is what happens from the perspective of the questionnaire designer or the interviewer.

6. Sacks describes the methods by which members of a culture identify persons in terms of so-called membership categorization devices (MCDs): "By the term 'categorization device,' we mean that collection of membership categories, containing at least one category, that may be applied to some population, containing at least one member, so as to provide, by the use of some rules of application, for the pairing of at least a population member and a categorization device member. A 'device' is then a collection plus rules of application" (1972a). Sacks (1972b) describes how references to a person in successive utterances can be interpreted consistently by means of MCD principles. Members of the collection of paired relational categories are, for example, spouse/spouse or parent/child.

7 I am grateful to my colleague Wil Dijkstra for providing me with these data.

6 GENERATING RECORDABLE ANSWERS TO FIELD-CODED QUESTIONS

1. In the Netherlands a "school concert" is a concert that is visited with the school.

2. This also holds true for *ja* in German (Stickel 1972).

3. The possible mistake by the interviewer is caused by the recent change in the Dutch school system. What used to be considered kindergarten is now the first two years of primary school, making primary school six years long instead of eight. When today's pupils are in sixth grade, they are about ten years old, rather than twelve. However, these respondents went to primary school in the old system.

4. See Mazeland and Ten Have (1996) on reformulations in semi-open research interviews.

5. See, for example, the studies by De Boer (1994) and Hak and De Boer (1996) on psychotherapy; Longman and Mercer (1993) on employment

training interviews; Smith and Whalen (1995), Whalen (1995) and others on calls to emergency services; Mehan (1984) on the categorization of students for special education programs; and Atkinson and Drew (1979) and Komter (1998) on court proceedings.

7 ESTABLISHING RAPPORT

1. See M. H. Goodwin (1980), Pomerantz (1984a), Goodwin and Goodwin (1992), and Jefferson (1993) on the organization of assessments in conversation.
2. In the Dutch fragments in this chapter I translate *ja* as "yes" or "yah," or I leave the *ja* untranslated, inserting a gloss of the English translation.
3. This aspect can be considered positive because on several occasions this respondent indicates that she dislikes other people knowing that she cannot write well.
4. See Maynard (1989: 56) on affiliation in the context of delivering bad news.
5. Sacks (1992) and more extensively, Watson (1987) discuss the "in-principle ambiguity" of the English "you." English uses the same linguistic form for both the singular and plural second-person pronoun, while Dutch makes a lexical distinction. *Je* is the singular pronoun and *jullie* the plural pronoun. In adddition *jij* is also used as a second-person singular pronoun. Roughly speaking, *jij* can only be used as an address form, whereas *je* can be used both as an address form and a generic personal pronoun, standing for "anyone," "everyone," and "one."

   Dutch further distinguishes between formal and informal address terms. *U* is the formal form, *je/jij* the informal form. Therefore, when a speaker addresses his or her co-participant with the formal *U*, the co-participant's use of *je* is most likely to be treated as a generic pronoun. In this respect, "you" is less ambiguous in Dutch than it is in English.
6. See Maynard (1992: 349–50) on the phenomenon of identifying in a medical context.
7. See Pomerantz (1984a: 87–8) on how self-deprecations are often undermined by recipients.
8. Note also that the interviewer joins in with the respondent's laughter about her unstated troubles when she places a laughter particle in her question utterance. Insofar as the respondent's turn foreshadows a troubles-telling, and thereby invites the interviewer's alignment as a troubles-recipient (Jefferson 1988), the interviewer may be seen as troubles-resistant when she joins in with R's laughter.
9. Abbenbroek, in her study on declarative questions, uses two types of data: standardized survey interviews and counseling interactions. She shows that when a questioner asks a declarative question, he or she already knows the answer. When this happens in the survey interview, it is often after the respondent has previously provided the requested information. In some cases, usually involving a counselor as questioner, the questioner may ask a declarative question requesting information that cannot be located on the tape. In these instances, however, the questioner seems to base her or his assumptions on generally shared knowledge and beliefs or on an inference that can be made based on what has been said previously.

10. Both the declarative structure and the optimistic wording mentioned in this section are also found in most of the *and*-prefaced questions in Heritage and Sorjonen's article. These phenomena occur in requests to which the health visitor already seems to have the information, as in, "And uh you're going to Doctor White for your (0.6) post-na:tal?" They also occur when the health visitors ask questions such as "An' you had a no:rmal pre:gnancy.; And a normal delivery.; And sh' didn't go into special ca:re," or "And you're feeling well?" They display the interviewers' assumptions that the mothers go through the normal routine. Therefore, formatting a question in a declarative syntax and using optimistic wording may further indicate that the question anticipates a "no-problem" answer.

11. Compare Bergmann (1992) on psychiatrists using "litotes formulations" in information-eliciting tellings. Litotes do not directly describe the object to which they refer, but rather they negate its opposite. Therefore, "a speaker's avoidance of a more direct or explicit description creates the possibility that the co-interactant will be the first to introduce such a description and, by doing so, show openness and honesty" (149).

9 IMPLICATIONS FOR SURVEY METHODOLOGY

1. Compare this to the study by Bolton (1991), who coded pauses only when they lasted longer than three seconds. He interpreted shorter pauses as indications of retrieval difficulties.

2. Compare with Mazeland (1992) on the information structure of interview questions.

3. See Schwartz 1996.

References

Abbenbroek, N. 1993. Voorinformatie en de formulering van vragen. Een onderzoek naar de verschillen tussen interrogatieve en declaratieve vragen. [Preinformation and the formulation of questions. Research into the differences between interrogative and declarative questions] MA Thesis, Utrecht University.

Antaki, C. and M. Rapley. 1996. "Quality of Life" talk: the liberal paradox of psychological testing. *Discourse & Society* 7, 3: 293–316.

Atkinson, J. M. 1992. Displaying neutrality: formal aspects of informal court proceedings. In P. Drew and J. Heritage (eds.). *Talk at work: interaction in institutional settings*. Cambridge: Cambridge University Press. 199–212.

Atkinson, J. M. and P. Drew. 1979. *Order in court: the organisation of verbal interaction in judicial settings*. London: Macmillan.

Auer, P. and A. di Luzio (eds.). 1992. *The contextualization of language*. Amsterdam: Benjamins.

Bassili, J. N. and J. F. Fletcher. 1991. Response-time measurement in survey research. A method of CATI and a new look at non-attitudes. *Public Opinion Quarterly* 55: 331–24.

Beach, W. 1993. Transitional regularities for "casual" "Okay" usages. *Journal of Pragmatics* 19: 325–52.

Beatty, P. 1995. Understanding the standardized/non-standardized interviewing controversy. *Journal of Official Statistics* 11, 2: 147–60.

Beckman, H. B. and R. M. Frankel. 1984. The effect of physician behavior on the collection of data. *Annals of Internal Medicine* 101: 692–6.

Belson, W. A. 1981. *The design and understanding of survey questions*. Aldershot: Gower.

Belson, W. A. 1986. *Validity in survey research*. Aldershot: Gower.

Bergmann, J. R. 1992. Veiled morality: notes on discretion in psychiatry. In P. Drew and J. Heritage (eds.), *Talk at work: interaction in institutional settings*. Cambridge: Cambridge University Press. 137–63

Biemer, P. P., R. M. Groves, L. E. Lyberg, N. A. Mathiowetz, and S. Sudman (eds.), 1991. *Measurement error in surveys*. Chichester: Wiley.

Boddendijk, A. 1991. Sprekende taal in telefonische interviews? Een exploratief onderzoek naar veranderingen in schrijftaalkenmerken. [Spoken language in telephone interviews. An explorative study of changes in written language.] MA Thesis, Utrecht University.

Boden, D. 1994. *The business of talk: organizations in action*. Cambridge: Polity Press.

Bolton, R. N. and T. M. Bronkhurst. 1996. Questionnaire pretesting: computer-assisted coding of concurrent protocols. In N. Schwarz and S. Sudman (eds.), *Answering questions*. San Francisco: Jossey-Bass.

Bradburn, N. M. and C. Miles. 1979. Vague quantifiers. *Public Opinion Quarterly* 43: 92–101.

Bradburn, N. M., S. Sudman, and Associates. 1979. *Improving interview method and questionnaire design: response effects to threatening questions in survey research*. San Francisco: Jossey-Bass.

Brenner, M. 1982. Response-effects of "role-restricted" characteristics of the interviewer. In W. Dijkstra and J. van der Zouwen (eds.), *Response behaviour in the survey interview*. London: Academic Press. 131–65.

Brenner, M. 1985. Survey interviewing. In M. Brenner, J. Brown and D. Canter (eds.), *The research interview: uses and approaches*. London: Academic Press.

Brenner, M., J. Brown and D. Canter. 1985. Introduction. In M. Brenner, J. Brown, and D. Canter (eds.), *The research interview: uses and approaches*. London: Academic Press. 1–7.

Briggs, C. L. 1986. *Learning how to ask: a sociolinguistic appraisal of the role of the interview in social science research*. Cambridge: Cambridge University Press.

Brown, P. and S. C. Levinson. 1987. *Politeness: some universals in language usage*. Cambridge: Cambridge University Press.

Butler, D. and U. Kitzinger. 1976. *The 1975 Referendum*. London: Macmillan.

Button, G. 1987. Answers as practical products: two sequential practices used in interviews. *Social Psychology Quarterly* 50, 2: 160–71.

Button, G. (n.d.). Some design specification for turns at talk in a job interview. Unpublished MS.

Cannell, C. F., F. J. Fowler and K. H. Marquis. 1968. The influence of interviewer and respondent psychological and behavioral variables on the reporting in household interviews. *Vital and Health Statistics Series* 2 (26).

Cannell, C. F., P. V. Miller, and L. Oksenberg. 1981. Research on interviewing techniques. In S. Leinhardt (ed.), *Sociological methodology*. San Francisco: Jossey-Bass. 389–437.

Cannell, C. G. and L. Oksenberg, 1988. Observation of behavior in telephone interviews. In R. M. Groves et al. (eds.), *Telephone survey methodology*. New York: Wiley. 475–95.

Chafe, W. L. 1982. Integration and involvement in speaking, writing, and oral literature. In D. Tannen (ed.), *Spoken and written language: exploring orality and literacy*. Norwood, NJ: Ablex. 35–54.

Churchill, L. 1978. *Questioning strategies in sociolinguistics*. Rowley, MA: Newbury.

Cicourel, A. V. 1964. *Method and measurement in sociology*. New York: The Free Press of Glencoe.

Cicourel, A. V. 1982. Interviews, surveys, and the problem of ecological validity. *American Sociologist* 17: 11–20.

Clark, H. H. 1992. *Arenas of language use*. Chicago: University of Chicago Press.

Clark, H. H. 1996. *Using language*. Cambridge: Cambridge University Press.

Clark, H. H. and M. F. Schober. 1992. Asking questions and influencing answers. In J. M. Tanur (ed.), *Questions about questions: inquiries into the cognitive bases of surveys*. New York: Sage. 15–48.

Clayman, S. E. 1988. Displaying neutrality in television news interviews. *Social Problems* 35, 4: 474–92.

Converse, P. 1970. Attitudes and nonattitudes: continuation of a dialogue. In E. R. Tufte (ed.), *The quantitative analysis of social problems*. Reading, MA: Addison-Wesley. 168–89.

Cradock, R. M., D. W. Maynard, and N. C. Schaeffer. 1993. *Re-opening closed questions: respondents' elaborations on categorical answers in standardized interviews*. CDE Working Paper 93–24.

Czaja, R. and J. Blair. 1996. *Designing surveys: a guide to decisions and procedures*. London: Pine Forge Press.

Davidson, J. 1984. Subsequent versions of invitations, offers, requests, and proposals dealing with potential or actual rejection. In J. M. Atkinson and J. Heritage (eds.), *Structures of social action. Studies in conversation analysis*. Cambridge: Cambridge University Press. 102–28.

De Boer, F. 1994. *De interpretatie van het verschil. De vertaling van klachten van mannen en vrouwen in de RIAGG*. [The interpretation of the difference. The translation of complaints of men and women in psychotherapy.] Amsterdam: Het Spinhuis.

De Sola Pool, I. 1957. A critique of the 20th Anniversary Issue. *Public Opinion Quarterly* 21, 1: 190–98

Dijkstra, W. 1983. *Beïnvloeding van antwoorden in survey-interviews* [Influencing answers in survey interviews]. Utrecht: Elinkwijk.

Dijkstra, W. 1987. Interviewing style and respondent behavior. *Sociological Methods and Research* 16: 309–34.

Dijkstra, W. (forthcoming) A new method for studying verbal interaction in survey interviews. In D. Maynard, H. Houtkoop-Steenstra, N. C. Schaeffer, and J. van der Zouwen (eds.), *Standardization and tacit knowledge: interaction and practice in the standardized interview*. New York: Wiley.

Dijkstra, W., L. van der Veen, and J. van der Zouwen. 1985. A field experiment on interviewer–respondent interaction. In M. Brenner, J. Brown, and D. Canter (eds.), *The research interview: uses and approaches*. London: Academic Press. 37–63.

Dijkstra, W. and J. van der Zouwen, 1988. Types of inadequate interviewer behavior in survey-interviews. In W. E. Saris and I. N. Gallhofer (eds.), *Sociometric research*, vol. 1: *Data collection and scaling*. Basingstoke: Macmillan. 24–35.

Drew, P. 1984. Speaker's reportings in invitation sequences. In J. M. Atkinson and J. Heritage (eds.), *Structures of social action: studies in conversation analysis*. Cambridge: Cambridge University Press. 129–51.

Drew, P. and J. Heritage. 1992. Analyzing talk at work: an introduction. In P. Drew and J. Heritage (eds.), *Talk at work: interaction in institutional settings*. Cambridge: Cambridge University Press. 3–65.

Drew, P. and M. L. Sorjonen. 1997 Institutional dialogue. In T. A. van Dijk (ed.), *Discourse as social interaction*. London: Sage. 92–119.

Drummond, K. and R. Hopper. 1993. Some uses of *Yeah*. *Research on Language and Social Interaction* 26, 2: 203–13.

Ferber, R. 1956. The effect of respondent ignorance on survey results. *Journal of the American Statistical Association* 51: 576–86.

Fienberg, S. E. 1990. Comment. *Journal of the American Statistical Association* 85, 409: 241–4.

Foddy, W. 1993. *Constructing questions for interviews and questionnaires: theory and practice in social research*. Cambridge: Cambridge University Press.

Ford, C. E. and S. A. Thompson. 1996. Interactional units in conversation: syntactic, intonational, and pragmatic resources for the management of turns. In E. Ochs, E. A. Schegloff, and S. A. Thompson (eds.), *Interaction and grammar*. Cambridge: Cambridge University Press. 134–85.

Fowler, F. J. 1989. The effect of unclear terms on survey-based estimates. In F. J. Fowler et al. (eds.), *Conference proceedings, health survey research methods*. Washington, DC: National Centre for Health Services Research. 9–12.

Fowler, F. J. and T. W. Mangione. 1986. *Reducing interviewer effects on health survey data*. Washington, DC: National Center for Health Services Research.

Fowler, F. J. and T. W. Mangione. 1990. *Standardized survey interviewing: Minimizing interviewer-related error*. Newbury Park: Sage.

Fowler, F. J. and C. F. Cannell. 1996. Using behavioral coding to identify cognitive problems with survey questions. In N. Schwarz and S. Sudman (eds.), *Answering questions*. San Francisco: Jossey-Bass.

Frankel, R. 1984. From sentence to sequence: understanding the medical encounter through microinteractional analysis. *Discourse Processes* 7: 135–70.

Frankel, R. 1989. "I wz wondering – uhm could RAID uhm effect the brain permanently d'y know?": some observations on the intersection of speaking and writing in calls to a poison control center. *Western Journal of Speech Communication* 53: 195–226.

Garfinkel, H. 1962. Common sense knowledge of social structures: the documentary method of interpretation in lay and professional fact finding. In J. M. Scher (ed.), *Theories of the mind*. New York: Free Press of Glencoe.

Garfinkel, H. 1967a. *Studies in ethnomethodology*. Englewood Cliffs, NJ: Prentice Hall.

Garfinkel, H. 1967b. What is ethnomethodology? In H. Garfinkel, *Studies in ethnomethodology*. Englewood Cliffs, NJ: Prentice Hall. 1–35

Garfinkel, H. and H. Sacks. 1970. On formal structures of practical actions. In J. C. McKinney and E. Tiruakian (eds.), *Theoretical sociology; perspectives and developments*. New York: Appleton-Century-Crofts. 338–66.

Gibbs, W. R. jr. 1987. *Mutual knowledge and the psychology of conversational English*. Cambridge: Cambridge University Press.

Glenn, P. J. 1995. Laughing *at* and laughing *with*: negotiations of participant alignments through conversational laughter. In P. ten Have and G. Psathas (eds.), *Situated order; studies in the social organization of talk and embodied activities*. Lanham, MD: University Press of America. 43–57.

Goffman, E. 1955. On face-work: an analysis of ritual elements in social interaction. In J. Laver and S. Hutcheson (eds.), 1972. *Communication in face to face interaction*. Harmondsworth: Penguin. 319–47.

Goffman, E. 1974. *Frame analysis: an essay on the organization of experience*. New York: Harper and Row.

Goffman, E. 1981a [1979]. Footing. In E. Goffman 1981. *Forms of talk*. Oxford: Blackwell: 124–60.

Goffman, E. 1981b. Radio talk. In E. Goffman 1981. *Forms of talk*. Oxford: Blackwell: 197–331.

Goldberg, J. 1978. Amplitude shift. A mechanism for the affiliation of utterances in conversational interaction. In J. Schenkein (ed.), *Studies in the organization of conversational interaction*. New York: Academic Press. 199–217.

Goodwin, C. 1981. *Conversational organization: interaction between speakers and hearers*. New York: Academic Press.

Goodwin, C. 1986. Between and within: alternative sequential treatments of continuers and assessments. *Human Studies* 9: 205–17.

Goodwin, C. 1992. Assessments and the construction of context. In A. Duranti and C. Goodwin (eds.), *Rethinking context: language as an interactive phenomenon*. Cambridge: Cambridge University Press. 147–91.

Goodwin, C. and M. H. Goodwin. 1987. Concurrent operations on talk: notes on the interactive organization of assessments. *IPrA Papers in Pragmatics* 1, 1: 1–52.

Goodwin, C. and M. H. Goodwin. 1992. Context, activity, and participation. In P. Auer and A. di Luzio (eds.), *The contextualization of language*. Amsterdam: Benjamins. 77–99.

Goodwin, M. H. 1980. Processes of mutual monitoring. *Sociological Inquiry* 50: 303–17.

Greatbatch, D. 1988. A turn-taking system for British news interviews. *Language in Society* 17: 401–30.

Grice, H. P. 1975. Logic and conversation. In P. Cole and J. L. Morgan (eds.), *Syntax and semantics*, vol. 3: *Speech acts*. New York: Academic Press: 41–58.

Groves, R., N. H. Fultz, and E. Martin, 1992. Direct questioning about comprehension in a survey setting. In J. M. Tanur (ed.), *Questions about questions: inquiries into the cognitive bases of surveys*. New York: Russell Sage Foundation. 49–64.

Gumperz, J. 1982. *Discourse strategies*. Cambridge: Cambridge University Press.

Haegeman, P. 1996. *Business English in Flanders: a study of lingua franca telephone interaction*. University of Gent.

Hak, T. (forthcoming). Survey interviewers as coders. In D. Maynard, H. Houtkoop-Steenstra, N. C. Schaeffer, and J. van der Zouwen (eds.), *Standardization and tacit knowledge: interaction and practice in the standardized interview*. New York: Wiley.

Hak, T. and F. de Boer. 1996. Formulations in first encounters. *Journal of Pragmatics* 25: 83–99.

Heath, C. 1982. Preserving the consultation: medical record and professional conduct. *Journal of the Sociology of Health and Illness* 4, 1: 56–74.

Heath, C. 1992. The delivery and reception of diagnosis in the general-practice consultation. In P. Drew and J. Heritage (eds.), *Talk at work: interaction in institutional settings*. Cambridge: Cambridge University Press. 235–68.

Heritage, J. 1984a. A change-of-state token and aspects of its sequential placement. In J. M. Atkinson and J. Heritage (eds.), *Structures of social action: Studies in conversation analysis*. Cambridge: Cambridge University Press: 299–345.

Heritage, J. 1984b. *Garfinkel and ethnomethodology*. Cambridge: Polity Press.

Heritage, J. 1985. Analyzing news interviews: aspects of the production of talk for an overhearing audience. In T. A. van Dijk (ed.), *Handbook of discourse analysis, Volume 3. Discourse and dialogue*. New York: Academic Press. 95–117.

Heritage, J. and J. M. Atkinson. 1984. Introduction. In J. M. Atkinson and J. Heritage (eds.), *Structures of social action: studies in conversation analysis.* Cambridge: Cambridge University Press. 1–17.

Heritage, J. and D. Greatbatch. 1991. On the institutional character of institutional talk: the case of news interviews. In D. Boden and D. H. Zimmerman (eds.), *Talk and social structure: studies in ethnomethodology and conversation analysis.* Cambridge: Polity Press. 93–138.

Heritage, J. and M. L. Sorjonen. 1994. Constituting and maintaining activities across sequences: *and*-prefacing as a feature of questioning design. *Language in Society* 23: 1–29.

Heritage, J. and A. L. Roth. 1995. Grammar and institution: questions and questioning in the broadcast news interview. *Research on Language and Social Interaction* 28, 1: 1–60.

Heritage, J. and D. R. Watson. 1979. Formulations as conversational objects. In G. Psathas (ed.), *Everyday language: studies in ethnomethodology.* New York: Irvington. 123–63.

Hippler, H. J. and N. Schwarz. 1986. Not forbidding isn't allowing: the cognitive basis of the forbid-allow asymmetry. *Public Opinion Quarterly* 50: 87–96.

Hirschberg, J. and G. Ward. 1995. The interpretation of the high-rise question contour in English. *Journal of Pragmatics* 24: 407–12.

Holleman, B. C. 1996. The nature of the forbid/allow asymmetry: two correlational studies. Paper presented at Essex '96, the Fourth International Social Science Methodology Conference, University of Essex, July 1–5, 1996.

Houtkoop-Steenstra, H. 1986. Summarizing in doctor–patient interaction. In T. Ensink et al. (eds.), *Discourse analysis and public life.* Dordrecht/Providence: Foris. 201–21.

Houtkoop-Steenstra, H. 1987. *Establishing agreement: an analysis of proposal-acceptance sequences.* Dordrecht/Providence: Foris.

Houtkoop-Steenstra, H. 1990. Normative and analytical perspectives on interviewing techniques. In H. Pinkster and I. Genee (eds.), *Unity in diversity: papers presented to Simon C. Dik on his 50th birthday.* Dordrecht/Providence: Foris. 133–51.

Houtkoop-Steenstra, H. 1991. Opening sequences in Dutch telephone conversations. In D. Boden and D. H. Zimmerman (eds.), *Talk and social structure: studies in ethnomethodology and conversation analysis.* Cambridge: Polity Press. 232–51.

Houtkoop-Steenstra, H. 1994. De interactionele functie van zacht spreken in survey interviews. [The interactional function of low volume in survey interviews.] *Gramma/TTT* 3, 3: 183–202.

Houtkoop-Steenstra, H. 1995. Meeting both ends. Between standardization and recipient design in telephone survey interviews. In P. ten Have and G. Psathas (eds.), *Situated order: studies in the social organization of talk and embodied activities.* Washington, DC: University Press of America. 91–107.

Houtkoop-Steenstra, H. 1996. Probing behavior of interviewers in the standardized semi-open research interview. *Quality and Quantity* 30: 205–30.

Houtkoop, H. and H. Mazeland. 1985. Turns and discourse units in everyday conversation. *Journal of Pragmatics* 9, 5: 595–619.

Houtkoop-Steenstra, H. and H. van den Bergh. 2000. Effects of introductions in large scale telephone survey interviews. *Sociological Methods and Research* 28, 3.

Houtkoop-Steenstra, H. and C. Antaki. 1997. Creating happy people by asking yes/no questions. *Research on Language and Social Interaction* 30, 4: 285–315.

Hyman, H. H. a.o. 1954. *Interviewing in social research.* Chicago: University of Chicago Press.

Hymes, D. 1972. Models of the interaction of language and social life. In J. J. Gumperz and D. Hymes (eds.), *Directions in sociolinguistics: the ethnography of speaking.* New York: Holt, Rinehardt & Winston. 35–71.

Jansen, C. and M. Steehouder. 1992. Forms as a source of communication problems. *Journal of Technical Writing and Commmunication* 22, 2: 179–94.

Jayyusi, L. 1984. *Categorization and the moral order.* London: Routledge & Kegan Paul.

Jefferson, G. 1972. Side sequences. In D. Sudnow (ed.), *Studies in social interaction.* New York: Free Press. 294–338.

Jefferson, G. 1978. Sequential aspects of story telling in conversation. In J. Schenkein (ed.), *Studies in the organization of conversational interaction.* New York: Academic Press. 219–48.

Jefferson, G. 1979. A technique for inviting laughter and its subsequent acceptance/declination. In G. Psathas (ed.), *Everyday language: studies in ethnomethodology.* New York: Irvington. 79–96.

Jefferson, G. 1981a. The abominable "Ne?": an exploration of post-response pursuit of response. In P. Schröder and H. Steger (eds.), *Dialogforschung.* Düssseldorf: Schwann. 53–89.

Jefferson, G. 1981b. "Caveat speaker": a preliminary exploration of shift implicative recipiency in the articulation of topic. Final report to the (British) SSRC. (mimeo)

Jefferson, G. 1984a. On a systematic deployment of the acknowledgement tokens "Yeah" and "Mm hmm". *Papers in Linguistics* 17, 2: 197–216.

Jefferson, G. 1984b. On the organization of laughter in talk about troubles. In J. M. Atkinson and J. Heritage (eds.), *Structures of social action. Studies in Conversation Analysis.* Cambridge: Cambridge University Press. 346–69.

Jefferson, G. 1984c. On the stepwise transition from talk about a trouble to inappropriately next-positioned matters. In J. M. Atkinson and L. Heritage (eds.), *Structures of social action: studies in conversation analysis.* Cambridge: Cambridge University Press. 191–222.

Jefferson, G. 1988. On the sequential organization of troubles-talk in ordinary conversation. *Social Problems* 35, 4: 418–42.

Jefferson, G. 1989a. Preliminary notes on a possible metric which provides for a "standard maximum" silence of approximately one second in conversation. In D. Roger and P. Bull (eds.), *Conversation: an interdisciplinary perspective.* Clevedon: Multilingual Matters. 156–97.

Jefferson, G. (ed). 1989b. Harvey Sacks – Lectures 1964–1965. Special issue of *Human Studies* 12: 3–4

Jefferson, G. 1990. List construction as a task and resource. In G. Psathas (ed), *Interaction competence.* Lanham, MD: University Press of America. 63–92.

Jefferson, G. 1993. Caveat speaker: preliminary notes on recipient topic-shift implicature. *Research on Language and Social Interaction* 26, 1: 1–30.

Jefferson, G. and J. R. Lee. 1981. The rejection of advice: managing the problematic convergence of a "troubles-telling" and a "service encounter." *Journal of Pragmatics* 5: 399–422.

Jefferson, G., H. Sacks, and E. A. Schegloff. 1987. Notes on laughter in the pursuit of intimacy. In G. Button and J. R. E. Lee (eds.), *Talk and social organisation*. Avon: Multilingual Matters. 152–205.

Jönsson, L. and P. Linell. 1991. Story generations: from dialogical interviews to written reports in police interrogations. *Text* 11, 3: 419–40

Joosten, A. 1995. De meervoudige betekenis van "hoe is 't?" in huisarts–patintgesprekken. [The multiple meaning of "How are you?" in doctor–patient interaction] In L. Meeuwesen and H. Houtkoop-Steenstra (eds.), *Studies naar mondelinge interacties*. Utrecht: Isor. 105–25.

Jucker, A. H. and S. W. Smith. 1996. Explicit and implicit ways of enhancing common ground in conversation. *Pragmatics* 6, 1: 1–18

Keith, K. D., R. L. Schalock, and K. Hoffman. 1986. *Quality of life: measurement and programmatic implications*. Lincoln, NE: Region V Mental Retardation Services.

Komter, M. L. 1991. *Conflict and cooperation in job interviews: a study of talk, tasks and ideas*. Amsterdam: Benjamins.

Komter, M. L. 1998. *Dilemmas in the courtroom: A study of trials of violent crime in the Netherlands*. Mahwah/London: Lawrence Erlbaum.

Kovar, M. G. and P. Royston. 1990. Comment. *Journal of the American Statistical Association* 85, 409: 246–7.

Krosnick, J. A. and D. F. Alwin. 1987. An evaluation of a cognitive theory of response-order effects in survey measurement. *Public Opinion Quarterly* 51: 201–19.

Labov, W. and D. Fanshel. 1977. *Therapeutic discourse: psychotherapy as conversation*. New York: Academic Press.

Lazersfeld, P. F. 1944. The controversy over detailed interviews – an offer for negotiation. *Public Opinion Quarterly* 8: 38–60

Levelt, W. J. M. 1989. *Speaking: from intention to articulation*. Cambridge, MA: MIT Press.

Levinson, S. C. 1987. Minimization and conversational inference. In J. Verschueren and M. Bertuccelli-Papi (eds.), *The pragmatic perspective*. Amsterdam: Benjamins. 61–130.

Levinson, S. C. 1988. Putting linguistics on a proper footing: explorations in Goffman's concepts of participation. In P. Drew and A. J. Wootton (eds.), *Erving Goffman: exploring the interaction order*. Cambridge: Polity Press. 161–227.

Lindström, A. 1994. When "Yes" means "No": the curled Ja as a preface to a dispreferred second pair part in Swedish conversation. Paper presented at the Sociology World Congress, Bielefeld, July 20, 1994.

Local, J. 1992. Continuing and restarting. In P. Auer and A. di Luzio (eds.), *The contextualization of language*. Amsterdam: Benjamins. 272–96.

Longman, J. and N. Mercer. 1993. Forms for talk and talk for forms: oral and literate dimension of language use in employment training interviews. *Text* 13, 1: 91–116.

Loosveldt, G. 1995. Interviewer–respondent interaction analysis as a diagnostic and validating instrument. In *Proceedings of the International Conference on Survey Measurement and Process Quality. Bristol, 1–4 April 1995.* Alexandria: American Statistical Association. 290–5.

Lyberg, L. and D. Kasprzyk. 1991. Data collection methods and measurement error: an overview. In P. P. Biemer, R. M. Groves, L. E. Lyberg, N. A. Mathiowetz, and S. Sudman (eds.), *Measurement error in surveys.* Chichester: Wiley. 237–63.

Lynch, M. (forthcoming). Standardized survey interviews: perspicuous settings of instructed action. In D. Maynard, H. Houtkoop-Steenstra, N. C. Schaeffer, and J. van der Zouwen (eds.), *Standardization and tacit knowledge: interaction and practice in the standardized interview.* New York: Wiley.

Marlaire, C. L. and D. Maynard. 1990. Standardized testing as an interactional phenomenon. *Sociology of Education* 63: 83–101.

Maynard, D. W. 1989. Notes on the delivery and reception of diagnostic news regarding mental disability. In D. T. Helm, W. T. Anderson, A. J. Meehan, and A. Warfield Rawls (eds.), *The interactional order: new directions in the study of social order.* New York: Irvington. 54–67.

Maynard, D. W. 1992. On clinicians co-implicating recipients' perspective in the delivery of diagnostic news. In P. Drew and J. Heritage (eds.), *Talk at work: interaction in institutional settings.* Cambridge: Cambridge University Press. 331–59.

Maynard, D. W. and C. L. Marlaire. 1992. Good reasons for bad testing performance: the interactional substrate of educational exams. *Qualitative Sociology* 15: 177–202.

Maynard, D. W. and N. C. Schaeffer 1997. Keeping the gate. *Sociological Methods and Research* 26, 1: 34–79.

Maynard, D. W. and N. C. Schaeffer (forthcoming). Ethnomethodology, Conversation Analysis, and survey research: toward a sociology of social scientific knowledge. In D. Maynard, H. Houtkoop-Steenstra, N. C. Schaeffer, and J. van der Zouwen (eds.), *Standardization and tacit knowledge: interaction and practice in the standardized interview.* New York: Wiley.

Maynard, D. W., N. C. Schaeffer and R. M. Cradock. 1993. *Declinations of the request to participate in the survey interview.* University of Wisconsin–Madison, Center for Demography and Ecology (Working Paper 93–23).

Maynard, D. W, N. C. Schaeffer, and R. M. Cradock. 1995. A preliminary analysis of "gatekeeping" as a feature of declinations to participate in the survey interview. Unpublished MS.

Mazeland, H. 1983. Openingssequenties van lesbeginnen. [Opening sequences in lesson beginnings]. In H. Mazeland and J. Sturm (eds.), *Onderwijs als interactieprobleem.* Special issue of *Toegepaste Taalwelenschap in Artikelen.* 77–101.

Mazeland, H. 1992. *Vraag/antwoord sequenties* [Question/answer sequences]. Amsterdam: Stichting Neerlandistiek.

Mazeland, H. 1994. *Woordbetekenis en sociale interactie.* [Word meaning and social interaction]. Paper for the Spiegel van de Samenleving. Zesde Sociaal-Wetenschappelijke Studiedagen 1994. April 7–8, 1994, Vrije Universiteit Amsterdam.

Mazeland, H. 1995a. Conversatie-analyse van communicatie in institutionele settings: te veel micro, te weinig macro? [Conversation analysis of communication in institutional settings: too much micro, too little macro?]. In C. Sauer and H. Mazeland (eds.), *Lezingen van de Studiedag Taalbeheersing Rijksuniversiteit Groningen*. Groningen: Rijksuniversiteit Groningen. 65–93.

Mazeland, H. 1995b. De gespreksorganisatorische status van verduidelijkingen en andere vormen van uitleggen. [The conversation-organizational status of explanations and other forms of accounts.] In E. Huls and J. Klatter-Folmer (ed.), *Artikelen van de Tweede Sociolinguïstische Conferentie*. Delft: Eburon. 419–35.

Mazeland, H. 1995c. Dissociating questioner and questioning in a survey. Paper presented at the Amsterdam Workshop on Interviewer-Respondent Interaction. November 18–21, 1995. Amsterdam.

Mazeland, H., M. Huisman and M. Schasfoort. 1995. Negotiating categories in travel agency calls. In A. Firth (ed.), *The discourse of negotiation: studies of language in the work-place*. Oxford: Pergamon.

Mazeland, H. and P. ten Have. 1996. Essential tensions in (semi-) open research interviews. In I. Maso and F. Wester (eds.), *The deliberate dialogue*. Brussels: VUB Press. 87–115.

McHoul, A. 1978. The organization of turns at formal talk in the classroom. *Language in Society* 7: 183–213.

Mehan, H. 1984. Institutional decision making. In B. Rogoff and J. Lave (eds.), *Everyday cognition: its developments in social contexts*. Cambridge, MA: Harvard University Press. 41–67.

Mishler, E. G. 1986. *Research interviewing: context and narrative*. Cambridge, MA, Harvard University Press.

Molenaar, N. J. 1982. Response effects of "formal" characteristics of questions. In W. Dijkstra and J. van der Zouwen (eds.), *Response behaviour in the survey interview*. London: Academic Press. 49–89.

Molenaar, N. J. and J. H. Smit. 1996. Asking and answering yes/no questions in survey interviews: a conversational approach. *Quality and Quantity* 30, 2: 115–36.

Moore, R. and D. W. Maynard (forthcoming). Achieving understanding in the standardized survey interview: respondents' and interviewers' uses of next-position repair techniques. In D. Maynard, H. Houtkoop-Steenstra, N. C. Schaeffer, and J. van der Zouwen (eds.), *Standardization and tacit knowledge: interaction and practice in the standardized interview*. New York: Wiley.

Morton-Williams, J. and W. Sykes. 1984. The use of interaction coding and follow-up interviews to investigate comprehension of survey questions. *Journal of Market Research Society* 26: 209–27.

Moser, C. A. and G. Kalton. 1978 [1971]. Question wording. In Bynner, J. and K. M. Stribley (eds.), *Social research: principles and procedures*. Longman and The Open University Press. 140–56.

Nieuwenkamp, A., A. van der Sloot, and E. Spanjer. 1997. "Wel leuk" of "vreselijk"? Wanneer gaat een interviewer na een unformatted answer door met de volgende vraag en wanneer probeert hij wel een formatted answer te verkrijgen?. ["Sort of nice" or "terrible"? When do interviewers proceed to the next question after an unformatted answer, and when do they probe for a formatted answer?]. Thesis, Department of Dutch, Utrecht University.

Nuckols, R. 1953. A note on pre-testing public opinion questions. *Journal of Applied Psychology* 37, 2: 119–20.

Oksenberg, L., C. Cannell and G. Kalton. 1989. New methods for pretesting survey questions. In C. F. Cannell, L. Oksenberg, G. Kalton, K. Bischoping, and F. Fowler (eds.), *New techniques for pretesting survey questions*. Ann Arbor, MI: Survey Research Center, University of Michigan. Unpublished report. 30–62.

Oksenberg, L., C. Cannell and G. Kalton. 1991. New strategies of pretesting survey questions. *Journal of Official Statistics* 7: 349–69.

Pomerantz, A. 1978. Compliment responses: notes on the co-operation of multiple constraints. In J. Schenkein (ed.), *Studies in the organization of conversational interaction*. New York: Academic Press. 79–112.

Pomerantz, A. 1984a. Agreeing and disagreeing with assessments; some features of preferred/dispreferred turn shapes. In J. M. Atkinson and J. Heritage (eds.), *Structures of social action: studies in conversation analysis*. Cambridge: Cambridge University Press: 57–102.

Pomerantz, A. 1984b. Pursuing a response. In J. M. Atkinson and J. Heritage (eds.), *Structures of social action: studies in conversation analysis*. Cambridge: Cambridge University Press. 152–64.

Pomerantz, A. 1984c. Giving a source a basis: the practice in conversation of telling "how I know". *Journal of Pragmatics* 8: 607–25.

Pomerantz, A. 1988. Offering a candidate answer. *Communication Monographs* 55: 360–73.

Psathas, G. 1995. *Conversation analysis: the study of talk-in-interaction*. Thousand Oaks: Sage.

Rapley, M. and C. Antaki. 1996. A conversation analysis of the "acquiescence" of people with learning disabilities. *Journal of Community and Applied Social Psychology* 6: 371–91.

Reddy, M. J. 1979. The conduit metaphor – A case of frame conflict in our language about language. In A. Ortony (ed.), *Metaphor and thought*. Cambridge: Cambridge University Press. 284–325.

Resnick, L. B. 1991. Shared cognition: thinking as social practice. In L. B. Resnick, J. M. Levine, and S. D. Teasly (eds.), *Perspectives on socially shared cognition*. Washington, DC: American Psychological Association. 1–20.

Rugg, D. 1941. Experiments in wording questions. *Public Opinion Quarterly* 5: 91–92.

Sacks, H. 1972a. An initial investigation of the usability of conversational data for doing sociology. In D. Sudnow (ed.), *Studies in social interaction*. New York: The Free Press: 1–31.

Sacks, H. 1972b. On the analyzability of stories by children. In J. Gumperz and D. Hymes (eds.), *Directions in sociolinguistics: the ethnography of communication*. New York: Rinehart and Winston. 329–45.

Sacks, H. 1984. Notes on methodology. In J. M. Atkinson and J. Heritage (eds.), *Structures of social action: studies in conversation analysis*. Cambridge: Cambridge University Press. 21–8.

Sacks, H. 1987. The preference for agreement and contiguity in sequences in conversation. In G. Button and J. R. E. Lee (eds.), *Talk and social organisation*. Clevedon: Multilingual Matters. 54–69.

Sacks, H. 1988/89. On members' measurement systems. *Research on Language and Social Interaction* 22: 45–60.

Sacks, H. 1992a/b (1964–1972). *Lectures on conversation*. 2 volumes, ed. Gail Jefferson. Oxford: Blackwell.

Sacks, H., E. A. Schegloff, and G. Jefferson. 1974. A simplest systematics for the organization of turn taking in conversation. *Language* 50, 4: 696–735.

Sacks, H. and E. A. Schegloff. 1979. Two preferences in the organization of reference to persons in conversation and their interaction. In G. Psathas (ed.), *Everyday language: studies in ethnomethodology.* New York: Irvington. 15–21.

Schaeffer, N. C. 1991a. Conversation with a purpose – or conversation? Interaction in the standardized interview. In P. P. Biemer, R. M. Groves, L. E. Lyberg, N. A. Mathiowetz, and S. Sudman (eds.), *Measurement errors in surveys.* New York: Wiley. 367–91.

Schaeffer, N. C. 1991b. Hardly ever or constantly? Group comparisons using vague quantifiers. *Public Opinion Quarterly* 55: 395–423.

Schaeffer, N. C. and D. W. Maynard. 1996. From paradigm to prototype and back again: interactive aspects of "cognitive processing" in standardized survey interviews. In N. Schwarz and S. Sudman (eds.), *Answering questions: methodology for determining cognitive and communicative processes in survey research.* San Francisco: Jossey-Bass. 65–88.

Schaeffer, N. C., D. W. Maynard, and R. M. Cradock. 1993. *Negotiating certainty: uncertainty proposals and their disposal in standardized interviewing.* University of Wisconsin–Madison, Center for Demography and Ecology (Working Paper 93–25).

Schalock, R. L. and K. D. Keith. 1993. *Quality of life questionnaire.* Worthington, OH: IDS Publishing Corporation.

Schank, R. C. and R. P. Abelson. 1997. *Scripts, plans, goals and understanding. An inquiry into human knowledge structures.* Hillsdale, NJ: Lawrence Erlbaum.

Schegloff, E. A. 1972. Notes on a conversational practice: formulating place. In D. Sudnow (ed.), *Studies in social interaction.* New York: The Free Press. 75–119.

Schegloff, E. A. 1980. Preliminaries to preliminaries: "Can I ask you a question." *Sociological Inquiry* 50, 3/4: 104–52.

Schegloff, E. A. 1982. Discourse as an interactional achievement: some uses of "uh huh" and other things that come between sentences. In D. Tannen (ed.), *Analyzing discourse: text and talk.* Washington, DC: Georgetown University Press. 71–93.

Schegloff, E. A. 1987. Between macro and micro: contexts and other connections. In J. Alexander et al. (eds.), *The micro-macro link.* Berkeley: University of California Press. 207–34.

Schegloff, E. A. 1989. From interview to confrontation: observations of the Bush/Rather encounter. *Research on Language and Social Interaction* 22: 215–40.

Schegloff, E. A. 1990. Comment. *Journal of the American Statistical Association* 85, 409: 248–9.

Schegloff, E. A. 1991. Conversation analysis and socially shared cognition. In L. B. Resnick, J. M. Levine, and S. D. Teasly (eds.), *Perspectives on socially shared cognition.* Washington, DC: American Psychological Association. 150–72.

Schegloff, E. A. 1992. Repair after next turn: the last structurally provided defense of intersubjectivity in conversation. *American Journal of Sociology* 98: 1295–345.

Schegloff, E. A. 1993. Reflections on quantification in the study of conversation. *Research on Language and Social Interaction* 26, 1: 99–128.

Schegloff, E. A., G. Jefferson, and H. Sacks. 1977. The preference for self-correction in the organization of repair in conversation. *Language* 53, 1: 361–82.

Schegloff, E. A. and H. Sacks. 1973. Opening up closings. *Semiotica* 8: 289–327.

Schiffrin, D. 1993. "Speaking for another" in sociolinguistic interviews: alignments, identities, and frames. In D. Tannen (ed.), *Framing in discourse*. Oxford: Oxford University Press. 231–59.

Schober, M. F. and F. Conrad. 1997. Does conversational interviewing reduce survey measurement error? *Public Opinion Quarterly* 61: 576–602.

Schuman, H. and S. Presser. 1981. *Questions and answers in attitude surveys: experiments on question form, wording, and context*. Orlando: Academic Press.

Schuman, H. and J. Scott. 1987. Problems in the use of survey questions to measure public opinion. *Science* 236: 957–9.

Schwarz, N. 1996. *Cognition and communication: judgemental biases, research methods, and the logic of conversation*. Mahwah: Lawrence Erlbaum.

Schwarz, N. and S. Sudman (eds.), 1992. *Context effects in social and psychological research*. New York: Springer.

Searle, J. 1969. *Speech acts: an essay in the philosophy of language*. Cambridge: Cambridge University Press.

Smit, J. H. 1995. *Suggestieve vragen in survey interviews. Voorkomen, oorzaken en gevolgen* [Leading questions in survey interviews. Occurrence, determinants, and effects]. Vrije Universiteit Amsterdam.

Smith, D. E. and J. Whalen. 1995. Texts in action. Unpublished MS.

Smith, N. (ed.), 1982. *Mutual knowledge*. New York: Academic Press.

Smith, T. W. 1984. Nonattitudes: a review and evaluation. In C. F. Turner and E. Martin (eds.), *Surveying subjective phenomena*, vol. 2. New York: Russell Sage Foundation.

Snijkers, G. and G. J. M. Conen. 1995. What is the total net household income? In-depth interviews and field test on income questions. Paper presented at International Conference on Survey Measurement and Process Quality, Bristol, April 1–4, 1995.

Sperber, D. and D. Wilson. 1986. *Relevance: communication and cognition*. Oxford: Blackwell.

Stalnaker, R. C. 1974. Pragmatic presupposition. In M. K. Muniz and P. K. Unger (eds.), *Semantics and philosophy*. New York: New York University Press.197–214.

Steehouder, M. and Jansen, C. 1992. Optimizing the quality of forms. In H. Pander Maat and M. Steehouder (eds.), *Studies of functional text quality*. Amsterdam: Rodopi. 159–73.

Stickel, G. 1972. "Ja" und "Nein" als Kontroll- und Korrektursignale. ["Yes" and "No" as control and correction signals]. *Linguistische Berichte* 17: 12–17.

Streeck, J. and U. Hartge. 1992. Previews. Gestures at the transitional place. In P. Auer and A. di Luzio (eds.), *The contextualization of language*. Amsterdam: Benjamins. 135–57.

Suchman, L. A. 1987. *Plans and situated actions: the problem of human–machine communication*. Cambridge: Cambridge University Press.

Suchman, L. and B. Jordan. 1990a. Interactional troubles in face-to-face survey interviews. *Journal of the American Statistical Association* 85, 409: 232–41.

Suchman, L. and B. Jordan. 1990b. Rejoinder. *Journal of the American Statistical Association* 85, 409: 252–3.

Sudman, S., N. M. Bradburn, and N. Schwarz. 1996. *Thinking about answers; the application of cognitive processes to survey methodology.* San Francisco: Jossey-Bass.

Tannen, D. (ed.), 1993. *Framing in discourse.* Oxford: Oxford University Press

Tannen, D. and C. Wallat. 1993. Interactive frames and knowledge schemas in interaction: examples from a medical examination/interview. In D. Tannen (ed.), *Framing in discourse.* Oxford: Oxford University Press. 57–74.

Tanur, J.M. (ed.), 1992. *Questions about questions: inquiries into the cognitive bases of surveys.* New York: Russell Sage Foundation.

Ten Have, P. 1987. *Sequenties en formuleringen: aspecten van de interactionele organisatie van huisarts–spreekuurgesprekken.* [Sequences and formulations: aspects of the interactional organisation of physician–patient interactions] Dordrecht/Providence: Foris.

Ten Have, P. 1991. Talk and institution: a reconsideration of the "asymmetry" of doctor-patient interaction. In D. Boden and D. H. Zimmerman (eds.), *Talk and social structure: studies in ethnomethodology and conversation analysis.* Cambridge: Polity Press. 138–63.

Ten Have, P. 1995. The spoken questionnaire: harvesting answers. Paper presented at the Amsterdam Workshop on Interviewer–Respondent Interaction. November 18–21, 1995. Amsterdam.

Ten Have, P. 1999. *Doing conversation analysis: a practical guide.* London: Thousand Oaks, New Delhi: Sage.

Thomas, J. 1995. *Meaning in interaction: an introduction to pragmatics.* London: Longman.

Treichler, P. A., R. M. Frankel, C. Kramarae, K. Zoppi, and H. B. Beckman (1984). Problems and problems: power relationships in a medical encounter. In C. Kramarae, M. Schultz and W. O'Barr (eds.), *Language and power.* New York: Sage. 62–8.

Uhmann, S. 1992. Contextualizing relevance: on some forms and functions of speech rate changes in everyday conversation. In P. Auer and A. di Luzio (eds.), *The contextualization of language.* Amsterdam: Benjamins. 297–337.

Van der Sloot, A., and E. Spanjer. 1998. "Wat IS een Q el service? Het vragen om toelichting in survey interviews. ["What IS a Q el service?". Requesting clarification in survey interviews]. MA Thesis. Department of Dutch. Utrecht University.

Van der Zouwen, J. (forthcoming) Why study interaction in survey interviews? A response from a survey researcher. In D. Maynard, H. Houtkoop-Steenstra, N. C. Schaeffer, and J. van der Zouwen (eds.), *Standardization and tacit knowledge: interaction and practice in the standardized interview.* New York: Wiley.

Van der Zouwen, J. and W. Dijkstra. 1995. Non-trivial question-answer sequences: types, determinants and effects of data quality. Paper presented at the International Conference on Survey Measurement and Process Quality, Bristol, April 1–4, 1995.

Van der Zouwen, J. and W. Dijkstra (forthcoming). Testing questionnaires using interaction coding. In D. Maynard, H. Houtkoop-Steenstra, N. C. Schaeffer, and J. van der Zouwen (eds.), *Standardization and tacit knowledge: interaction and practice in the standardized interview.* New York: Wiley.

Waterplas, L., J. Billiet, and G. Loosveldt. 1988. De verbieden versus niet toelaten asymmetrie. Een stabiel formuleringseffect in survey-onderzoek? [The forbid versus allow asymmetry: a stable wording effect in survey research?]. *Mens en Maatschappij* 63, 4: 399–415.

Watson, D. R. 1987. Interdisciplinary considerations in the analysis of pro-terms. In G. Button and J. R. E. Lee (eds.), *Talk and social organisation.* Avon: Multilingual Matters. 261–89.

Weber, E. 1993. *Varieties of questions in English conversation.* Amsterdam: Benjamins.

Whalen, J. 1995. A technology of order production: computer-aided dispatch in public safety communications. In P. ten Have and G. Psathas (eds.), *Situated order: studies in the social organization of talk and embodied activities.* Lanham, MD: University Press of America. 187–231.

Willis, G. B. and S. Schechter. 1997. Evaluation of cognitive interviewing techniques: Do the results generalize to the field? *Bulletin de Méthodologie Sociologique* 55: 40–66.

Wilson, T. P. 1971. Normative and interpretative paradigms in sociology. In J. D. Douglas (ed.), *Understanding everyday life: toward the reconstruction of sociological knowledge.* London: Routledge & Kegan Paul. 57–80.

Wilson, T. P. 1985. Social structure and social interaction. Paper presented at the International Conference on Ethnomethodology and Conversation Analysis. Boston University.

Zimmerman, D. H. 1969. Record-keeping and the intake process in a public welfare agency. In S. Wheeler (ed.), *On record: files and dossiers in American life.* New York: Sage. 319–45

Zimmerman, D. H. and D. Boden, 1991. Structure-in-action: an introduction. In D. Boden and D. H. Zimmerman (eds.), *Talk and social structure: studies in ethnomethodology and conversation analysis.* Cambridge: Polity Press. 3–22.

Subject index

Page numbers in bold type indicate definitions or main discussions.

absence 9, 23, 29
 noticeable/observable absence **19**
acknowledgment (tokens) 24, **25**, 124, 130,
  131
action projection **89**, 90
Action Projection Component (APC) 102
activity components **89–90**
adequate and inadequate behavior **17**, 35
 conversationally (in)adequate behavior
  12
adjacency pairs 22–5, 33
 first- and second-pair parts 22–3
affiliation 137, 140, 141, 144
agenda-based interaction 19, 20, 40
agreement 33
 see also disagreement and preference
  organization
ambiguity 67, 121, 175–7, 188n5
animator (as a production role) **44**, 45
answers
 accountable answers 77, 116
 adequate answers 4, 185n1
 answer instruction **33**, 116, 121
 answers vs. responses 26, **51**, **109**
 appropriate vs. correct answers 31
 candidate answers **30–1**, **109–12**, 116,
  177; as searching instruction 110
 categorical answers vs. instances 118–19
 collecting answers 51, 131
 descriptive answers **54**, 69, 71, 75
 formatted answers **4–41**, 51, 185n1
 near-formatted answers **53**
 next-positioned new answers 93
 no-problem answers 146, 147, 149, 152,
  153
 optimistic/positive answers 160, 161,
  165, 167–9, 172
 probing answers 10–11
 vague answers vs. precise responses 68,
  125–6

 yes–no answers 24, 65
  see also responses
APC, *see* Action Projection Component
approximations 53, **125–6**
assessable (statements) **131–2**, 144, 151
assessments 24, **25**, 28, 49, **130**, 131, 135,
  144, 188n1
audience design (vs. recipient design) 67,
  85, 186n4
author (as a production role) **44–5**, 48–9,
  60

behavior coding studies 5, 17, 21, 42, 99,
  174, 175

candidate analysis 23
candidate solution 23
categorical terms (vs. instances) **116–17**
categorization (problems) **116–17**, 119, 120
change-of-state token (*also* "oh"-receipt)
  26–7
claiming (vs. demonstrating) **141**
classification, *see* categorization
closure implicativeness **25**
coding answers 121
cognitive interviewing 14, 175, 180
collaborative questionnaire completion 77,
  83
common ground **65–7**
complete enough 35, 96, 101
completed-for-response **94**
conditional relevance **23**
conduit metaphor 180, 181
connectives 101, 105, 111, 102
context
 and meaning **20–1**
 context-sensitivity 21
 conversational context, *see also* sequential
  context 63, 87
 interpretative context 21

205